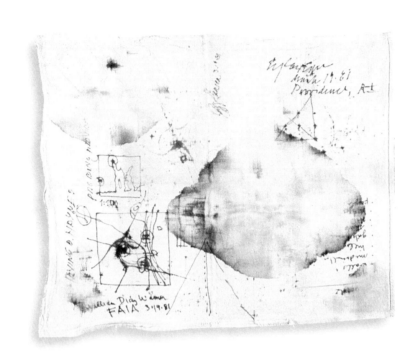

Providence,

NORTHEASTERN UNIVERSITY PRESS ■ *Boston*

Francis J. Leazes Jr.
Mark T. Motte

the Renaissance
City

The photograph on the opening page is from the 19 March 1981 doodlings of three renowned Providence architects on a napkin at their favorite Providence restaurant. From these casual sketches came the idea that moving the rivers might solve downtown Providence's traffic problems and reconnect the city to its historic maritime past. Courtesy of Friedrich St. Florian, AIA

The title page photograph is courtesy of Thomas Payne, WaterFire Providence.

Northeastern University Press

Library of Congress Cataloging-in-Publication Data
Leazes, Francis J.
   Providence, the Renaissance city / Francis J. Leazes Jr., Mark T. Motte.
     p. cm.
  Includes bibliographical references and index.
  ISBN 1-55553-604-2 (cloth : alk. paper)
   1. Urban renewal—Rhode Island—Providence—History—20th century. 2. City planning—Rhode Island—Providence—History—20th century. 3. Urban policy—Rhode Island—Providence—History—20th century. 4. Providence (R.I.)—Social conditions—20th century. 5. Providence (R.I.)—Politics and government—20th century. 6. Providence (R.I.)—Economic conditions—20th century. I. Motte, Mark T., 1962– II. Title.
  HT177.P76L43 2004
   307.3'416'097452—dc22   2004001098

Designed and composed in Optima and Adobe Jensen types by Gary Gore.

Printed and bound by Thomson-Shore, Inc., Dexter, Michigan. The paper is Fortune Matte, an acid-free stock.

MANUFACTURED IN THE UNITED STATES OF AMERICA

08 07 06 05 04   5 4 3 2 1

To our families

Contents

Illustrations

List of Tables and Figures

List of Abbreviations

CCC   Capital Center Commission
CCRI   Community College of Rhode Island
CDBG   Community Development Block Grant
COLA   cost-of-living adjustment
CPC   City Plan Commission
DBCC   Downtown Business Coordinating Council
DEM   Rhode Island Department of Environmental Management
DEPCO   Depositor Economic Protection Corporation
DPD   Providence Department of Planning and Development
DRC   Design Review Committee (of Capital Center Commission)
EIS   Environmental Impact Statement
EPA   Environmental Protection Agency
ERA   Economics Research Associates
FHWA   Federal Highway Administration
FRA   Federal Railway Administration
GRS   general revenue sharing
HNTB   Howard, Needles, Tammen and Bergendoff
HOV   high-occupancy vehicle
HSGT   High Speed Ground Transportation [Act]
ISTEA   Intermodel Surface Transportation Efficiency Act
MOCD   Mayor's Office of Community Development
NEA   National Endowment for the Arts
NECIP   Northeast Corridor Improvement Project
NEH   National Endowment for the Humanities
P&W   Providence and Worcester Railroad
PASS   People Against Stadium Shenanigans
PBA   Public Building Authority
PILOT   Payment in Lieu of Taxes
PPAC   Providence Performing Arts Center

PPG	Providence Place Group
PPS	Providence Preservation Society
PRA	Providence Redevelopment Agency
R&D	research and development
RIC	Rhode Island College
RIDOT	Rhode Island Department of Transportation
RIEDC	Rhode Island Economic Development Council
RIHPHC	Rhode Island Historical Preservation and Heritage Commission
RIPA	Rhode Island Port Authority
RISD	Rhode Island School of Design
RISDIC	Rhode Island Share and Deposit Indemnity Corporation
SOM	Skidmore, Owings and Merrill
SWAP	Stop Wasting Abandoned Property
TIF	tax increment financing
UDAG	Urban Development Action Grants
URI-CCE	University of Rhode Island College of Continuing Education
VMAPA	Veterans Memorial Auditorium Preservation Association

Acknowledgments

Many people have contributed to the development of this book. The encouragement we received from Bob Gormley at Northeastern University Press came at just the right time. The staff, including Ann Twombly, Angela Dombroski, and copy editor Lori Rider, have been remarkable. The early comments and encouragement of Tim Hennessey at the University of Rhode Island (URI) and Bill Hudson at Providence College were greatly appreciated, as were the insights of Scott Simoneau and Bill Coughlin.

The Rhode Island College (RIC) community fully supported our efforts and we thank our faculty colleagues Victor Profughi, Chet Smolski, Milburn Stone, John Perrotta, and Laurence Weil for their reading, comments, and interviews at various times. The RIC Faculty Research Fund provided some financial assistance. RIC photographer Gordon Rowley and assistant David Cranshaw were always available to come up with a last-second photograph. Charles Allsworth helped us create innumerable photograph files on CD-ROMs. Marlene Lopes was gracious enough to allow us to use the elegant Special Collections Archive room at RIC's Adams Library for interviews. Kim Reynolds helped move paper along. Early on Marcia Marker Feld and Gayla Gazerro of the URI Urban Field Center and David Smith Winsor encouraged the idea for a book on Providence, as did John R. Mullin of the University of Massachusetts. A special note of thanks is given to all of our students who asked questions and wrote papers that helped us shape the book.

The following individuals also deserve mention: Daniel Brown (Office of the Governor); Mark Brown (Rhode Island Statewide Planning Program); Gary Calvino and Thomas Payne (WaterFire Providence, Inc.); Jennaca Davies (William D. Warner, Architects and Planners); Phyllis A. Ferreira (Office of Municipal Affairs); Robert Godin (Rhode Island Division of Taxation); Glenn Helliwell (Rhode Island Department of Labor and Training); Christopher Ise (Providence Department of Planning and Development); Peter Marino (Rhode Island Public Expenditure Council); Deborah Melino-Wender (Capital Center Commission); Alden Raine (DMJM Harris, Inc.); Jim Savage (Rhode Island

Office of Municipal Affairs); Gwenn Starn (Rhode Island State Archives); Tim Tyrrell (Office of Tourism, University of Rhode Island); and Rhode Island oral historian Linda Wood.

The book would not have been possible without the cooperation of everyone we interviewed on multiple occasions: Governors J. Joseph Garrahy and Bruce Sundlun; senatorial aides Kenneth Payne (Senator Claiborne Pell) and Keith Lang (Senator John Chafee); former mayor Joseph R. Paolino Jr.; William E. Collins (policy director for Mayor Vincent A. Cianci Jr.); Patricia McLaughlin (legal counsel and chief of staff for Mayor Vincent A. Cianci Jr.); former Providence Foundation directors Kenneth Orenstein and Romolo "Ron" Marsella; Daniel Baudouin (executive director, the Providence Foundation); Edward "Ted" Sanderson (director of the Rhode Island Historical Preservation and Heritage Commission); Joseph DiStefano (former president of Capital Properties); James R. Capaldi (director of Rhode Island Department of Transportation); retired Rhode Island administrators Joseph Arruda (assistant director of planning, Rhode Island Department of Transportation) and Edward Wood (director of Department of Environmental Management and Department of Transportation); Gordon Hoxie (retired federal transportation administrator, Federal Highway Administration); Samuel Shamoon (Providence Department of Inspections and Standards); Thomas Deller (Providence Department of Planning and Development); architects William D. Warner, AIA, and Friedrich St. Florian, AIA; Barnaby Evans (WaterFire); Richard Oster (former chair, Rhode Island Convention Center Authority); David Brussat (*Providence Journal* editorial board member and columnist "Dr. Downtown").

Foreword

Rhode Island College Professors Francis J. Leazes Jr. and Mark T. Motte have written a very important and detailed record of the greatest period of development for the city of Providence, Rhode Island. In the period from 1976 to 1994, a time during which we served as governor for a total of twelve years, the city was literally transformed. The litany of successful projects is familiar to many: renovating the Biltmore Hotel; rehabilitating the Loews Theater as the Providence Performing Arts Center; constructing three new bank buildings; creating Capital Center (seventy-plus acres of land) by moving railroad tracks and tearing down the local "Chinese Wall," a railroad embankment that cut through the heart of the city; opening and expanding university campuses; building the Rhode Island Convention Center and Westin Hotel; developing the Providence Place mall; and—certainly the most dramatic aesthetic moment—rediscovering and opening up the Providence rivers and waterfront, inspiring the nationally renowned WaterFire displays. How these and other projects came to fruition is chronicled in detail in this book.

In our opinion none of what has been called the "Providence renaissance" would have happened without the existence of a group of business leaders, including the heads of the state's four major banks plus Textron, the Providence Journal Company, and the Outlet Company, working collaboratively with public representatives, including governors, mayors, the state's congressional delegation, top administrators, architects, and creative developers. Looking back, it is amazing that business leaders, politicians, and bureaucrats could produce the stunning buildings and parks that are now part of the downtown landscape. The media—local, regional, and national—have nominated Providence as one of the most desirable cities in the United States in which to live and work. None of this would have come to pass without sustained cooperation between key leaders in both the private and public sectors working with a talented group of Rhode Island artists, architects, and developers. Their collective vision has physically and functionally transformed the city.

As former governors we are both grateful to all those whose contributions made Providence's redevelopment a reality. We are both thankful to Professors Leazes and Motte for their work. Everyone who is interested in the dynamics that have shaped American cities in recent decades and, in particular, the success story of Providence should read this book.

J. Joseph Garrahy
Bruce Sundlun
Former Governors, State of Rhode Island

Introduction

On the evening of 23 August 2003, thousands of people from all across New England and far beyond gathered together in downtown Providence to walk the city streets, enjoy the balmy night air, and exchange pleasantries with strangers. A decade earlier you would have been hard put to find even a dozen people walking downtown on a Saturday night. Back then not a single person would have believed that such a dramatic transformation was about to bloom over this somewhat forlorn, industrial city sandwiched between the powerhouses of Boston and New York.

That August night in 2003, the Bruner Foundation honored the city of Providence with the 2003 Rudy Bruner Silver Award for Urban Excellence—a prestigious national award given in recognition of the city's resurgence and its success in the complex process of urban placemaking. That night the glowing golden light of one hundred blazing bonfires reflected off the surfaces of three restored riverways and illuminated the renovated granite stonework of the river walks and the city's historic buildings. The Providence Place mall was bustling with commercial activity not seen downtown in decades. The Bajnotti Fountain was once again resplendent in Burnside Park, now accompanied by elegant contemporary sculpture, a handsome ice-skating rink, and a modern intermodal transportation center. The hotels and restaurants were packed, and the music in the air was mixed with the fragrant scent of cedar smoke from WaterFire. Cape Verdean Capoeira flashed on Union Plaza, swing dancers crowded the financial district, fire dancers balanced above the dark water, and six thousand people received colorful origami cranes or flowers. The contrast to the Providence of a generation before was profound.

The noted Providence-based architect Friedrich St. Florian, in his address to the Transforming Providence conference on 22 November 2000, captured the decline and the despair that previously characterized the city and the stunning recovery that is under way:

During my thirty-seven years in and out of Providence I witnessed the closure of its movie palaces, the closure of its department stores, and the closure of the last food market downtown. When the venerable Biltmore Hotel closed its doors and was boarded up, the old city was ready to die.

The renaissance that we have good reasons to celebrate today occurred outside the boundaries of the old city core. Good things have many fathers, and indeed the Providence renaissance has many authors.

It was the city's fortune to be too poor to suffer the insult of urban renewal that ravaged other American cities. Its remarkable stock of nineteenth-century and early-twentieth-century buildings were boarded up rather than leveled to make room for parking lots. The rage of urban renewal largely bypassed Providence.

Providence was one of the first cities in the nation literally to invent historic preservation. It was at the home of J. Carter Brown's parents on Benefit Street that one evening John Nicholas Brown and Antoinette Downing first discussed historic preservation as a tool of city planning that was to profoundly influence the course of the city's redevelopment efforts.

I also like to think that the evening of March 19, 1981, was another blessed moment. Three architects met at the Blue Point Oyster Bar for after-work cocktails. That evening, the future of Providence was contemplated and on a linen napkin the idea of the river relocation was born and manifesto-like confirmed by the signatures of the authors. That night a full moon was shining upon Providence.

One of those architects, William Warner, went home and set into motion what arguably became the cornerstone of Providence's renaissance: the restoration and relocation of its rivers. Later, upon its completion, Barnaby Evans created the crowning achievement of this historic enterprise—and WaterFire Providence became the symbol for a reborn city.

Providence, Rhode Island, has much to celebrate, and our current successes stem in part from seeds planted over the centuries: from the energy of our many excellent colleges, from the beauty of our architectural heritage, from a respect for art and craftsmanship brought here by immigrants from many lands, and from the tolerance and mutual respect we inherited from the state's founder, Roger Williams. But in this book, Francis Leazes and Mark Motte rightly focus on the past twenty-five years as a period of dramatic resurgence.

The Rudy Bruner Award for Urban Excellence was given to Providence in recognition of "The Providence River Relocation Project: Creating a Place for Community and Art." In organizing the Bruner Foundation application I had the privilege of meeting many of the people involved in rebuilding Providence, and I came to a deep appreciation of the truth of Friedrich's words—the city's renewal has indeed had many authors. *Providence, the Renaissance City* chronicles the many people whose vision, creativity, hard work, cooperation, and leadership made possible the rebirth of Providence.

Twenty-five years ago the downtown we see today would have been almost unrecognizable. The photographs on the pages that follow dramatically show the vast wasteland of train sidings, parking lots, and raised track beds that characterized downtown Providence from the 1940s to the 1980s. These blemishes have now been replaced with Capital Center, Station Park, a new train station, an upscale shopping mall, hotels, and restaurants. The notorious Suicide Circle, with its frenzied traffic and one of the widest bridges in the world, has been replaced with a graceful series of parks with quiet walkways lining the three rivers that used to pass unseen beneath rusted traffic overpasses. Empty department stores now house lively universities, and commercial activity has returned to downtown at Providence Place, where a dramatic, multistory glass atrium spans both the river and the railroad, linking the State House to the "old downtown." A new airport, the Convention Center, and hotels welcome visitors from afar, and our downtown parks host the International Convergence Arts Festival, which fills them with sculpture, theater, and music.

In this book you will learn that the accomplishments achieved in Providence are exemplary for many reasons. They embody creative and imaginative solutions within an urban vision of ambitious scale. There is a consistent commitment to excellence of design and the inclusion of art, informed by an engaged dialogue with all sectors of the community. Providence avoided the interim "quick fix" that was characteristic of so many American cities. Instead, we have dared to pursue a vision, embarking on long-term solutions with the civic-minded support of our citizens, institutions, and political and business leadership.

In their analysis of the Providence renaissance, Professors Leazes and Motte acknowledge that, while Providence still has problems to tackle, we are approaching them with fresh energy, with rekindled pride, and with renewed resolve—and, as I like to say, perhaps with a hint of cedar in the air.

Barnaby Evans
WaterFire Providence

Preface

During the mid-1990s the plastic surgeon Dr. Sydney Hansen left Los Angeles and went home to Providence. At first she did so reluctantly, but soon she realized that her roots meant more to her than doing facelifts for the stars. She reunited with her family, fell in love with her old haunts, made friends, and practiced family medicine at a community clinic somewhere in less affluent Providence. Like Dorothy (and E.T.), she had found home.

Of course, Sydney Hansen was just a television character brought to life by actress Melina Kanakaredes, who captured in her role the yearning felt by many Americans: a desire for belonging, roots, and an authentic place to call home. The writers and producers of NBC's *Providence* presented a dreamy image of a city "back east," complete with perpetual autumn colors, rowers on rivers, and colonial facades. The TV version of Providence was a city one could hardly imagine Dr. Hansen having left in the first place. Los Angeles—what was she thinking?

The metaphor of a movie (Providence has appeared in several films in recent years, including such disparate delights as *There's Something about Mary*, *Amistad*, and *Federal Hill*) or television series is a useful one in understanding New England's renaissance city. Urban rebirth is appearance and substance, image and reality. One of the many Providence residents who spoke to us for this book said he felt as if he was living and working on a movie set. Everything was being transformed around him. It almost looked too good to be real. He feared that if he looked too closely he would find that the entire set was being supported by two-by-fours, as were innumerable towns in Old West movies. Like many professionals living and working in the downtown, he wondered as we drove from Boston in snarled Southeast Expressway traffic whether the so-called Providence renaissance amounted to anything more than smoke and mirrors; if you scratched the surface of the shiny domes, white cupolas, and graceful river walks, the grit and grime of the industrial age would be revealed once again. Is Providence a real renaissance city or just a Rust Belt city with an elegant postmodern veneer?

Our investigation into the politics and policies of urban transformation in Providence was driven by similar questions: What is an urban renaissance, how does it start, and can it be sustained? All around Providence are New England cities whose downtowns have decayed, despite brave efforts to "save" them. In the neighboring states of Connecticut and Massachusetts, Bridgeport, Hartford, New Haven, Waterbury, Springfield, and Worcester experienced incipient urban decline. But here in Providence we saw that something tangible was changing for the better and wondered why.

Providence was different. Unlike many of its sister cities in the northeastern United States, Rhode Island's state capital was spared the wholesale redevelopment of its downtown core in the postwar period. The federal highways did cut off the inner ring of the city from its neighborhoods, but instead of ripping out the guts of the city using urban renewal money, successive Providence city administrations merely allowed deindustrialization to play out before their eyes. Through a combination of pandering to ward constituencies over downtown interests and a type of passive inattention by mayors and their appointees, downtown Providence weathered the vagaries of urban renewal by keeping its physical fabric virtually intact. The nineteenth-century commercial architecture was certainly obsolete, but it survived until trends toward adaptive reuse took hold in the 1980s. An emerging urban historic preservation movement, which became a national model, ensured that authenticity and integrity of facades and streetscapes would play a strong role in the design motifs adopted for the renaissance to come. Still, its rivers and waterfront were virtually nonexistent by 1980, and abandoned railroad yards, tracks, and sidings were a dominant feature of downtown Providence, as any passerby on I-95 could attest.

So how did this city of covered rivers, cut up by rails and roads, abandoned in large measure by droves of its residents, come to be the renaissance city? That's what compelled us to write this book. Good ideas and opportunities stimulated leadership within the public and private sectors, leading to projects that have been labeled renaissance policy. Good fortune plays a role, but it is to some degree a self-made good fortune. Providence was able to take advantage of opportunities because many people who gave some thought to the future were committed to staying in the city.

Which brings us to former mayor Vincent A. "Buddy" Cianci Jr. No prefatory comments about the Providence renaissance would be complete without reference to Buddy. We have been asked many times during our research for this book if the story of Providence's renaissance is predominantly the story of this flamboyant mayor, who was perhaps the most dominant individual on the Providence political landscape from 1974 to 2002. Cianci was an ebullient mayor whose high-profile appearances on the *Today Show* and *Imus in the Morning* during the 1990s reinforced his carefully crafted persona of the quick-witted, affable rogue who saved a city.

Everyone in Providence, it seems, has a favorite Cianci anecdote, and we heard many—some humorous, some troubling—in our interviews and just by being residents of the city. Since most are unverifiable we do not dwell on them in the book. Cianci was a civic booster who almost single-handedly marketed the city and served as the bellwether for its population's burgeoning collective self-esteem during the 1990s and the first years of the twenty-first century. Buddy stood for Providence's spirit of renewal. In 2001 he said, "We have moved more than railroad tracks and rivers. We have moved the heart and soul of an entire city."[1]

The political career of Buddy Cianci is a colorful one, and he was proud to accept the accolades that came his way for the renaissance of Providence. (Mike Stanton, a journalist for the *Providence Journal*, has written an informative, enjoyable biography of Cianci titled *The Prince of Providence*.) Unfortunately, and tragically to some, Cianci's career and reputation foundered on the rocks of a conviction related to civic corruption and bribe taking by members of his administration under the federal RICO statutes. He currently is serving a sentence in a federal penitentiary in New Jersey.

But Buddy Cianci, for all of his deal making and ebullient spirit, is *not* the story of the Providence renaissance. His was a very important role, but in several important ways it was secondary to the parts played by others. A number of individuals at different times can lay claim to being just as important to the Providence renaissance story. If "saving cities" was done by electing colorful mayors, the answer to how to start and sustain an urban renaissance would be quite simple: elect the right person as mayor.

We have found that what matters is ideas around which a consensus is formed among government, business, and residents, perhaps years in advance—ideas that finally get the chance to be tried out because an opportunity presents itself in the form of change in the political or economic environment. We found that temporary coalitions are important to Providence, as is the terrier-like persistence of public and private officials to get projects completed. These officials need not be in the public eye. In many ways the Providence renaissance is about the creativity and dedication of career civil servants and appointed officials as much as elected ones, although two elected individuals, former U.S. senators Claiborne Pell and John Chafee, deserve much more attention than they have received to date in the story of the Providence renaissance. The convergence of talent in Providence and the state, motivated by *civitas*, by a chance to use professional expertise, by profit, or by electoral success, is unmistakable.

We see the Providence renaissance as an unfinished policy agenda. The

2003–4 municipal budget had a projected deficit of $59 million, a gap that faced the city's new mayor, David Cicilline. A politician not tied to city hall in the past, Cicilline took the oath of office in January 2003 in the wake of the corruption scandals and continual fiscal crisis that plagued city hall under Cianci. With a slowed pace of development in the downtown, a stagnant property tax base, and neighborhood activists claiming that the neighborhoods have been neglected in favor of downtown glitz, his policy agenda is full. Yet another wave of private and public consultant reports (nothing new to Providence) has blitzed the policy environment decrying the fiscal, economic, and social state of the city. We, too, assess these aspects of the state of the city, but we do so within the context of the decades of work creating the Renaissance City.

One last point: We made no a priori assumption that indeed a Providence renaissance has occurred. The city's appearance has changed. There is a different "feel" to the city. We encountered many former residents who have returned and remarked, "We just can't believe it," or words to that effect. At a recent political science convention in Providence we encountered a 1973 Brown alumna who had not returned to the city since that date, took a bus in, got off at the bus terminal, and thought she was in the wrong city! Still, the question remained for us: Has the emphasis been placed on image over substance? In the end do we have a wonderful backdrop for TV shows and movies, but not yet the underlying conditions that promote economic growth? In this book we take the reader through how Providence got to where it is, those elements associated with change, and the lessons we have taken from this experience. We keep in mind, though, one cautionary note on the ephemeral nature of "image": In 2003 *Providence* the TV series was canceled.

Providence: A Renaissance City by Accident or by Design?

In every period when civilization has achieved a kind of homogeneity,
the city is the most revealing physical expression of the social and political
realities of the age.

F. Roy Willis, *Western Civilization: An Urban Perspective*, vol. 2 (1981)

Small opportunities are often the beginning of great enterprises.

Demosthenes

I was the ugliest girl in Providence, Rhode Island.

Lola in *Damn Yankees* (1955)

A Smudge, a Fire on the Rivers, a Renaissance

■ Until very recently it would have been hard to imagine that the national
media would bother to mention the gritty New England city of Providence,
Rhode Island, at all, not the capital city of a state once identified as a "smudge" on
the side of the fast lane from New York to Cape Cod.[1] Rather than the "destination city" for tourists and business people it aspired to become, Providence was
the embodiment of Gertrude Stein's urban lament upon reaching Oakland, California, in 1947: "When you get there, there is no there, there!"

Stein and others during the last half century bemoaned the demise of the
North American city, their pessimism well founded.[2] Central cities suffered
losses in jobs, population, capital, buildings, housing, and prestige. Cars, the
movement of capital abroad, the competition from suburbs and their mythic
"Mayberry" dream, struggling schools, high taxes, crime, and racial and class ten-
sions contributed significantly to the perception and reality of an urban economic and social decline. David Rusk's *Cities without Suburbs*, John Norquist's *The
Wealth of Cities*, and many others point to a general social implosion within cities
characterized by middle-class flight, disparities of income between city dwellers
and suburbanites, the loss of jobs and businesses, and a pervasive general blight.[3]

Yet there is hope. Nowhere is that hope more loudly proclaimed than in

Providence, Rhode Island. Decades after Bette Midler sang here and left, proclaiming it "the pits," Providence claims to be experiencing renewal, revitalization, reinvention—in a word, renaissance. *Money* magazine buried the "smudge" image in December 2000 by naming Providence the best place to live in the East.[4] From his seat in city hall Vincent A. "Buddy" Cianci Jr., the city's longest-serving mayor, proudly proclaimed Providence as the "Renaissance City." He enthusiastically hosted community leaders from around the nation, in this, the city where in 1974 monkeys that had escaped from the decrepit Roger Williams Zoo roamed the city streets. As Cianci described it: "My first night there were animals running all over the city. I'm not kidding. Friggin' monkeys running across the city. Factories were closing, people were moving out and the roads were falling apart. It sucked."[5] Today that same zoo is nationally renowned. The completed downtown river relocation project has won architectural awards, including the International Downtown Association's Award of Merit and the National Endowment for the Arts Presidential Award for Design Excellence.

Were he alive today Roger Williams, who founded the city in 1636, could stand on the banks of the newly reclaimed Moshassuck River at the national memorial marking the site of his homestead and respond to the Narragansett sachem's "What news, Netop [friend]?" by saying, "We got a hit network television series!" NBC televised five seasons of a popular series entitled simply *Providence*. The title sequence and location shots revealed an elegant New England city replete with brick sidewalks, Victorian wrought-iron streetlights, and elegant colonial architecture. Those location shots, and some of the scenes actually filmed in Providence, appear to have been captured on film with sepia gauze filters at the peak of fall colors when the crimson and bronze leaves along Blackstone Boulevard are truly breathtaking.

If there is a "comeback city," then Providence seems to fit the bill.[6] The public relations excitement and pace of projects in the city of the Providence-born showman George M. Cohan are dizzying. No project seems too small or too large. In his 1995 *Downcity Plan* written for Providence, the renowned Florida-based architect and urban planner Andres Duany predicted a downtown renaissance. Duany praised innovative urban design and public works "infrastructure" projects that included moving not one but two rivers, reconfiguring roads and bridges, and eliminating elevated railroad tracks as activities that would lure private investment back into the traditional downtown core. Constructing a large downtown urban mall, building a convention center/hotel complex, and encouraging many other hotels and retail and commercial projects are part of the Providence renaissance. Land taking and clearance have begun to make way for the moving of a federal interstate highway to free up acres of prime waterfront property. A tax-friendly arts and entertainment zone has been created. A new train station to greet high-speed rail service, an outdoor skating rink rivaling Rockefeller Center's, new downtown loft apartments for artists, and a gondola service on the relocated rivers are amenities the city now offers. The reclaimed rivers are set afire, not by chemicals or other toxins but as the central moment in a work of public art dubbed WaterFire, which has achieved national artistic recognition for its creator, the local artist Barnaby Evans, and for Providence. There was even talk of an urban canal project, presumably to increase the fledgling gondola fleet. And there is much, much more. The extent of the physical transformation of Providence is best understood by viewing the city itself as it was and as it is today.

Before and after the renaissance: A stunning physical and functional transformation of the transportation network and land use pattern, overlooking the railroads and Memorial Boulevard.

Courtesy of Rhode Island Department of Transportation (Before) and WaterFire Providence (After)

Somewhere woven among these projects, mayoral civic boosterism, and the imaginative and whimsical plot lines of a television series is a compelling story of a city's attempts to redefine itself as it had done many times before in its history. Once agrarian, then maritime, then industrial, and now—well, evolving—Providence is not a stranger to change. Whether the city will be successful is a concern for the future. How it has gone about achieving its renaissance is of interest now.

The excitement of the self-proclaimed renaissance of Providence begs for answers to two general questions. First, what is an urban renaissance, and how does it start and sustain itself? Second, has all the effort made a difference for the well-being of the city, or is it all just a massive case of civic cheerleading, good salesmanship, marketing, or, worse, the self-aggrandizing or enriching behavior of a privileged few? The goal of this book is to answer those questions. Our contribution to an understanding of urban America lies in this intersection of the genesis of a renaissance, the expression of it through multiple projects, and the actual measurement of change in the city's fortunes.

Defining an Urban Renaissance

To historians, the Renaissance is the period between the fifteenth and seventeenth centuries that saw the revival in Europe of classical influences in literature, art, architecture, and design. During the Renaissance Western civilization literally emerged from the chaos and anti-intellectualism of the Dark Ages, a time when knowledge retreated into the inner sanctums of monasteries. This first great urban rebirth occurred at a time when Europe's religious and secular leaders could exploit emerging economic surpluses and relatively stable polities to consolidate their own power.

Cities became the canvases upon which bishops, kings, princes, and aristocrats celebrated their power and wealth through urban beautification projects and architectural grandeur. Entrenched residential poverty was overlooked in the scramble to build palaces, cathedrals, and monuments that would both impress and deter potential adversaries as well as consolidate dynasties. Michelangelo, Leonardo da Vinci, François Mansart, and other artists and architects were given unprecedented creative freedom by their patrons. Public art and urban design received patronage and funding on a scale not seen in Europe since the Roman Empire.

The contemporary term "urban renaissance" generally refers to the economic development policy of a particular locale fighting hard to reverse sometimes decades-long declines: their own Dark Ages. "Renaissances" are proclaimed on a seemingly regular basis. Baltimore's Mayor William Schaefer (1971–86) may have been the first chief executive of a large U.S. city to use the term "renaissance" to describe an urban rescue effort. The phrase "urban renaissance" accompanied the central business district projects and the attendant extensive civic boosterism in Los Angeles (First Interstate World Center), Miami (Bricknell Avenue: "the Wall Street of Latin America"), San Diego (Horton Plaza), New York (South Street Seaport and Battery Park City), and Detroit (Renaissance Center). High-end office, retail, and advanced business service sector renaissances were proclaimed in Boston (Faneuil Hall), Philadelphia (The Gallery at Market East), Milwaukee (Grand Avenue), and St. Louis (St. Louis Center).

The renaissance in these locales often focused on the central business district and the creation of festival marketplaces filled with boutiques, upscale restaurants, and specialty shops. Coordinated events on historical themes, activities, festivals, new permanent exhibits in museums and galleries, and public art and sculpture are basic renaissance activities. An office of tourism and conventions with a strong, image-making "sales pitch" ("I Love New York") and a "ringleader" mayor usually are associated with these urban rebirths. The attempt is to market the city as a product, a tourist attraction.[7]

The term "urban renaissance" is not lonely for companions: saving cities has been on the public agenda for a long time, it seems. *Urban renewal* has a long, sad history in the United States, stretching from the 1940s through the 1960s. The idea of using bulldozers to clear vast tracts of urban "wastelands" to make way for new projects had its heyday in the 1950s, leaving the cores of many cities as distant memories relegated to "Vanishing (fill in the name of the city)" coffee-table books.

Since then, however, efforts to revive cities have shied away from bulldozers and have focused more on financing and other forms of assistance to the private sector. An attempt at a renaissance might involve *urban regeneration* projects that are fast paced, entrepreneurial in focus, and designed for a "quick hit" to stimulate activity in the central business districts of cities. *Entrepreneurial planning* is a five-step recipe for urban change requiring municipal control over downtown parcels; site preparation and land renewal; confidence-building public-sector demonstration projects; development financing packages; and private and public-private projects to produce jobs and tax revenue. *Leveraged planning* emphasizes the need for public-sector financing to access private financing in difficult investment climates.

While useful, those descriptions and prescriptions fall short of a definition of "renaissance" that permits policy makers to judge when a city has been successful in achieving its development goals. We developed a concise definition of urban renaissance derived from nearly three decades of ideas contained in academic and practitioner writing on the subject of urban economic development, which we summarize in chapter 2. An urban renaissance is a sustained effort by private and public individuals, groups, and institutions that for a variety of reasons act to reverse urban physical, fiscal, economic, and social decline often brought on by forces outside their control. These collective efforts result in projects that when taken in the aggregate produce a measurable change in a city:

- The city's physical appearance improves—the canvas looks different;
- Enough revenue is generated to provide a satisfactory level of city service and the city remains solvent;
- Commercial and residential property values are stabilized and increased as the local economy improves;
- An improved economic environment promotes business retention and attracts new business; and
- City residents realize real jobs, changes in income, and an improved quality of life.

The end result is a "livable city."

Renaissance Policy in Providence

The Providence attempt at a renaissance is a three-decade-long story of sustained effort by individuals and organizations that refused to permit the city to fail physically, fiscally, economically, or socially by taking advantage of opportunities. Our central theme is that the set of activities associated with what is called the Providence renaissance evolved somewhat serendipitously and often hinged on critical events over which participants may have had little control but which they were well positioned to take advantage of decisively. In other words, Providence renaissance policy is to a large extent the product of the right people being in the right place at the right time with the right project idea.

The renaissance in Providence as it currently is perceived is not, however, a product of accident.[8] Plans were important, but no one plan was the driving force behind the renaissance. Many plans and reports written over the years contained ideas, some more important than others, whose execution became possible at opportune times. For example, moving railroad tracks was proposed in an urban renewal report in 1960, but the tracks were not moved until between 1982 and 1985. The reason and timing had nothing to do with urban renewal plans and everything to do with the persistence of a policy entrepreneur. In another instance, the Capital Center project that began in the late 1970s as a comprehensive plan to lure the financial industry to set up shop in an economically collapsing Providence evolved into the now more familiar attempt to rebuild the city on the collective backs of retail, arts and entertainment, and intellectual capital. This changed thinking stalled one part of Providence's renaissance in Capital Center, but it also led to a renewed effort to adapt the old core of the city into a place of high-end residences, higher education institutions, and arts and entertainment venues. However, without the assemblage of Capital Center the river projects most likely would never have been undertaken and the "smudge" image of Providence might never have been erased and replaced by its persona as an innovative, energetic city on the move with a new downtown symbolized by the Providence Place mall and a revitalized downcity. "Downcity" generally refers to the rectangular area in downtown Providence bounded by Empire, Dorrance, Sabin, and Pine Streets.

People were also significant, as leaders from the public and private sectors played critical roles at important times. The story of the Providence renaissance is filled with policy entrepreneurs, advocates willing to invest their time, resources, and talents to promote a policy position in the hope of some future return. Often these entrepreneurs led community "elites" to see an idea through to conclusion. In many instances those elites could not spring into action until something else in the project environment occurred. While certainly profit and election credit were important motivators for some, often it appeared that a sense of *civitas* in both the public and private actors took hold, at least for many of the projects that came on line. Civil servants as often as not played key roles in successful projects.

Organizations were important as rallying points for individual and group stakeholders; as idea incubators; as financing vehicles; and as mechanisms for airing differences concerning projects and the politics surrounding them. These organizations sometimes were highly visible and at other times were barely detectable. Some organizations remained active throughout the renaissance period, while others came and went with projects.

These plans, people, and organizations interacted in ways that made it difficult to discern a uniform approach to renaissance policy formation over the decades. However, five factors associated with successful Providence Renaissance projects became conspicuous.

(1) Accidents of location, economics, and policy often produced markets and money to sustain a project.

(2) The ability of public- and private-sector elites and organizations to mobilize rapidly when an opportunity to undertake a renaissance-advancing project appeared was an important characteristic.

(3) The formation of "contingent coalitions," temporary, shifting alliances in support of a project with the ability to sustain cooperation over the life of longer projects, was ever present.

(4) Dedicated, tenacious individuals—policy entrepreneurs—who believed strongly in their "good ideas" and could sustain momentum and act as policy advocates were a constant presence.

(5) The importance of the federal-state-local intergovernmental financial system in sustaining urban economic development cannot be minimized.

Measuring an Urban Renaissance

Despite the excitement and the plethora of projects associated with the concept of urban renaissance, practitioners and academics still struggle to define what specifically characterizes a successful urban renaissance. How does a locale know when it actually has experienced change in more than its image? The focus still remains on the prescription to save cities rather than on the fiscal, economic, or social outcomes of urban revitalization efforts.[9] Using our definition as a guide, we gathered from many sources more than a decade's worth of information that helped gauge the actual physical, fiscal, economic, and social changes that have occurred in Providence as renaissance activities unfolded. In that way we could judge whether the multiple public and private projects conceived and implemented over an extended period of time actually were associated with a measurable change in the city's physical, fiscal, economic, and social welfare—that is, whether the Providence renaissance whole is greater than the sum of its individual parts.

The results to date are mixed. The city's central business district, the focus of much of the renaissance physical activity, clearly is improved architecturally and aesthetically, and commercial retailing has returned to Providence. The identity of the old retail section of downtown Providence is still unclear, although this area is increasingly dominated by higher education institutions; arts and entertainment and tourism; a fledgling growth of residential living; and perhaps by some as yet unidentified possibility. The city's fiscal health remains uncertain even as some indicators point to an improved city economy. There is still a considerable distance to go before the welfare of all its citizens realizes the promise of renaissance policy.

What is unmistakable is the impression that changes have occurred in Providence. The many events that create crowds in the city, the ever-present college students, the new look, and the increased population of immigrants bringing to Providence a renewed ethnic flavor and political impact also are part of this renaissance. A walk through the food court at the Providence Place mall, apparently the new community gathering place on any weekend of the year, is clear testament that something positive has changed in Providence.

Why Study Providence?

In urban case studies such as ours there will always be claims of exceptionalism—that the city is unique, so that what is learned is not generalizable to other places. As Massey (1996) suggests, "when the particularities of place are well accounted for, case study results are more genuinely transferable to other locales."[10] Clearly the type of political regime and the characteristics of local policy environments in U.S. cities can provide endless permutations of economic development policies that defy easy classification. However, for several reasons Providence as a case study in economic development provides an excellent opportunity to examine the processes and policies associated with an urban renaissance and to examine ways of measuring the various impacts of those policy decisions. Some of those reasons point to Providence as representative of mainstream urban America, while others point to Providence as unique.

The first reason to pay attention to the Providence story is that many features familiar to students of contemporary urban America are present in the city. Providence is not an exceptional city somehow free from urban difficulties. The frenzy of renaissance activity took place against the backdrop of a struggle to cope with a declining tax base, entrenched poverty, school funding woes, and continuing challenges to its traditional economic base. Further, for many years Providence was considered a bastion of patronage and corruption.[11]

Second, with a highly diverse population of more than 170,000, Providence is a "medium-sized" city by the U.S. Bureau of the Census definition, making the lessons from a case study of Providence potentially more generalizable to the majority of urban places in the United States. Case studies of larger cities such as New York, Los Angeles, and Chicago undoubtedly are important to understand, but the scale of most cities in the United States tends to be much smaller.

The Providence story also offers insight into the continued important role that intergovernmental relations plays in contemporary urban revival. A state-city "alliance," not always cordial, not always successful, but always in place, accompanied and at times superimposed itself on a pattern of constantly shifting, project-specific, public-private partnerships. Federal assistance is evident everywhere in the Providence renaissance story. In the late 1970s an alliance of city, state, and national officials was mobilized, allowing the city to access vast sums of federal money just when municipalities across the nation were experiencing a withdrawal of federal aid.

A fourth reason to study Providence in detail is that, as is the case of the many other proclaimed urban renaissance areas, Providence's redevelopment effort was led by the public sector and remained so until quite recently. Hundreds of millions of dollars in public planning and expenditure occurred before a single private investment dollar was realized. Public money was invested, among other projects, in the construction and realignment of streets, bridges, lights, sewers, and highway interchanges and on- and off-ramps; State House ground work; the creation of a new urban park; and the building of a new train station to welcome travelers on the newly upgraded electrified commuter train system.

While proactive private elite and business-sector involvement was evident, more aggressive forms of private-sector activity have yet to emerge. No privately financed office building has broken ground in downtown Providence since the 1980s, despite all of the renaissance activity. The lack of willingness of national private lenders to finance hotel construction is holding up no fewer than three hotel projects in Providence, even though numbers show that Providence does not have enough hotel beds to support demand.

Another significant reason to study Providence nationally is the lessons it contains about the potential for exploiting natural resources within the built environment—in this case uncovering and relocating rivers. With the possible exception of San Antonio, Texas, few other urban resuscitation efforts in the United States have depended to such a great extent on moving and refocusing on urban natural resources. Providence's massive relocation of railroad tracks clearly can instruct others about the ability of large-scale infrastructure projects to yield "virgin" land. The area became a relatively clean slate of more than seventy-five acres, allowing additional renaissance activities to be proposed and debated. As a result of these land development efforts, Providence has redeveloped almost a third of the entire downtown area as a viable alternative to the older downcity commercial core. This approach stands in contrast to many local economic development efforts in underutilized but densely built-up central business districts.[12]

In the early 1990s the city's infamous Suicide Circle made way for the uncovered and relocated river channels as well as a much-improved system of roads and bridges.

Courtesy of Rhode Island Department of Transportation (Before) and Thomas Payne, WaterFire Providence (After)

The Providence renaissance story has a duality about it. The city has built in increments a partial "tourist bubble,"[13] with a mall and a convention center. The area possesses a historic and entertainment theme centered on its rivers, especially when WaterFire is lit. However, the effort to build a professional football stadium collapsed, there is massive resistance to a casino, and building hotels has proven to be a formidable, at times futile undertaking. Instead, the current hope for a sustained renaissance lies on some combination of higher education; retail; arts, entertainment, and tourism; health services; and a general "style" of urban living downtown: elegant and ethnic, vibrant and stable.

Central to the Providence story is that over three decades a remarkably steady set of public, quasi-public, and private institutions and actors have played key roles in these activities. During the prime redevelopment phase (1980–2000), well-forged alliances among private sector individuals and organizations and local, state, and federal appointed and elected officials materialized. The idea of a renaissance was firmly implanted among these various actors. While they might not all have agreed on a single "vision" and perhaps had differ-

ent motivations, there was enough combined strength in these alliances to bring some projects to fruition. Opponents emerged not because they opposed revitalization, but because their idea of renewal was different.

Providence's economic development efforts can be differentiated functionally from mainstream urban economic redevelopment policy. The city was spared the worst vagaries of federal urban renewal and slum clearance programs of the 1950s and 1960s that typified other similarly sized New England cities such as Hartford, Connecticut, and Worcester, Massachusetts. However, Providence faced the challenge of developing a central area of the city that for nearly a century was devoid of buildings. Roads and railroad tracks, dirt parking lots, and covered rivers occupied the land as a result of history, and, to a certain extent, of fifty years of private disinvestments compounded by policy neglect from both city hall and the State House.[14]

A last reason to study the Providence renaissance is that the geography and the time periods for redevelopment are clearly delineated over a twenty-five-year period, a convenient crucible for analyzing the hows, whys, and wherefores of the policies that were enacted. A "pre-renaissance" phase occurred between 1970 and 1980, when a long-dreamed-about project of local planners and public and private civic boosters became possible with a change in federal transportation and energy policy. Dormant plans and wish lists began to look promising as a way to reverse the city's noticeable decline. Sources of public and private capital became available. The right local people seemed in place at the right time to help the city. After this initial phase, infrastructure projects dominated the policy stage between 1980 and 1990 and were followed after 1990 by more glamorous moments, for example, building of Providence Place, and a flirtation with the National Football League.

Lessons Learned

There are a number of important lessons taught by a study of Providence. These lessons begin with the realization that government can make a positive difference. Without the capital provided by the federal government (and the state, to a more limited degree) what is called the Providence renaissance would not have happened. The second, somewhat surprising, lesson is that government is often the entrepreneur—that is, government must take risks in order to lure the more conservative private sector into making renaissance investment decisions. A third lesson is that the Providence renaissance is the product of people who varied in their motivation, but that policy entrepreneurs were critically important to the successful completion of projects and to sustaining momentum. Whether by birth, by profession, or by a sense of obligation, a leadership elite who mostly lived in the city and was committed to the future of Providence surfaced to play important roles at varying times. A fourth lesson is that the activity leading to physical and aesthetic rebirth does not determine the meaning of success. While physically a city may change, ultimately a successful renaissance must be measured against positive fiscal, economic, and social changes that occur. The fifth lesson is that a renaissance is not a linear, planned event, or the product of a policy regime. More than a little luck and happenstance are involved: the right people with the right ideas are in the right place at the right time. The sixth lesson is that the ability of public- and private-sector elites and organizations to mobilize rapidly when an opportunity appears adds to likely renaissance project success, as long as these contingent coalitions are focused on well-vetted ideas where a consensus exists about the merit of any idea.

The Organization of the Book

Chapter 2 explains our theoretical framework. We pay special attention to competing ways of thinking about city development, including regime theory and an ideology of "privatism," the theory of elites, rationalism, and the importance of planning and policy making in what euphemistically is called the "garbage can." We also detail how we developed our definition of urban renaissance and the many observations of those who have studied urban economic development.

Chapter 3 is a narrative of Providence renaissance activities over nearly three decades. Many of the projects that came to fruition had their origins in plans, politics, and personalities within the eddy of Providence and Rhode Island politics that date back as far as the 1960s. The history, geography, demographics, and architecture of the city are sketched for obvious contextual reasons. The local economy and city government are similarly described. The chapter chronicles the relationship between city and state as well as Providence's history of financial difficulties.

Chapter 4 outlines the planning activities and efforts to physically rebuild the city. The local organizations, personalities, pre-renaissance plans, and early public-private endeavors most often associated with Providence renaissance projects are depicted. We differentiate between three types of project: fairly traditional projects where the hope is that private development will be lured by providing infrastructure and other amenities (moving railroads, building highway interchanges, and creating acres of land for Capital Center); endeavors that encourage further development, usually involving some city image-building element (the rediscovery of the rivers and waterfront); and projects that are expected to produce sustained, tangible economic benefits (the Providence Place mall and the Rhode Island Convention Center).

While we do not chronicle every project associated with the Providence renaissance, chapters 5 through 10 tell the story of endeavors that capture how the renaissance unfolded. Two projects—railroad relocation and the formation of Capital Center—are chronicled in chapter 5. The stories of three critically important projects, the highway interchange, river relocation, and the creation of an urban water park system, including Waterplace and its signature event, Water-Fire, are recounted in chapter 6. Chapters 7 through 9 contain the fifteen-year saga of the Providence Place mall as well as that of the recession-driven Conven-

The overall impact of the Capital Center and river relocation projects on downtown Providence is best revealed from the air. Between the mid-1960s and the mid-1990s the Rhode Island State House remained one of the few recognizable landmarks.

Courtesy of Providence Foundation (Before) and Capital Center Commission (After)

tion Center/Westin Hotel complex. Not all renaissance projects came to fruition. Chapter 10 narrates the failure to build a professional football stadium in Providence.

In each of the above cases we put individual projects under the microscope using the factors often utilized to analyze economic development projects: motives, expectations, impelling forces, and policy constraints. The full array of plans, financing mechanisms, administrative tools, and other arrangements that accompanied a renaissance undertaking are detailed in each chapter. For each type of endeavor we determine the amount of public and private investment. Policy constraints facing officials, government-business partnerships, varying levels of public participation, types of decision making, and conflict resolution processes are revealed.

The fiscal, economic, and political pressures to succeed are high and come from many sources. Motivations vary from project to project and even for undertaking the effort at all. The unitary interests of the city, including the need for elected officials to "claim credit," "get elected," "avoid blame," and "do something," are noted in some detail. The different outcomes sought by Providence and other public and private decision makers consistently reappear, primarily the desire for fiscal stability, improved income for residents, and jobs.

Chapter 11 answers the question whether fiscal, economic, and social changes occurred as the physical renaissance was under way. We constructed a series of trend analyses of the city's fiscal, economic, and social health covering the period 1987–2000. The chapter is thus a detailed "still life" of recent conditions of the city compared to those that existed in 1987, when the last property tax revaluation took place within Providence and when two seminal events in the renaissance were either completed or in progress: moving the railroads and rivers.

Chapter 12 first describes in summary terms what the Providence renaissance actually is and then goes on to explain in analytical terms how the Providence renaissance came to be in theory and practice. We then describe what is under way in Providence currently and how that meshes (or not) with what has characterized the Providence renaissance to date. Among those new efforts are the moving of I-195 to open the Providence waterfront to development; the ongoing attempts to renovate the Masonic Temple into a much-needed hotel; renewed downcity efforts to create a higher education and residential presence; high-end condominium projects outside both downtown and Capital Center; and other smaller undertakings. These projects may represent the real hope for a sustained and citywide renaissance by contributing to a change in fiscal, economic, and social indicators of success.

We also suggest policy elements that will be important for the city to consider as it continues its efforts to undergo a renaissance, including the emergence of new leadership elites, the formation of new coalitions, strategies for garnering resources, and a set of indicators of success. This concluding chapter contains a more detailed summary of the lessons we learned about urban public policy than outlined in the previous section of this chapter. The chapter concludes with a general assessment of the usefulness of the term "renaissance" in the modern urban context.

The fifteenth- through seventeenth-century Renaissance allowed the political and economic leadership to exploit economic resources and relatively stable polities to consolidate their own power. It provided a backdrop against which bishops, kings, princes, and aristocrats celebrated their power and wealth through beautification projects and architectural grandeur. It was in some ways a scramble to build palaces, cathedrals, and monuments to deter political adversaries and to consolidate dynasties while ignoring social ills. It also was a period during which artists and architects were given unprecedented creative freedom and public money by their patrons. Whether the contemporary American urban renaissance is a distant replay of the much earlier European Renaissance is an open question. Recent intense development activity in Providence provides an opportunity to help answer that question.

Machines, Elites, and the Garbage Can

2

It [the Providence renaissance] was the result of a convergence of ideas and money and people.

Joseph F. Arruda, Assistant Director for Planning, Rhode Island Department of Transportation, 1960–89

■ The Providence renaissance unfolded over a twenty-five-year period. That time span presents a challenge to anyone trying to explain the hows, whys, and wherefores of transforming a declining city into something fresh. Plans and projects, people and organizations, political and economic circumstances swirled together, sometimes guided by a "vision" and sometimes pushed forward by an immediate opportunity. To the extent that the Providence renaissance was a product of a comprehensive vision, that visualization had little chance of becoming a policy reality without a number of seemingly random events falling into place. The manners in which specific projects came to be pursued varied. Economic and political environments constantly shifted. Elaborate plans took unanticipated turns. Policy directions shifted. The policy actors, institutions, coalitions, plans, and financing tools had to demonstrate a high degree of flexibility over the decades-long time span.

Alternative frameworks for studying urban policy making are readily available for reaching an understanding of the way the city's rebirth found its way onto the policy agenda, how decisions were made, and which individuals, institutions, and circumstances were principally responsible for the projects associated with the renaissance. The dominance of elites; competition among groups; global capital mobility; the emergence of urban growth machines and urban regimes; and the unitary interests of city dwellers are sometimes competing, sometimes complementary theoretical explanations of how urban redevelopment takes place. The role of business, the variety of power relationships, and what actually makes it onto the policy agenda are three issues used to differentiate among these different policy explanations. We chose to apply what is inelegantly called policy making in the "garbage can" as a broad framework to study the Providence renaissance because, as we explain, the garbage can context does not preclude the presence of other policy-making explanations.

In this chapter we briefly go over the traditional explanations for the distribution of community power in urban settings, primarily the concepts of elites, pluralism, regimes, urban unitary interests, and the alleged dominance of global capital. We also describe the basic tenets of the rational, incremental, and institutional choice models of policy decisions. Taken together, these descriptions enable us to detail why in our view it is helpful to use the "garbage can" policy framework to understand twenty-five years of events and decisions that often hinged on circumstances outside the control of public- and private-sector decision makers and interested groups; where motivations to act varied considerably; and where results were sometimes successful, sometimes mixed, and sometimes out-and-out failures.

Elites and Group Competition for Community Power

Rhode Island's small geographic size and the relative ease with which policy makers come in contact with each other suggest the possibility that a well-organized *governing elite* could command urban policy. The classic governing elite is a small number of people drawn disproportionately from the upper strata of society who operate the major businesses and economic institutions in a community and who serve as opinion shapers. This *stratificationist* theory claims that elites are able to manipulate government to allocate resources in a way that serves their own agenda, thereby keeping power in their social and political spheres and insulating them from the general public's demands. Newcomers enter the elite slowly and only after the elite's basic values are accepted. The policy process is very incremental, designed to minimize threats to the existing social system.[1]

Pluralists counter that power is located in many different centers in a community, is not cumulative, and exists only when used by competing groups. These power centers may or may not overlap, and power in one arena does not necessarily lead to power in another. Pluralists argue that the role of business, varied power arrangements, and the ability to reach the decision agenda help define the differences between the elite theorists and pluralists.[2] In this context, the presence of national and international corporations, rather than locally owned companies, as key elements of a local business community and the variation of business sectors (utilities, financial, retail, etc.) in a given locale argue against a unified "business community." Further, business is not the only locus of power, because there are a wide variety of power arrangements in each community, those relationships can change over time, and differing groups are able to affect what decisions actually make it onto the decision agenda.

Urban Growth Machines and Global Capital

The elite and pluralist viewpoints are part of the discussions centering on the presence or absence of an "urban growth machine" and the role global capital plays in the fate of cities. As a conceptual umbrella, the theory of urban growth machines is well entrenched in the writing about cities. A growth regime is a system whereby local elites with substantial property holdings dominate community policy making, set the decision agenda, specify what is acceptable, make policy choices, and then see to it that implementation occurs. Individuals and institutions most favorably disposed to aggressive economic development try to lure investors and major corporations back to the central city and thereby guarantee the success of machine participants. Any property owner, large or small, whose holdings stand to increase in value readily joins the growth machine.[3]

In regime analysis growth is said to occur because local real estate owners and agents, downtown bankers, developers, property management firms, ad agencies, accountants, attorneys, construction unions, newspapers, philanthropic foundations, universities, and elected officials work together to produce development. These groups constitute governing coalitions that produce decisions with a favorable impact for the alliances. Success is measured by maximized return on the property they hold. For public officials the reward is electoral success, which is predicated on successful economic development.[4]

Urban growth regime analysis is based on an ideology of "privatism," which places local business at the center of local economic development politics. Urban areas become dependent on private business for jobs, income for residents, and adequate local revenue to provide public services without high tax burdens to residents. The assumption is that business dictates decisions or at least holds a privileged position in economic development activities, implying that public officials pursue policies that primarily benefit private business. Growth machine allies define economic development needs; persuade local officials to pursue certain projects; increase economic development activity; define sought-after outcomes; and constrain decision making. The deck is stacked in favor of business because information regarding the level of effort that is needed to maintain or attract a firm is in the hands of the private sector. Opposition is from weaker, less organized, and generally poorer and neighborhood-based individuals and organizations more concerned with the use of their property and neighborhood quality of life issues than with the economic exchange value of their property.[5]

The urban growth machine viewpoint differs from the more neo-Marxist view that the dominance of global capital is the determinant of urban fortunes in the United States. Cities are at a disadvantage because capital has proven to be mobile, making cities less competitive because they are built for labor-intensive industries that no longer exist. National and international corporations dictate the decisions localities will make as they pursue profits and exhibit less concern about local land use, except to the extent it has an impact on their corporate bottom line.[6]

Unitary Interests and Urban Regimes

The idea that business and political leaders and ordinary residents of a city have a *unitary interest* in protecting local business and attracting new investment capital to create new jobs is yet another view of the genesis of urban redevelopment. This theory does not view growth machines as driving economic development decisions but recognizes that it is in everyone's interest to ensure that the city succeeds economically.[7] Alternatively, Clarence Stone argues that there is no unitary interest of the public, elected officials, and business, but that elected officials are skilled at convincing voters that cities will benefit if an alliance between elected leaders and their appointees and pro-growth business is strong. Stone calls this an *urban regime of systemic power*. Mayors in particular want a successful economy and the prestige that comes with real and perceived success. So mayors are dependent on a pro-growth business elite for capital and jobs, and on voters to keep them in office.[8]

Institutional Choice, Rationalism, and Incrementalism

Choosing to use a particular agency structure, or financing arrangement, or set of regulations over another often has a subsequent impact on the policy outcome or results in favoring one interest over another. The *institutional choice* view is that institutions, structures, and rules and regulations to develop and implement policy are not neutral and help explain in part policy outcomes.[9] The political appointees and civil servants who have access to public funds, or who make regulations, or who are charged with implementation details can be as important to policy outcomes as are the more public "movers and shakers," because they can use their expertise to bridge the gap that often exists between concepts and the ability to bring a project to a successful conclusion.

The idea that self-interest is the motivating force in policy choices, that politics offers rational choice opportunities to maximize gains and avoid irrational, confused choices, weaves in and out of elite, pluralist, and regime theory analysis. Public choice theory springs from the view that government ought to create conditions that permit individuals to maximize their ability to make policy choices. Even the individual's choice of community is based on a rational calculation of personal costs and benefits. There is little room for the notion that while choices might result in individual benefit, decisions actually might be based more on a nonrational community of interests rooted in loyalty to place than on profit or return.[10]

That loyalty does not imply keeping the status quo. Almost by definition a city undertaking an aggressive urban redesign is not engaged in *incremental* policy making. Significant change would be hard to achieve in a policy environment where the expected outcome is little change from current conditions while holding dear existing consensus and past compromises. Incrementalism requires "give and take" or mutual adjustment by participants in the policy process as all parties try to reduce the uncertainty about the future consequences of their current actions.[11] Decisions can produce dramatic policy results, but the decision making itself can be the product of diverse motivations that are both incremental and rational in nature. That is, over many years, the motivations that undergird individual, group, and institutional decisions are varied and the results unpredictable.

Renaissance Making in the Garbage Can[12]

The rather inelegant "garbage can" policy framework offers a way to understand twenty-five years of renaissance decision making in Providence: how the renaissance appeared on the decision agenda; the way alternatives got specified; and ultimately why certain choices were made and then sometimes successfully implemented and sometimes not. The garbage can policy framework accommodates well what we came to view as the policy hallmark of the Providence renaissance: that when opportunities arose, the right people in the right place at the right time had what appeared to be the right idea and were willing to show the requisite amount of leadership to try to bring that idea to fruition. Motivations varied considerably, including the advancing of self-interests and profit, electoral success, professional ambition, and achieving legislative, executive, and administrative goals. But among many of the individuals who had to make decisions, a common, powerful (if unspoken), unifying theme of *civitas*, of doing the right thing for Providence, was clearly present over the decades. That theme emerges only through a comprehensive study of events rather than a focus on a single project or a series of plans.

In the garbage can, issues, politics, and policies sit in jumbled fashion alongside each other. Policy problems come to the attention of policy makers in various ways: statistical indicators; precipitous events; and attention-grabbing complaints, perhaps in the form of a government report or a best-selling book. Ideas originate, compete, evolve, prosper, and perish in unpredictable ways in a primordial soup. Ideas and alternatives, and their practicality, are pondered in think tanks, at conferences, at executive and legislative staff meetings, and in other public and private forums, and often appear in print somewhere. The vagaries of public sentiment and the ideological preferences of the public may shift, or elections may change the executive or legislative makeup. Specialist knowledge, new technology, fads, or gradually built ideas appear and disappear. Participants are from both within and outside government.

Then, somewhat serendipitously, issues, politics, and policy come together at opportune points and open a *policy window*, allowing interested participants to specify the alternatives that are chosen to address the suddenly available policy issue. All of the long periods of discussion, studies and reports, shelving of ideas, and consideration of more alternatives finally acquire a purpose, where at one time they were ignored or were not relevant to a policy choice. Political support gels in favor of a particular policy.

Despite the appearance of ambiguous, somewhat chaotic policy making, in the garbage can there is actually a great deal of focus on ideas and their likely success or failure. Extensive bargaining and conflict among competing interests does occur. Decisions are made when the right problem arises and when the right decision makers are receptive to an available solution at an opportune time. Policy makers and implementers develop the capacity to perform effective assessments of the political feasibility of their actions and the array of political forces shaping or curtailing various opportunities.

Policy entrepreneurs bring these streams of policies and processes together. These individuals can be found in many positions and places. They might be motivated by personal ambition, or by the opportunity to promote their values, or simply because they love "the game." Policy entrepreneurs share certain qualities. They may be experts who deserve to be listened to, or they may have an ability to speak for others or may be sitting in a position of authority. Another common characteristic is their political connections or negotiating skills. Most important of all, they are persistent, tenacious, and willing to spend enormous amounts of their own resources on the policy issue of importance to them.

As will become evident in this book, the concepts of a growth machine, an urban regime, and governing elites are not antithetical to the garbage can policy framework. In the case of Providence, relying on the garbage can framework does not preclude the idea that elements of an active growth machine and an active governing elite were taking advantage of opportunities to promote policy agendas friendly to various coalitions or individuals. Certainly elites were involved in decisions. A few prominent individuals appeared again and again at crucial decision points. However, some projects favored by elites never were accomplished or continue to languish. At other times elites appeared firmly in control, but only temporarily, seemingly at the mercy of events that swirled around them. Certainly various interests sold ideas on the basis that the city or state should undertake the expense because "everyone" would benefit.

However, over and over again it became apparent that the Providence renaissance fell into place not because a growth machine created it; or because an elite was in such control it could make things happen; or because group competition produced the changed city; or because the planners and bureaucrats drove the agenda; or as the result of incremental policy choices. Discrete events, sometimes far apart, opened windows of opportunity for policy entrepreneurs, civic elites, elected and appointed officials, and others to reach back for ideas that had long been discussed but for which no opportunity had existed for implementation. Policy logjams were broken, new ideas flowed, past plans were resurrected, long public debates were held, and other policy events unfolded, sometimes in unpredictable, fortuitous waves.

Bold, informal planning as well as individual decision making designed to "break the mold" generally dominate the Providence story, rather than the tiny steps associated with incremental thinking. A surprising aspect of the Providence story is the nonconservative choices that a number of nonelected government bureaucrats took to make things happen in the city. In addition, a number of institutional arrangements were created to bring together on a regular basis private and public decision makers. The civil servants, particularly those with access to public funds, were often as important to the Providence renaissance as were the more public movers and shakers. These implementers were close to the decision-making processes, so there was never a great distance between ideas and those responsible for putting them into action.

Building a Renaissance Definition

Sorting through the range of theories and concepts associated with policy making confirmed for us the importance of developing a working definition of urban renaissance. Several areas of inquiry associated with urban economic development were available to us in constructing our definition.

Local official *motivation* to pursue economic development policies is one area of inquiry. Public officials do not shy away from economic development activity. Often the pressure to do something about a city's future is intense and motivates officials to act. The decision to undertake economic development often seems to be the rational thing to do, because the risk of not doing something is greater than the risk of trying and perhaps not succeeding.[13] Political decision makers spend a considerable amount of time thinking about economic development, believe they can have an impact, and expect electoral rewards for real or symbolic success.[14]

The *catalysts* that impel urban economic development activity in the United States are other subjects to be examined. For city policy makers to protect the fiscal base of the city and to provide a reasonable level of services, they must confront the threatening realities of economic change. Urban policy makers are forced to act as swiftly as possible because of increased capital mobility, a changed international marketplace where manufacturing capacity shifts across borders, and the vagaries of a global domestic economy. These economic changes compel local officials to engage in the politically popular behavior of trying to increase property values and generate jobs by securing new businesses and building projects, providing tax breaks, and so on.[15]

The *outcomes* sought by those advocating economic development reside within an ambiguous, uncertain, and tumultuous environment. The question is still unanswered regarding the set of effects urban decision makers desire the most.[16] Whether officials know what they want, what business really needs, or what other urban competitors are prepared to offer often is unclear. Survey results indicate a blending of an improved fiscal picture and more jobs as desired outcomes in the minds of policy makers.[17] Fiscal outcomes focus on an improved tax base and a resulting increase in local tax revenue. Employment-related outcomes are usually expressed as an increase in the number of jobs available within the city or, in some instances, specifically for city residents.[18] Certainly, local revenue can increase without local employment increases and vice versa.

Economic development is risky political business with no guarantees of success. Adopting bureaucratic rules and established ways of doing things become methods for coping with risk and uncertainty. Elected officials retain control over nonroutine matters such as granting tax abatements. The symbolic political credit claimed by elected officials when outcomes are favorable, whether or not the politician had anything to do with the economic development activity, can precipitate clashes with those professionals responsible for planning and implementing economic development policy.[19]

Economic development *tools* vary considerably. A distinction is made between conventional public intervention to attract economic activity and the more entrepreneurial intervention that requires risk taking, public-private ventures, public strategic investment, and government flexibility. As such, the tools of economic development often are divided into supply-side, demand-side, or market-based devices.

Supply-side tools include tax incentives, debt financing arrangements, infrastructure investment, regulatory policy, tax increment financing, enterprise zones, land rezoning, and site development. Demand-side policies focus more on fostering new businesses, creating new markets, or encouraging new product development through R&D or targeted investment. Business incubators, venture capital financing, export market development, job training for small business, and R&D support are typical examples. Empirical studies have uncovered clusters of market-based tools that attract and retain businesses, involve regulatory reform, create lending and financial incentives, promote historic preservation and aesthetic improvement, and enhance land management. Economic development costs such as tax abatements and loan guarantees or tax-exempt bonds are used to measure the success of economic development policy relative to benefits derived.[20]

Measuring the extent of economic development activity is somewhat problematic. Although the presence or absence of a type of activity or a simple tallying of the number of tools used typically is employed to measure the scope of activity, neither description adequately measures the extent of economic development activity. Resources deployed, such as tax dollars abated, can potentially better measure the extent of government activity.[21] Case studies, then, are valuable because this type of data is difficult to gather and generally is not available in national data sets. Fiscal and economic distress, the loss of an industrial base and its jobs, increased regional competition, the size of the city, and intangible factors such as strong leadership are possible impetuses for cities to engage in extensive levels of economic development activity.

The *constraints* that confront local economic development policy makers are legion. Whether local government economic development policy is a product of relatively unconstrained local political choices or is determined by mobile capital economics that force cities to adopt policies favorable to urban growth machines is debated. Local officials are thought to make choices in one direction only: favorable to business regimes owing to the mobility of capital.[22] Those less inclined to that fatalism argue that local decision makers do not simply make knee-jerk, panicky decisions favorable to growth machines. Rather, they are acutely aware of resource allocation concerns and the competition for resources and that there are winners and losers.[23]

Local governments do have market-based "bargaining chips" such as desirable location, economies of agglomeration, and existing fixed capital. Other advantageous conditions for city governments occur when intergovernmental mechanisms for intervention and support exist, and are used, or when there is strong popular control such as interparty competition, extensive public participation opportunities, and so on.[24] So when the advantage is to business, city governments tend to get what they want, while the locality absorbs more cost and risk. When the city has the advantage, the municipality will place demands on the private sector.

Many factors are thought to permit localities to overcome constraints and engage in successful economic development efforts. These factors include the locality's size, mayoral formal and political strength, a professional bureaucracy, strong community-based activities, the actual degree of economic distress, and certain demographic factors such as a high number of renters, a low number of married households, and a low number of families with children. The degree of centralization also is a constraining factor. Economic development can be lodged in any number of government units ranging from cabinet-level agencies to specially created corporations. It can be scattered among many departments or be

Between 1980 and 1999, the principal gateway to downtown was transformed from a rail corridor surrounded by vacant lots to a highway corridor abutted by an upscale shopping mall, renovated office buildings, and luxury hotels.

Courtesy of Rhode Island Department of Transportation (Before) and Thomas Payne, WaterFire Providence (After)

put in the hands of semipublic agencies with a degree of legislatively authorized independence. Nonprofit partnership arrangements and even a chamber of commerce might be utilized.[25]

Mayors within a centralized executive power structure are key actors in overcoming constraints. They can lead the effort, negotiate deals, and develop effective coalitions. For routine development issues, however, the responsibilities fall to the bureaucrats, where established routines rule. These routines minimize public scrutiny, value closed decision making, and focus on elites. Examples of routines include symbolic economic development programs; universal incentives rather than need-based ones; and adoption of policies as they emerge in other jurisdictions that are perceived as competitors.[26]

Deciding on economic development policy is not free of conflict. The absence of conflict can appear to represent consent, but in fact it reflects a screening out of opposing views. The kind or degree of conflict varies. Distinctions are made between economic development decisions made in a style dominated by business, in a populist style where the elite is challenged in a more pluralistic setting, or in a mix of the two models. The degree of public participation is related to the degree of conflict and to the strategies used by public officials in deciding which activities to pursue and the structural arrangements used.[27]

Summary

An established theoretical framework guides our foray into the world of the Providence renaissance. The garbage can model permits us to take into account the role of elites, groups, and institutions, the mix of individual and organizational motivations, and the role of chance in the Providence story. The economic development literature provided the elements that we used to develop our working definition of urban renaissance presented in chapter 1.

The new built environment defines much of the discussion about change in Providence—the way the city looks in the downtown area. There is also a more amorphous sensation in the air that something has changed in Providence. The definition of renaissance we employ is designed to provide substance to this feeling rather than solely to focus on the physical changes in the city. Our analysis of individual renaissance projects provides detailed evidence of what the city hoped for by changing the built environment. A number of individual projects undertaken over twenty-five years were put under the microscope to examine the history, motives, catalysts, constraints, expected outcomes, and tools associated with each. From these individual analyses emerges the aggregated story of how the Providence renaissance unfolded. A subsequent analysis of fiscal, economic, and social change in the city helps place the Providence renaissance in a broader context. The rest of this book tells the story of how this city has succeeded in developing an image, and perhaps the reality, of an urban renaissance.

Providence: The Place and Its People

3

The River Relocation Project of the early 1990s has rediscovered the rivers that flow through the city center and exploits them to glue the city back together in a modern but thoroughly urbanistic fashion.

Providence Preservation Society, *Guide to Downtown Providence: Celebrating the Past, Meeting the Future*

A Brief History of Providence

■ Even among older East Coast cities, Providence, the capital city of the State of Rhode Island and Providence Plantations (the smallest state with the longest name) is filled with history. Its founder, the religious nonconformist Roger Williams, chose the name Providence (it means "loving care") because he believed "God has showed merciful Providence unto me in my distresse."[1] Williams founded the city in 1636 as a sanctuary for religious refugees from the Massachusetts Bay Colony. The presence of the religious dissenters during the seventeenth century earned the region the title of Rogues Island and established the area as a destination for rebels, nonconformists, and outright villains.[2]

Providence's founding foreshadowed the real estate adage "location, location, location." Williams first settled in Seekonk Cove. Unfortunately for Williams, this land was considered part of Plymouth and the Massachusetts Bay colonies, both of which as a matter of policy found Williams undesireable. Heeding the advice of his friend Edward Winslow, governor of Plymouth, and of his friends among the local Narragansetts, Williams shifted his settlement to the west bank of the Seekonk River. Debarking from the boat, Williams stepped foot onto a very large granite boulder. The local Narragansett sachem advised Williams to settle slightly farther to the west, on the eastern shore of the Moshassuck River.

Williams took the advice. The Roger Williams National Memorial, established in 1973, is a 4.5-acre urban park in Providence that marks the spot of this latter settlement more or less on the east side of what was once called the Great Salt Cove. The little-known site marking Williams's arrival on the granite boulder (much of which was blown up as part of an effort to create a small park in his honor) is in an area untouched by the renaissance. It did, however, become the center of an East Side neighborhood dispute over the aesthetics of a drive-through Dunkin' Donuts. Location, location, location!

Providence's history is tied to sea and land commerce. The city's location at the head of Narragansett Bay made it an attractive port. By the early half of the eighteenth century, wharves were built along the river waterfronts and at the head of the bay. Shipbuilding took place along Weybosset Neck. A sizeable portion of the city's growth during the eighteenth and nineteenth centuries is attributable to its maritime orientation: "The west side of North and South Main Streets—followed by India Point and the West Side of the Providence River—filled with wharves and warehouses. The income from the sea trade provided the means for construction of the mansions for merchants as well as dense residential development in Fox Point for sailors, chandlers and other tradesmen."[3] By the end of the American Revolution, Providence had eclipsed Newport, its chief maritime and political rival, as Rhode Island's principal port. Providence's location provided easy access to the hinterland and its markets, giving the city a distinct advantage over Newport, which is located at the far end of Aquidneck Island.

Near the close of the eighteenth century, Providence oriented more toward land commerce as other cities along the eastern seaboard developed. The city became the center of America's textile industry following Samuel Slater's development of the first water-powered cotton mill in 1794 in neighboring Pawtucket, Rhode Island. Until the nineteenth century Providence remained home by and large to New England shipping and textile manufacturing families. Names such as Brown, Tillinghast, Goddard, Waterman, and Chafee dominated the social and political life of the city and state, controlling the economic growth of Providence and the Rhode Island portion of the Blackstone River Valley until well into the 1880s.[4]

The city's growing land orientation was mirrored in its treatment of its rivers and the Great Salt Cove. By the 1780s the city was filling in the rivers. Following the Great Gale of 1815, which destroyed the last drawbridge across the rivers connecting Weybosset with Providence, the city built a permanent bridge effectively closing off the cove from navigation. By the time the city was incorporated in 1832 (population 17,000) the steam locomotive was prevalent. Railroads more than ships became important vehicles for commerce. By 1844 the Providence and Worcester Railroad reduced the Great Salt Cove to a small basin, where a waterfront park was created along with promenades and trees. Unfortunately, the basin became a rather large cesspool, and the cove park was accessible only by crossing railroad tracks. Riverfront filling progressed so much that by the 1860s, when the Woonasquatucket and Moshassuck were canalized, the rivers became for all intents and purposes waste receptacles. In the end the park was abandoned and by 1895 was filled in to accommodate yet more railroad tracks. By 1904 the Crawford Street Bridge, begun in the 1870s, was completed, effectively paving over much of the Providence River that forms from the confluence of the Woonasquatucket and Moshassuck. While it still had a waterfront, Providence was no longer a city whose economic fortune rested on access to the ocean. Providence's commercial land orientation was clear.

Extensive mill development along the upper Woonasquatucket and Moshassuck Rivers created an environment conducive to growth. The rapidity of manufacturing and technological innovation, growing international demand for textiles, and intensifying interregional competition forced mill owners to import large quantities of cheap labor from southern and central Europe in order to remain efficient.[5] During the latter portion of the nineteenth century and through

The Great Salt Cove dominates the landscape in early-nineteenth-century Providence (Painting by Alvan Fisher, 1818).

a good deal of the early part of the twentieth, Roger Williams's quiet fishing village established its regional primacy as a textile, jewelry, machine tool, steam engine, and metals fabricating center.[6] Gorham Silver, Corliss Steam Engine Company, Nicholson File Company, American Screw Company, and Brown and Sharpe Manufacturing were Providence industrial giants employing many thousands of Providence workers.

Architecture, Neighborhoods, and Urban Design

The city's history has left its architectural imprint on its neighborhoods in an urban design story not unfamiliar to those who study cities in the Northeast. Providence's downtown is compact and relatively well preserved despite the flurry of recent development in and around the central core. The downtown contains clusters of architecturally significant, high-quality, nineteenth- and early-twentieth-century commercial structures, and neighborhoods are filled with impressive Federal-style, Greek Revival, Italianate, and Victorian houses. This architectural mélange was assembled without much planning on anybody's part, as there was no zoning code in Providence prior to 1923. This impressive array of residential structures at both ends of the affordability spectrum has been preserved through the work of a well-organized historic preservation lobby.

Providence's streets and neighborhoods are not museum set pieces. They exhibit the variety created by a long history and a diverse population. This lack of uniformity is a part of Providence's charm, for the city's social, economic, and architectural history can be read in the physical form of individual buildings and in the differences among neighborhoods.[7] This multiplicity of form and style can be viewed from the city's geographic highpoints.

To the east is College Hill, where at Prospect Park stands an imposing statue of Roger Williams extending his hand over the city, offering dramatic views of the old commercial core, the new Capital Center, the state capitol, and the riverfront. Merchant and professional houses are arrayed on the slopes of College Hill, which, in turn, rises to the compact campus of Brown University and the impressive mansions of Rhode Island's eighteenth-century "oldest families" at its crest.

Heading down College Hill to the area bounded by Main and Benefit Streets, where the first permanent settlement occurred, is an impressively well-preserved stock of eighteenth- and early-nineteenth-century buildings. Immediately across the Providence River is downtown, a nineteenth- and early-twentieth-century commercial district dominated at its eastern end by a cluster of tall postwar office buildings. To the north and west of downtown, the rivers are lined with huge industrial buildings, remnants of the city's early strategic role in the Industrial Revolution. South of downtown and along the west side of the Providence Harbor are docks and warehouses, legacies of the city's nineteenth-

These maps from 1744 to 1940 show how Providence turned its back on the waterfront. With the arrival of the railroads and commercial pressure to develop downtown land, the Great Salt Cove was filled and the Providence River almost completely decked over by 1940.

Courtesy of Providence Department of Planning and Development

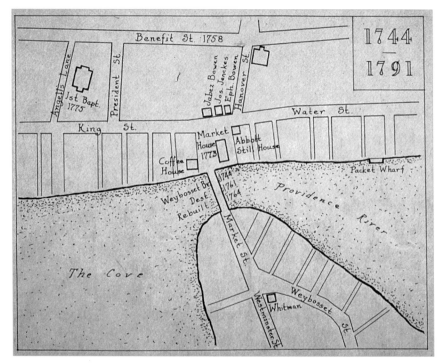

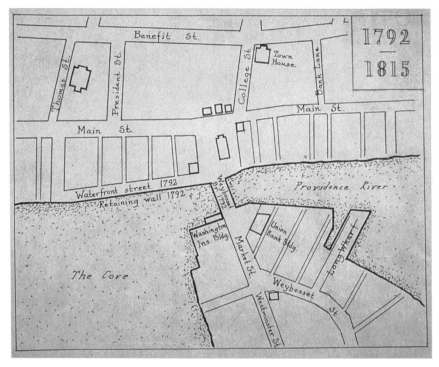

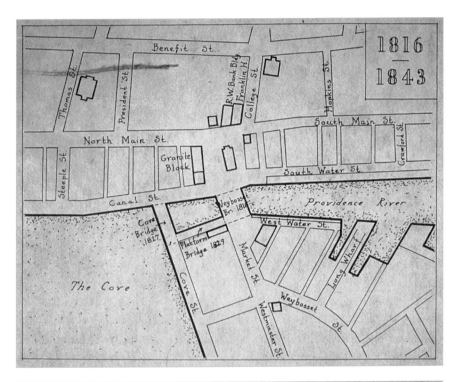

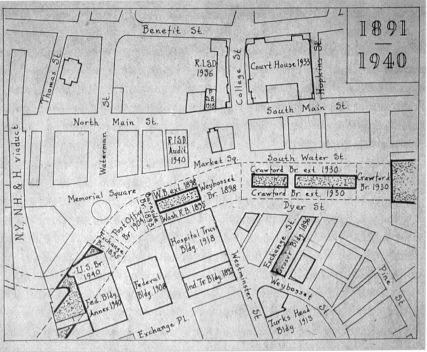

up and out. The lowest level of cheap housing has since disappeared, but the sturdier tenements of the nineteenth century remain in significant numbers, a physical reminder of the rapidly changing socioeconomic profile of the city during these years."[9]

Streetcars enabled housing growth to occur far beyond walking distance from the inner-city mills and factories. The streetcar lines extended to Cranston to the south and Pawtucket to the north, enabling skilled workers to rent or purchase homes several miles from where they worked. Open spaces began to fill rapidly. By the outbreak of World War I Pawtucket, Providence, and Cranston represented a seamless, continuously built-up urban region.

From the 1920s onward the automobile diminished reliance on streetcars and later the public bus system. Cars and improved roads made residential development feasible at greater and greater distances from principal work destinations. Pressure to maintain, modernize, and redevelop the inner-city neighborhoods evaporated as new communities sprang up beyond the city limits. Throughout the mid- to late twentieth century, deterioration of the urban core and surrounding neighborhoods continued virtually unabated as the focus of developers shifted to the suburbs.

Following World War II, Providence underwent a profound restructuring of its economy, suffering what has been deemed an economic hardening of the arteries.[10] In a story familiar to the Northeast, industry moved to the suburbs or southern states where labor and land acquisition costs, municipal taxes, and utilities were cheaper. City residents also "suburbanized," taking advantage of the single-family-home subdivisions built in neighboring towns. Between 1940 and 1980 Providence lost about 100,000 people.

Growth in car ownership strained the city's established infrastructure, requiring road widening, new road construction, and the creation of large parking lots, the last cropping up on the sites of demolished and obsolete industrial, commercial, or residential structures. During the 1960s the interstate highway network divided the city along north-south and east-west axes. Interstates 95 and 195 were superimposed upon established transportation corridors and, in many instances, required large-scale demolition of houses, businesses, and roads. The downtown was literally severed from its neighborhoods as the highways cut a swath through the city. Abrupt cul-de-sacs were created where once arterial roads had linked the inner-city residential neighborhoods to the central business district.

This process accelerated the blight and decline in the residential neighborhoods of Elmwood, Federal Hill, Olneyville, Smith Hill, Upper South Providence, Valley, and the West End, leading to much discussion of the need for sound city planning and urban revitalization. By 1980 Providence found itself with a legacy of obsolete, deteriorating buildings with no chance for their imme-

world economy, and the passage of time, turned many of those assets into weaknesses.

Transportation Network

Roger Williams's chosen location for his new settlement proved to be advantageous to the city for much of its history, but only recently has the city rediscovered that geographic reality. Geographically, Providence is a city "on the water" located in southeastern New England at the head of Narragansett Bay, one of the best deep-water harbors on the Atlantic coast. The bay has more than ten miles of commercial waterfront, with piers and wharves that can accommodate deep- and medium-draft vessels. The Port of Providence serves as a major oil and gas terminal for the New England region. Its rivers and the uncovered and restored remnants of the old cove flow into Narragansett Bay along with the neighboring Seekonk River. Much of the city's renaissance revolves around these rivers and the cove, with ambitious plans to recover the entire waterfront extending into Narragansett Bay still in the making.

In addition to its water access, an extensive road network has been an invaluable asset upon which the city can draw in its renaissance efforts. Providence is the junction for six highways: I-95, I-195, I-295, and state highways 146, 6, and 10. With the exception of I-295, these roadways meet in downtown Providence. This configuration of roads places 65 percent of the New England region's total population within a seventy-five-mile driving radius of Providence. Providence is less than an hour's drive from Boston and approximately three hours by car from New York City along Interstate 95, which bisects the city on a north-south axis. When I-95 was completed in 1965, the five exit ramps into Providence were considered a coup for such a small city.[14] I-195 links Providence to southeastern Massachusetts, making Cape Cod barely an hour's drive away. Route 146 from Worcester, Massachusetts, flows directly into I-95 in Providence.[15] Route 10 provides commuters an additional entry and exit point from the wealthier suburbs along I-95 south of the city. Other highways were planned but not approved, a circumstance that would prove fortuitous for the Providence renaissance.

The rail service that carried much of the commerce of Providence throughout the nineteenth century is still part of the downtown transportation system. Freight trains regularly pass through Providence. Amtrak provides frequent rail passenger service from downtown Providence along the entire Northeast Corridor.

Theodore Francis Green Airport

Through much of the period between 1980 and 2000, Providence benefited from the state and federal decision to expand Theodore Francis Green Airport in Warwick, Rhode Island, to become a major regional airport.[16] Officially opened in 1931, it was the country's first state-owned airport. In 1938 the airport was named after former Rhode Island governor and then U.S. senator Theodore Francis Green, who became the state's longest-serving U.S. senator and the oldest person to serve in the Senate before Strom Thurmond of South Carolina. The airport provides lower-cost domestic and limited international passenger service on seven major airlines and serves as the northeast hub for Southwest Airlines and a subregional hub for other air carriers. Boston's Logan Airport is a one-hour drive from Providence, which permits connections to the rest of the world.

Located just twenty minutes from downtown Providence, the airport has undergone innumerable expansions. The expansion of the airport began in earnest in 1979, at about the time the idea of a revived Providence was being contemplated. To a number of observers the airport expansion is critical to the success of the state in attracting business and tourists and consequently is an important element in the renaissance story. By 1987 the runways at Green were greatly expanded. The new parking garage and Bruce Sundlun Terminal were built and opened by 1997, financed by state bond money and federal funds. Further federally financed improvements were made in the 1990s. An exit ramp from I-95 takes arriving passengers directly to the departure terminals. Additional expansion of the runways is under consideration, drawing significant local opposition because of the airport's location in the middle of a residential neighborhood in Warwick.

Business, Employers, and Economic Sectors

Some of these very communication links that served the city strategically for so long proved to be economic threats to the city before they would become potential assets again. The railroads and growing road networks opened up the United States for development. During the interwar years the textile mills began to move south, where land and labor were less expensive. Cotton no longer had to be shipped north, and labor was less well organized in states like Georgia and South Carolina. The cheap immigrant labor of southern New England turned into more expensive and successful organized labor. The nation's transportation network meant finished goods could reach market much more quickly.[17]

The painful shift experienced by downtown economies in many northeastern cities like Providence was offset nationally by a flourishing post–World War II national economy, whose transformation from a manufacturing to a service orientation conferred significant benefits on the emerging suburban and exurban communities of the Northeast and the new cities of the western and southwestern United States.[18] People, industry, and retail activity suburbanized and moved interregionally in a nationwide decentralization trend, particularly from those older cities located in the northeastern Rust Belt. Providence, like other north-eastern cities, found itself in a rather bleak situation.

> Central city population growth first slowed relatively then declined ab-solutely in relation to that of the suburbs. Accompanying these well-known social changes was the relative economic decline of the central cities unable to replace obsolete industries and associated disinvestments from their built environments. . . . Older American cities became vehicles for the en-capsulation of minority groups and low-income whites in obsolete sectors of the economy and deteriorating physical environments.[19]

Intraregional competition also affected Providence. With declining indus-trial jobs and obsolete factories in the dense inner city, industrialists sought op-portunities for development on the metropolitan fringe. Jobs went to the suburbs, and people moved from Providence to access them. Between 1940 and 1980 Providence experienced a precipitous population decline. First industry, then residents, and eventually retail activities moved out of the city to greenfield sites in Cranston, Lincoln, and Warwick, Rhode Island, and the "golden mile" of Route 6 in Seekonk, Massachusetts.

The transformation of the Providence industrial landscape through inter- and intraregional competition resulted in an economy dependent on govern-mental, medical, educational, and financial services. The nonprofit sector emerged as a major component of the Providence local economy. In 1950 the greatest sector of employment in Providence was manufacturing. By the 1990s more than 50 percent of Providence jobs were in the service sector, with another 14 percent in the retail and wholesale trades. Manufacturing had shrunk to slightly more than 10 percent of all jobs in the city.

The single largest employment sector in Providence is health care. Rhode Is-land Hospital, by far the largest health care institution in the state, occupies hun-dreds of acres in South Providence. Miriam Hospital, Roger Williams Medical Center, Hasbro Children's Hospital, Women and Infant's Hospital, Butler Hos-pital, and the federal Veterans Administration Hospital all are located in Provi-dence. More than 19,000 workers, about 20 percent of Providence's jobs, are in health-related fields. The second-largest employers in Providence are personnel supply and computer service businesses. Retail makes up 10 percent of city jobs. Once the dominant industry, jewelry producers are the only large manufacturing sector remaining in the city, representing about 40 percent of the manufacturing jobs, which equals barely 6 percent of total jobs in the city.[20]

Higher education is another dominating presence in the Providence econ-omy. Private and public universities and colleges, which are noticeable in virtually every section of the city, employ nearly seven thousand people in Providence, accounting for almost 7 percent of the total Providence workforce. Brown University and the Rhode Island School of Design (RISD) are situated on the east side of the city. Johnson and Wales University has become the major property owner in the old downcity and jewelry district of the city. The University of Rhode Island Feinstein College of Continuing Education and Roger Williams University urban campus share in the revitalization of the Washington Street streetscape, one of the major thoroughfares into the central city. The private Dominican institution Providence College anchors the middle-class Elmhurst neighborhood. Rhode Island College, the state's principal urban presence and the college with the largest contingent of Rhode Island students, is anchor to the other major middle-class neighborhood of Mount Pleasant. The Community College of Rhode Island (CCRI), with its many job training and remedial programs, has satellite campuses in the largely immigrant and lower-income neighborhoods of South Providence.

The decline of well-paid manufacturing employment and the rise of the service sector left many Providence residents with low-wage employment. As a result, by 1990 Providence ranked below both the state and national averages for median family and household income. More than 25 percent of Providence households had incomes lower than $10,000 in 1990. The official poverty level for that year was $12,091.[21]

Providence found itself in an odd position in the late 1980s. It had most of its physical attributes still in place, including superb architecture, a large population within its sphere of influence, and a growing strength in service industries and the nonprofit sector. Yet the city's residents were becoming poorer as industrial jobs disappeared. So was the city's tax base.

The Political Backdrop of the Providence Renaissance

The Providence renaissance has occurred within the structure and swirl of Rhode Island and Providence politics. While a comprehensive political history of the city and of its relationship to the state is beyond the scope of this book, the structure of city government, the city and state relationship, the city's finances and its continued fiscal stress, and mayoral politics are important contexts for understanding some of what occurred in Providence from 1980 to 2000.

The Structure of Providence Municipal Government

The Providence Home Rule Charter, adopted in 1980 and fully effective in January 1983, provides for a strong mayor/council form of government.[22] The voters of the city elect concurrently the mayor and a ward-based fifteen-member city council for a four-year term. As chief executive the mayor prepares the annual budget for submission to the council; has the authority to veto or to sign ordinances passed by the council; and has a line-item veto. The council's major responsibilities are to alter, amend, and approve a Rhode Island–mandated balanced city budget before passage and to pass ordinances within the scope of authority granted by the Home Rule Charter.

The mayor appoints all department heads and most of the members of the agencies, boards, and commissions that directly affect city operations and serves ex officio on many of these bodies. While the council must approve some of the appointees, the mayor generally has wide latitude in selection of these department heads. Providence provides a typical range of services, including police, fire, sanitation, parks and recreation, and a large school system. The State of Rhode Island, not the city, is responsible for such services as Medicaid, general public assistance, public health, and transportation, among others.

The planning function of city government has long been under the direct aegis of the mayor, and the Department of Planning and Development (DPD) has at various times been an important agency as the Providence renaissance unfolded. The director of in the DPD serves at the pleasure of the mayor. The department's early roots lay in the 1950s, but it was nearly obliterated during the administration of Mayor Joseph Doorley (1964–74). Mayor Vincent Cianci (1975–84; 1991–2002) resurrected a planning department during the 1970s. Mayor Joseph Paolino Jr. (1984–90) created the DPD in 1985 by consolidating the Department of Planning and Urban Development, the Mayor's Office of Community Development, and the Office of Economic Development. This large, administrative arm of government provides ideas; grant-seeking expertise; technical support for project implementation; and technical support for the City Plan Commission (CPC), which was established in 1951 as the body that provides final legislative approval for zoning.

An array of quasi-public boards and commissions with differing appointive relationships with the mayor and city council are responsible for other city functions that have been associated at times with the Providence renaissance. The Providence Public Building Authority (PBA) was created by the state legislature in 1987 to issue bonds for Providence that were limited to an amount equal to 15 percent of the city's most recently adopted budget for a single issue and 50 percent in the aggregate. An annual appropriation from the city to the PBA in the form of a lease-rental payment is equal to the amount necessary to cover payment of Authority bonds or notes. The PBA is a distinct legal entity from the city with no taxing authority, but it does report annually to the mayor and city council. The Providence Redevelopment Agency (PRA) is responsible for aiding the mayor in economic development activities. ProvPort, a nonprofit corporation that was created in 1994 to bail the city out of a tight fiscal year, leases the municipal wharf. On 28 September 1994 the city entered into a thirty-year lease agreement with ProvPort that enabled the city to garner $16.6 million in upfront lease payments to balance the city budget and avoid a tax increase in the 1994 election year.[23]

The city's school system dwarfs any of the other thirty-six school districts in this state of thirty-nine cities and towns, where local control of schools is guarded fiercely.[24] There are 28,000 children in the twenty-seven elementary schools, seven middle schools, and four large high schools that make up the Providence school system. In recent years a few charter schools and alternative public schools have come into being. A large number of Providence students live in family settings that fail to meet the federal government's poverty standards and where English is not the first language spoken at home.

The system's governance is highly politicized. The Providence School Board is composed of nine mayor-appointed members, which ensures that the degree of control of the school board and of the superintendent by the mayor's office is an issue never far from the political surface. The board is responsible for the operation, management, control, and maintenance of the schools, including curriculum, budget preparation, and appointment, promotion, and compensation of teachers and other departmental personnel. The superintendent is appointed by the board and acts as the chief operating officer. The school system's budget is developed by the school board and superintendent, is submitted to the city's finance director, and undergoes a mayoral review before being sent to the city council. The council acts on the school budget to the same extent it deals with other city departments. The city's finance department is responsible for holding school expenses to the appropriated amounts.

Municipal Finances: Fiscal Stress in Providence

Providence renaissance policy unfolded during a twenty-five-year period of fiscal trial and tribulation in which the city lurched from one short-term period of fiscal stress to another. When woven together, these truncated periods constitute consistent fiscal strain punctuated by short periods of financial calm. Providence and Rhode Island recently have touted themselves as "Hollywood East," so we might think of these stressful periods as fiscal "cliff-hangers," with the latest threat beaten back just in the nick of time.

Fiscal stress means the city revenues are insufficient to maintain existing service levels, thereby creating a potential budget deficit.[25] While circumstances peculiar to a given period can positively or negatively alter fiscal circumstances, the city has had a pronounced long-term structural deficit. Numerous task forces over three decades have issued report after report detailing the heart of Providence's fiscal troubles: the city chronically fails to generate enough revenue to support its level of spending, making state assistance necessary to prevent financial failure. So while a physical renaissance is under way, the city's basic financial structure has been on unstable ground.

Many northeastern communities have confronted the basic fiscal concern: a shrinking or slow-growing tax base, exponentially growing costs, and increasing skepticism among taxpayers about their willingness to endure tax increases.[26] Certainly one eagerly awaited result of all of the renaissance activity is the ability to generate enough revenue to alleviate a greater portion of the fiscal stress the city routinely experiences trying to pay for its range of services.

Property Tax Dependence and State Aid

There are two basic facts of fiscal life for Providence. The first is that to pay its bills Providence must rely heavily on property tax revenues. The fiscal stress in Providence is exacerbated by Rhode Island's well-documented overreliance on the property tax. Rhode Island relies more heavily on the property tax for revenues than is typical in the United States. Rhode Island's property tax collections per $1,000 of personal income were fifth in the nation in 1996. The state ranks in the bottom half of all states in terms of property tax capacity, yet like many other New England states ranks in the top ten in its efforts to collect revenue from that tax.[27]

Providence is the capital city of a state where it is expected that local communities will pay for a large share of their expenditures through the property tax. In fiscal year 2000 Providence required a high level of property tax effort to obtain resources from a seriously constrained tax capacity. That effort was exceeded only by Central Falls, Rhode Island, a community so financially bereft that the state took over complete funding of its public school system.[28] Recent statewide property tax reform efforts recognized this dependence by requiring more frequent local property revaluations.[29]

State efforts at reforming the property tax bring into sharp focus the second basic fiscal fact of life for Providence: it is increasingly at the mercy (quite literally, some say) of state policy makers for decisions regarding taxes, schools, and economic development. Providence is the state capital and primary city in a very small state. Its problems cannot be ignored. There is an old Rhode Island adage reflecting the similarity to a medieval city-state: "As goes Providence, so goes the state."

True or not, it is a tense relationship: less a cooperative "city-state" as some policy makers are fond of saying, and more of a complex city sometimes versus state, in a relationship growing uneasy in its dependency. Providence's twenty-member state house delegation, while the largest in the state's one-hundred-member General Assembly, is hard-put to elicit sympathy from an increasingly suburbanized state legislature.[30] In these ways the political relationship of Providence mirrors the historical, often difficult relationships between states and their largest cities. Successive governors and the legislature have made efforts to help revitalize the city's core. Statehouse Democrats, the party that has overwhelmingly dominated Rhode Island state legislative politics for decades, do share a common economic and political stake with Providence, because the city is a reliable source of Democratic votes in statewide elections.

Some of the city's fiscal difficulty lies with state policy and some with city policy. For instance, the state regularly fails to adopt a budget until near the beginning of the coming fiscal year, usually late in May or June, making it difficult to determine the precise level of aid to support essential services such as public education. City leaders routinely make the case that school aid in particular is inadequate. State and federal tax policy exempts nonprofit organizations from paying property taxes. As Providence is the state capital, many municipal, state, and federal offices are located there and, of course, are also tax exempt. The city for its part has enacted a homestead provision that reduces by 33 percent the taxable value of residential real estate of six dwelling units or less. The consequence is that, combined with nonprofit tax-exempt property, slightly more than 50 percent of the city's property cannot be taxed.[31]

The Politics of Stress

The voters in the city have shown remarkable electoral tolerance of the fiscal stress phenomenon and reliance on state aid by routinely re-electing incumbents. Neither the two mayors of Providence between 1975 and 2002 nor city council members have paid the ultimate political price for financial uncertainty. The voters have a seemingly endless ability to digest, or ignore, the numerous study commissions that have documented the fiscal instability of Providence. For example, in 1975, shortly after winning the 1974 mayoral race by a mere 709 votes over the Democratic incumbent, Joseph Doorley, Mayor Cianci submitted the first of many controversial budgets to the city council, asking that year for a seven-dollar increase in the tax rate. There followed two years of acrimonious budget battles with a sharply divided twenty-six-member city council: fifteen councilors consistently opposed to Cianci, and a bloc of eleven in support of him.

This type of division of the city council would be a hallmark of many of the Cianci years. At the time Cianci commented, "We could send them the cure for cancer and the vote would be 15 to 11 against."[32] Cianci also tried to impose a unilateral five-dollar increase and endured subsequent litigation and a brutal strike by municipal sanitation workers in 1976. Yet the mayor was re-elected in 1978 after rallying the public to his war on a "corrupt" city council.[33]

Mayor Cianci refused to raise taxes for the two years prior to the statewide election of 1980, the year he made his ill-fated run for the governorship of the state midway through his second term as mayor. To help balance the city's budget he counted on the sale of a local housing project to yield $4 million, a sale that never materialized. His gubernatorial campaign foundered on a series of indictments of city employees and the looming fiscal crisis that threatened layoffs and prompted an unofficial, brief, sanitation workers strike.

Payback came in 1981 when it became apparent that revenues and expenditures were far out of balance. In January a task force appointed by the mayor documented a nearly $24 million projected deficit. To stave off threatened insolvency that year, Mayor Cianci proposed to the city council an $11.43 supplemental tax increase, which sent shock waves through the entire community. Again the city council, despite its sound and fury, gave the mayor most of what he wanted, as they too faced the fiscal reality posed by too much spending and a shrinking tax base. Mayor Cianci survived both his gubernatorial debacle and obvious budget woes and was re-elected following a "no increase in taxes" budget in the 1982 mayoral election year. He won by a slightly improved margin of one thousand votes.

Mayor Cianci resigned from office in April 1984 following his conviction over personal matters unrelated to his running of the city, but budget woes continued. Mayor Joseph R. Paolino Jr., as president of the city council, assumed the mayor's duties until he was elected to his own term in the 1986 election. In 1987 Paolino appointed a Special Commission on Alternatives to the Property Tax "in recognition of the ever increasing burden the property tax places on the property taxpayers of Providence, and the need to find alternative methods of funding city services."[34] The commission's 1989 report was the policy response to the public outcry following the revaluation effort that produced a manyfold increase in property values, which threatened a major hike in the tax liability of longtime Providence taxpayers.

To soften the tax blow, a two-tiered, and much maligned, tax classification system separating the tax on real estate from taxes on personal property, primarily autos, was approved by voters in the city. As part of the referendum, the current homestead provision was approved, requiring that the city for property tax purposes reduce by 35 percent the assessed value of all residential property of six units or less, whether the owner lived in the unit or not.[35] The new classification was put into effect in 1988.

For Paolino, like Cianci, the lure of the governorship proved too strong to resist. He launched a losing campaign for that office in 1990. After four years as a local radio talk show host, former mayor Cianci won a hotly contested three-way race by the minuscule margin of 317 votes and promptly found himself confronted in 1991 with yet another large budget deficit. A new mayoral task force was appointed in early 1992 that continued the lament of out-of-control spending and a tax base inadequate to cope with built-in spending requirements.

Between 1992 and 1996 Mayor Cianci was unable to extract a tax increase from the city council and was unwilling to submit a tax increase budget during the 1994 election year. Following his 1994 re-election, Cianci announced a deficit reduction program in his 1995 State of the City Report that included eliminating two hundred city jobs, a wage freeze, a 20 percent cut in health insurance costs, and a plan to charge nonprofit organizations for fire calls.

The program had little lasting impact. In 1997 the Providence city council appointed a Special City Council Commission to Restructure Providence Finances. The same issues that were raised as far back as 1975 were addressed: a shrinking tax base and increasing expenditures required either hard spending choices or new revenue sources. The required ten-year revaluation effort in 1997 was postponed beyond the 1998 election, in which Mayor Cianci ran unopposed, and would not be completed until the year 2000.

Over the last decade some contentious institutional executive-legislative battles broke out. During the 1990s the city council flexed new political muscle, often granted after lengthy courtroom battles, over such matters as the authority

Providence's elegant French Revival–style city hall.

Photograph by the authors

to sign collective bargaining agreements; budget development; neighborhood improvement bond issues; the size of the fire department; the residency requirement for city employees; and the cost-of-living adjustments (COLAs) for retired municipal employees. In recent years yet another "anti-Cianci" faction maintained a slim majority on the council after years of a council predominantly favoring the mayor, further complicating city politics. While Democrats hold every city council seat, partisanship plays a more minor role in city political life than do the battles over neighborhood shares of development funds and other ward-based concerns.

Further complicating political life in the city have been the various federal and state investigations of city hall corruption during Cianci's terms. Mayor Cianci himself resigned the office in April 1984 as a result of a conviction of assault on his estranged wife's alleged lover. He received a five-year suspended sentence. In the 1980s thirty Cianci subordinates and other city workers and contractors were found guilty of a variety of felonies and sent to prison or forced to resign. In a case of "déjà vu all over again," Mayor Cianci, his chief of staff, and a number of lesser officials were indicted in April 2001 in what the local media outlets dubbed "Plunder Dome." In June 2002 Buddy Cianci was convicted of engaging in a racketeering conspiracy under the federal RICO statute and sentenced to a lengthy term in federal prison, ending his long tenure in Providence city hall.

Summary

This abbreviated general description of Providence points to an important characteristic of the community: it is accustomed to change. Its history was linked to water for a time, but the city eventually turned its back on that resource, putting its faith in the railroad as the technology to ensure its manufacturing commerce a place within the nation's economy. The city's post–World War II decline is typical of that experienced by many medium-sized cities, characterized by loss of population, manufacturing jobs, and wealth. These changes forced another round of adaptation on the city.

Providence retained its architecture and geography as assets and is well situated as an economic node in the region. It is a city that provides a full range of services under a strong mayor-council form of government that has proven to be relatively stable throughout more than two decades of renaissance activity. Its economy is undergoing a transformation, as manufacturing long ago lost its primacy to health and other industries.

The city had to confront systemic fiscal challenges caused by a shrinking tax base, large-scale spending, and an increasing reliance on state aid from a legislature not always friendly to its capital city. Still, within this context Providence sought to redefine itself in the new national and world economy. Policy makers hoped that making a renaissance would aid in that transformation. Politically it was equipped to do battle with a strong mayor-council form of government. "A critical element to rebuilding cities is leadership (strong mayor form of government). It's been an indispensable element here."[36] A renaissance is expected to play a key future role in resolving the long-standing fiscal stress the city has experienced, as will a strengthened state-city relationship that is based on recognition by state policy makers of the importance of Providence to the state's economy.

By 1975 downtown Providence had been carved into dislocated segments by railroads and highways. Between 1980 and 2000 it would take a small cadre of visionary policy entrepreneurs to stitch the fabric of the city back together again.

Courtesy of Providence Department of Planning and Development

Renaissance Planning, Partnerships, and People

4

When the Biltmore was boarded up in 1974, I thought
the city was going to die.

Friedrich St. Florian, 7 April 2003

■ The physical renaissance of Providence is sometimes the result of plans for
which opportunities were seized and in other instances a product of more
momentary, fragmented, inspired development. This fragmentation may have
worked to the city's benefit. Renaissance "planning," such as it was, ensured by design or default that no single agency accrued sufficient power to impose a singu-
lar vision on policy makers. At different times ideas jostled for position and
prominence. Some ideas, and their advocates, waited for decades before seeing
the concept become a reality.

Plans are best seen as a rational systemic response to demands that something be done, some action taken to reverse decline.[1] An early hallmark of the
Providence renaissance was the existence of a number of plans for the city's
"comeback." These plans constituted rational choice opportunities or system in-
puts for public and private decision makers. While planning played an important
role in the renaissance at times, some plans were never implemented; elements of
others were adopted; a few were opportunistic, drawn in response to an immediate need; and others still hope to guide significant change in Providence.

Plans focusing on the physical rebirth of Providence's downtown have not
been in short supply. In the words of the architect Friedrich St. Florian, "Providence had more master plans than any other city of its size that I am aware of."[2]

Planning was not done in Providence in the traditional sense but rather by opportunity, by what became available. Some planning efforts were drawn by public agencies and others assembled through the auspices of the private sector. While there were "master plans," none can be considered *the* master plan for the renaissance.

These planning efforts do share common characteristics. With a few exceptions, the plans are geographically discrete. They generally focus on a geographic subarea (Capital Center, jewelry district, downcity) or a feature of downtown (rivers, harbor, highways) and tend to ignore somewhat the surrounding area. The plans are functionally disparate, that is, they embrace different visions of what role the downtown should play in the city and regional economy. Consequently, one plan does not necessarily build on another. The plans also serve to highlight a competition that has emerged among the developers and advocates of those working to reconstruct the northern Capital Center and those in the traditional, and troubled, downcity core. Planning has been done in both the private and public sector and been supported by a mix of public and private funding streams. The plans often build on what appears to be possible, or on what appeared as an opportunity, rather than reinventing the city from scratch. In some instances projects emerged that were part of no plan at all. The Providence Place mall came on the policy agenda without consideration as the focal point in a plan. The mall might be considered an antiplan element. It came to exist in spite of plans that forbade that type of project in downtown Providence.

Many of the officials we interviewed commented that Providence has seen the development—and subsequent shelving—of more land use, revitalization, and economic development plans than any other medium-sized city in America.

Courtesy of Providence Department of Planning and Development

Pre-Renaissance Planning

The College Hill Plan[3]

The rescue of College Hill from the wrecking balls hired by Brown University and the Rhode Island School of Design, while not focused on downtown rebirth, is a notable event in the Providence renaissance for three reasons. First, it fostered the formation of the Providence Preservation Society (PPS) in 1957 in reaction to these higher education plans and urban renewal ideas that emerged and as a result brought historic and architectural preservation prominently onto the policy agenda. Second, the PPS became a way to reengage the old elite in the civic life of the city. Third, the College Hill effort captured the attention of such policy entrepreneurs as the architectural historian Antoinette F. Downing and William Warner, a former Providence city planner and urban architect.

The expansion plans of Brown University and the Rhode Island School of Design became a cause célèbre in Providence in the 1950s because of the planned demolition of historic homes on College Hill on the East Side of Providence. The PPS was organized to oppose the plans of Brown and RISD. Many of the women of the "first families" of Providence, such as Beatrice "Happy" Chace, Elizabeth Allen, Frances Sloan, and Mary Elizabeth Sharpe, led the fight to save College Hill's historic architecture. Another first family member, John Nicholas Brown, a descendant of Roger Williams and a member of the family that founded Brown University, was the chair of the society from 1956 to 1979.

An early renaissance social barometer was the PPS's efforts toward a collective decision by the city elite to stay and help, not abandon, the city. This effort would produce tangible results for the city. It successfully sought a federal demonstration grant to document significant and historic resources in the city and to develop a preservation plan. One society member, Beatrice Chace, was urged to buy deteriorating properties on and around Benefit Street—a main East Side thoroughfare, then considered a veritable slum—and restore them as a demonstration of what preservation could yield. Chace bought fifteen such properties, and others followed her lead.[4] There never was an evacuation of Providence by its old elites like that experienced by Hartford and Philadelphia.[5]

Professionals such as Antoinette F. Downing entered the preservationist fray. Downing, from Texas and New Mexico, would become a legend in Providence preservation politics, a voice for historic preservation in the city until her death in May 2001. She fought hard to spare Providence the private higher education–driven wrecking ball and worked with Bill Warner and others such as Laichlin Blair, a former Rhode Island state planner, to write the 1959 HUD-financed and city-sponsored "College Hill plan" formally titled *College Hill: A Demonstration Study and Plan for Historic Area Renewal*. The American Institute of

An underestimated factor in the Providence renaissance was the well-preserved legacy of historical architecture in the neighborhoods abutting downtown, particularly such gems as these on College Hill on Providence's East Side.

Courtesy of Gordon Rowley, Rhode Island College

Architects awarded Downing a prize in 1961 for developing a way to measure and quantify the value of historic architecture, the direct result of the Preservation Society's efforts to save College Hill. Downing pushed hard for Rhode Island to establish what would become the Rhode Island Historical Preservation and Heritage Commission (RIHPHC), which embarked on an ambitious historic preservation survey program for the entire state that was completed in the mid-1980s. This work later would become part of the fabric of decisions regarding future development projects in Providence: the city had a historic and architectural quality that ought to be considered in future development.

The College Hill plan and subsequent work eventually yielded a historic district and a design review committee to oversee development in the neighborhoods on College Hill, as well as city ordinances requiring that private institutions disclose their master plans and seek approval from the CPC. The result was a historic, aesthetically pleasing College Hill backdrop to a future Providence renaissance. Today Benefit Street is one of the posh addresses in the city sometimes featured in travel magazines, and it was often a location shot for the television series *Providence*.

Urban Renewal Planning: Downtown Providence 1970 *and the Interstate Highways*

As preservation efforts began on College Hill, federal urban renewal was rearing its head in Providence. There was a growing concern among Providence businesses that the city needed a planning shot in the arm to revitalize the Providence downcity. The Downtown Business Coordinating Council (DBCC), an offshoot of the Chamber of Commerce, obtained a federal urban renewal matching grant to add to the council and city's own funds to study a cooperative private-public effort to renew downtown.[6] The DBCC created an advisory board and a series of task forces to assist the City Plan Commission in drawing up a master plan for the city.

The result was that in 1960, with its downtown core continuing to stagnate and citywide out-migration of the middle class gaining momentum, the City Plan Commission published the first comprehensive examination and strategies for revitalization of the Providence urban core. Entitled *Downtown Providence 1970*, its author, the city planner Dieter Hammerschlaag, using the federal Urban Renewal Administration planning grant, planned for widespread demolition and complete rebuilding of the city center between 1960 and 1970. In its proposals for downtown Providence the plan claimed "good grounds for optimism that Rhode Island's stagnation is more a product of local psychological depression than of national forces. . . . Rhode Island can hope to participate in national economic progress without undue pessimism concerning its ability to compete."[7]

At the heart of *Downtown Providence 1970* was classic 1950s-style urban renewal: wholesale redevelopment of the urban core by demolition of the historic commercial center, including the French Revival–style Providence City Hall. The new central business district would become a single-use environment focused on office development, punctuated by pedestrian zones, parking lots, large public spaces, a heliport, and numerous Le Corbusier–inspired modernist office and residential towers linked by multilevel walkways, plazas, and acres of satellite parking lots. *Downtown Providence 1970* proposed realigning the railroad tracks in downtown to create numerous new land parcels and a new "government center" in the Union Station area that would include sports and convention centers and retail space.[8] The plan ran into numerous obstacles, not the least of which was the objection of the president of the New York, New Haven and Hartford Railroad to the idea of moving railroad tracks, the plan's centerpiece.[9]

The political establishment within the city, in particular Mayor Joseph Doorley (1965–74), showed little interest in matters relating to downtown development.[10] In 1970 the chair of the CPC, Edward Winsor, blasted the mayor for being "uninvolved in city planning, especially in long-range city planning" and criticized the mayor's limited project-by-project approach to the city's recovery. The mayor responded, "I wouldn't waste time planning for 25 years in the future."[11]

Mayor Doorley's term of office was predicated on a political belief that providing essential city services and jobs was enough to ensure re-election, the classic urban ward patronage machine and neighborhood politics frame of reference. "No Dough Joe" was the city labor union description of Doorley's approach to raising taxes and asking for bond approvals for capital planning purposes.[12] His electoral success was testament to his political judgment, if not his vision for the city's future.

Doorley's lack of interest in downtown economic development stands in stark contrast to his affinity for federal urban renewal, his embrace of the Model Cities Program, and his insistence on pushing for fair housing and antipoverty funding.[13] Mayor Doorley was trying to build a new political base, a strategy that would lead to trouble among former supporters who were concerned about loss of patronage jobs. Doorley himself fed some of this disenchantment by his flirtation with national politics, chairing the Democratic Party credentials committee at the 1968 Democratic National Convention and running for Democratic National Chair in 1970.[14] The intra–Democratic Party struggle that was still festering in 1974 opened the door to a possibility of a strong challenge, an opportunity eventually taken by Vincent A. "Buddy" Cianci.

In the meantime the *Downtown Providence 1970* plan effectively disappeared as a comprehensive blueprint for downtown. No advocate stepped forward to keep it alive. The federal urban renewal bulldozers destined to clear downtown Providence never revved their engines. The lack of public and private advocacy, the outright opposition to it from some quarters, and the disappearance of federal urban renewal money that had never really been secured resulted in only a very small part of *Downtown Providence 1970* being implemented. A few artifacts of this urban renewal plan are the University Heights complex and the current Marriott at Orms Street. Demolition occurred in what is now called Moshassuck Square (then Randall Square) outside of the hub of today's renaissance Providence. Consequently, Providence and much of its historic architecture was spared wholesale demolition, and the space occupied by rails and parking lots remained. "It was good that we never implemented the 1960 plan."[15] The plan's railroad relocation idea would remain in the background waiting for another day.

Providence was spared the worst vagaries of 1950s and 1960s federally funded urban renewal and its attendant wholesale land clearance. Two unfortunate exceptions are University Heights and Cathedral Square, both on the fringes of the downtown core.

Courtesy of Gordon Rowley, Rhode Island College (University Heights); photograph by the authors (Cathedral Square)

The failure of the *Downtown Providence 1970* plan to generate interest contains an important early lesson concerning renaissance activities: sometimes the decision *not to do something* is more important than actions undertaken. In the early history of urban renewal in Providence there are two such instances. The first is that the genesis of the Providence renaissance rested not on vigorous advocacy of a master plan. It was a fortunate *inattention* paid to downtown renewal planning and the eventual demise of federal urban renewal that would mark the 1960s as a critical epoch in the future of renaissance Providence. Downtown Providence remained intact.

The second instance of fortunate inaction centered on interstate highway construction. While Providence policy makers sparred over the city's future, there was little hesitation among federal highway planners as to what they intended to do: continue the federal interstate system. The federal interstates that bisected the city both north-south (I-95) and east-west (I-195) were completed by the mid-1960s, claiming houses, neighborhoods, and factories, an occurrence not uncommon in American cities at that time. However, a crucial, forgotten choice in the 1950s was the decision not to fill in the Providence River and bring I-95 down the riverbed to link it with I-195. There was a decided lack of interest in moving the principal power facility, the Manchester Street power station, and its adjacent coal yards and electric generating plant from the location where the

The architect and city planner William D. Warner envisioned the relocation of I-195 as part of a plan for carrying the benefits of the Capital Center and river relocation plans downriver to the Old Harbor. The new road is currently under construction; more than forty acres of prime land will be available for open space and commercial development once the existing downtown sections of I-195 are demolished.

Courtesy of William D. Warner, Architects & Planners

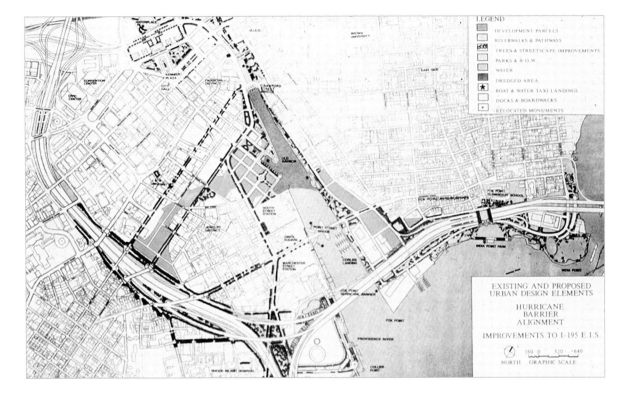

highways would have to converge.[16] Consequently, the Providence River remained, albeit covered and neglected.

In the absence of development leadership during this pre-renaissance period, the city did not have the political will or capital to undertake redevelopment on the scale envisioned in the *Downtown Providence 1970* plan. Mayor Doorley even rejected the idea of building a retail mall at the corner of Charles and Orms Streets.[17] Still, something had to be done to reverse what most observers noted was a decline in the city's fortunes. The city needed a jump-start. Symbolic of this pre-renaissance approach to revitalization is the fifteen years (1958–1973) it took to complete a single project: the Providence Civic Center. While some sewer and street work was done in the jewelry district and the federal interstates plowed through the city, the city and state embarked on a plan to bring people into the city by building a new focal point for entertainment.

The Providence Civic Center[18]

The Providence Civic Center project foreshadowed renaissance-era projects in three ways. The idea for a civic center surfaced in 1958 as a cooperative federal-state-city project, reflecting the need for intergovernmental coordination that would become one important feature of the later renaissance. The project was touted as a job creator to "relieve the unemployment situation."[19] Geographically, the locale for the proposed civic center was the state-owned site of the Rhode Island College of Education (the location that eventually would become the Providence Place mall in the future).

This proposed civic center never got built. What did ultimately emerge after fifteen years of bitter fighting was a stand-alone building constructed with no federal assistance and a great deal of opposition from state policy leaders and the Rhode Island public. A civic center was not contained in the *Downtown Providence 1970* plan except as an exhibition hall. Efforts by Mayor Doorley and the state to secure federal economic development funds for a civic center feasibility study failed. Recognizing the increasingly dire straits of the city, Governor John Chafee (1962–1968) in 1967 agreed to share the expense of hiring the Arthur D. Little Company to undertake a feasibility study. The report was encouraging enough for Chafee to announce his willingness to commit state resources to help the city build a civic center if the local Chamber of Commerce thought it was a good idea.

Within the city's boundaries, the Civic Center generally was seen as a hope for the future. The "eggs" were being placed in this one development project basket. Jobs, economic spin-offs, and votes from the construction trades were expected to materialize. Many suburban voters did not share that vision. The suburban-urban political split in Rhode Island was evident in the voting for a civic center bond issue in the general election of 1968. Voters statewide rejected the referendum: only three of the thirty-nine cities and towns supported it.[20]

The civic center idea did not die, however. Former Providence mayor Walter Reynolds, Mayor Doorley, organized labor, and other city and state officials managed to pressure the legislature to approve a civic center bond issue ballot item for a special referendum in Providence only. This limited bond issue passed overwhelmingly in 1969, but it proved to be an inadequate source of capital. A second municipal bond referendum question supported by Doorley was submitted to the voters of Providence in 1971 and passed, thus securing enough financing to build what by then was labeled "Doorley's Dream."

Since its opening on 3 November 1972 for a Providence Reds hockey game, the facility's usage has been mixed. Although sometimes filled with Providence College basketball fans, rock concertgoers, Providence Bruins devotees, religious revival meeting attendees, and the smells and sounds of circuses, at other times it stands empty and deteriorating, in constant need of city bailouts. Even today it is not considered to be part of the renaissance but rather a financial problem that renaissance policy makers must address. In 2000 Dunkin' Donuts bought the

The Providence Civic Center, renamed the Dunkin' Donuts Center for its current corporate sponsor.

Photograph by the authors

naming rights to the facility, prompting the nickname "The Dunk." Public policy makers hope that this financial shot in the arm will help with a much-needed modernization.

So while the events that resulted in the Providence Civic Center foreshadowed renaissance-era projects, they also stand in stark contrast to much of what occurred in the period between 1980 and 2000. The Civic Center's tortured roots demonstrated the importance of state-city cooperation and of political leadership (or the lack of it) to rally the public, the business community, and elected officials in a revitalization effort. The failure to secure federal feasibility study money stands in contrast to the flow of federal dollars into Providence within just a decade. Federal dollars would make politics less contentious by avoiding the need to obtain public bond approvals. The fifteen years it took to decide to erect this single building is almost farcical when compared to the time it took to remake the entire physical structure of the central business district by moving railroads and rivers less than a decade later.

Providence in Crisis, 1970–1978: Necessity Is the Mother of Invention

As elsewhere in the United States, the suburban challenge pressed on Providence throughout the 1960s and 1970s. The rapid development of suburban retail shopping plazas and office parks springing up in close proximity to I-95 posed a serious threat to the city's ability to reverse its declining prosperity. In the early 1970s the Rhode Island and Midland Malls, just eight miles south of Providence, seized a large share of the state's retail dollars. Concomitantly, the three largest downtown department stores in Providence, Shepard's, Gladding's, and the Outlet, announced their closing.

The built environment in Providence was passing through the same kind of difficult transition that other medium-sized cities in the United States experienced. New office parks, some supported by the state, were established on virgin suburban sites tailored to the reorientation of Rhode Island's economy to emerging global communications industries and financial services. These locations were convenient to computer hardware, software, telecommunications, and defense-related R&D companies taking hold along Route 128 around Boston, just a short ride from Providence.

The Providence business community, prompted by two precipitous, nearly calamitous, events in 1973, began to organize a response to the potential wholesale disintegration of the functional and physical fabric of the central business district. The announced relocation of Rhode Island's largest independent insurance group, the Allendale Insurance Company, from Providence to neighboring Johnston, Rhode Island, heralded the loss of a key financial sector business. At nearly the same time the state revealed a plan to move its court complex from Providence to the suburbs, threatening the disintegration of a principal government presence in the city, along with its associated law offices, libraries, and other legal support services.[21]

A pervasive feeling among the business and political leadership was that the Providence economy was on the verge of an implosion and that something needed to be done quickly. The "plan" seemed to be to let parking lots proliferate and hope that malls, stores, and retail would come back.[22] On the eve of Vincent Cianci's debut as mayor in 1975, the *Providence Journal*, the state's largest newspaper, summed up Doorley's decade-long tenure: "[Mayor] Joseph Doorley often seems to look only at the bottom line, checking the cost figures, and often ignoring what are sometimes termed civic needs or social benefits. . . . Neighborhoods are deteriorating, yet it seems the Doorley administration's only response is to tear down more abandoned houses. The mayor has never demonstrated much interest in urban planning of any kind."[23] The inaction that characterized the 1960s was replaced by a growing sense of urgency.[24] The city council created its Committee on Urban Redevelopment, Renewal and Planning in 1973 to help the council deliberate urban development issues. Bruce Sundlun, as chair of the Chamber of Commerce, began to lead lobbying efforts directed at the state to save downtown.[25]

Sundlun over the next two decades would become a pivotal Providence renaissance activist. As CEO of Outlet Communications, chair of numerous nonprofit boards, including the Providence Foundation and Greater Providence Chamber of Commerce, and eventual governor of the state, he was continually in a position to assist others, push along reluctant partners, cajole private sector contacts, including the *Providence Journal*, and make allocative decisions benefiting the city. He had contacts with the Old Yankees, with their embedded values of place, and with the Jewish community and their connections to many civic institutions.[26]

The 1974 mayoral campaign in large measure focused on the central city development issue and brought Vincent Cianci to the mayor's seat in Providence. Candidate Cianci, a state organized-crime prosecutor who grew up in the heart of Rhode Island Italian-American politics in Providence's Silver Lake neighborhood, relentlessly charged that the Doorley administration had abdicated its responsibility to downtown Providence, notwithstanding the completion of the Providence Civic Center. Taking advantage of the brutal internal battle within the Democratic Party over control of city patronage between Doorley and his one-time mentor Larry McGarry, a Smith Hill Irish-American political boss, Cianci chose to run as a Republican and avoid a primary. He won his first mayoral election by 709 votes.

A Crucial Partnership: The NEA, *Interface Providence,* and the Providence Foundation

As the 1974 electoral politics in the city unfolded, halfway up College Hill, RISD professor of architecture Gerald V. Howes and his colleagues worked with the Urban Systems Laboratory at MIT to address the road traffic problems that Providence confronted. At that time energy was high on the policy agenda nationally. Ideas to move traffic efficiently were in demand, as the energy crunch of 1973–74 was taking its toll. RISD had been incorporated in 1877 "for the purpose of aiding in the cultivation of the art of design," and its mission was "the instruction of artists in drawing, painting, modeling and designing, that they [students] may successfully apply the principles of art to the requirements of trade and manufacture."[27] Howes and his students were called upon to apply the principles of art to create a vision of the transportation revitalization of the city's central business district.

The resulting report, *Interface Providence,* was published in 1974. If judged by its direct design impact, the *Interface Providence* study was only somewhat more influential than the *Downtown Providence 1970* plan. The central idea was to create an intermodal transportation and improved vehicular and pedestrian traffic system to alleviate congestion in the inner financial, retail, and government core through a system of ring roads, satellite parking garages, and pedestrian links connected to the surrounding neighborhoods of Smith and College Hills. A few of the ring roads actually were constructed. The report also pointed out the possibility of making use of the city's waterfront and creating a small lake.

However, if viewed as a catalyst for awakening the potential for public-private partnerships and for a reinvigorated federal role in assisting Providence, the *Interface Providence* plan assumes much more importance. The *Interface Providence* report itself was the product of a federal grant that brought the state's congressional delegation into an emerging consensus that something had to be done to save Providence. The financing for the 1974 RISD study was provided by a National Endowment for the Arts (NEA) challenge grant highlighting urban design and intermodal transportation strategies, bringing together two of the strong areas of policy interest of U.S. senator Claiborne Pell. Underlying the *Interface* plan was Senator Pell's advocacy of public transportation and railroads; he had written an influential book on transportation policy, *Megalopolis Unbound: The Supercity and the Transportation of Tomorrow* (1966). Senator Pell also was a strong patron of the arts, an interest that was sparked by a conversation he had with Jacqueline Kennedy when she was first lady.[28] He was the chief Senate sponsor of the 1965 legislation that resulted in the establishment of the NEA and the National Endowment for the Humanities (NEH). Several of Pell's staff went on to become administrators for the NEA.[29]

Senator Pell would remain in the background of the renaissance story in

Providence, as was his style. His "cultural logic" as a member of a very wealthy old New York family was that one could talk to anyone about anything. He told his staff often, "The art of politics is letting the other person have your way."[30] However, the senator was not beyond letting his preferences be known, so when he was alerted about the RISD grant proposal, he indicated his "strong support" for the grant application to his former staff, now in place at the NEA. They warmly received the grant proposal and ushered it through.[31]

An important condition of the NEA grant was that there be matching funds raised by a local nonprofit sponsoring agency. That grant requirement was fortuitous for the renaissance story because it brought about an early partnership with the then-fledgling Providence Foundation, an offshoot of the Greater Providence Chamber of Commerce. This foundation would prove to be a rallying point for the Providence renaissance for more than two decades. The idea of creating the Providence Foundation, as a 501(c)(3) nonprofit public–private partnership, was first floated in Providence in 1974 during discussions between the Mayor's Office of Community Development (MOCD) and the executive board of the Greater Providence Chamber of Commerce.[32] Unlike the Greater Providence Chamber of Commerce, whose spotlight was on metropolitan regionwide development issues, the Providence Foundation's goal was to "create, plan and facilitate feasible downtown development projects which can then be implemented by others."[33] The foundation raised operating funds by soliciting contributions from large downtown corporations and garnering grant support from government agencies. The founding principles signaled the intent of the organization's advocates that the foundation was to stimulate strong interest in Providence by individuals who could make decisions (consequently, only the CEO or highest local official could be a member), that it was to be a politically neutral organization, and that there had to be a direct business interest in the success of the foundation.[34]

The genesis of the Providence Foundation is characteristic of the unplanned, crucially important policy events associated with the ultimate unfolding of the Providence renaissance. Since 1975 the foundation has played a key role in a number of projects associated with the Providence renaissance, including the creation of Capital Center, the relocation of rivers, and the moving of I-195. So without the "gentle, almost invisible nudging" of Senator Pell and his former staff working at the NEA, the *Interface Providence* grant may not have been obtained and the Providence Foundation might not have been able to act as a catalyst to rally the civic and business elite to develop a vision for Providence.[35]

Changing the Policy Framework in Providence

Buddy Cianci, who ran as the "anticorruption" candidate, was inaugurated in January 1975 and immediately embarked on what would become a nearly three-decade effort to revitalize Providence.[36] His memories of watching workmen taking the jazz piano from the Biltmore ballroom almost literally as he was being inaugurated and of moving into City Hall and seeing a janitor breaking up old furniture to stoke the furnace were repeatedly told to staff and the press as a way to describe just how far the city had come.[37]

Cianci sought out useful allies, among which were the Providence Preservation Society and the Providence Foundation. He contacted Antoinette Downing, who was still an activist for neighborhood preservation on College Hill and across the city at a time when historic preservation was having a "hard time getting the respect of the business community."[38] Cianci sent a limousine to her East Side home to bring her to City Hall for a discussion on ways she could help to decide how to use the federal Community Development Block Grant (CDBG) funds the mayor's office controlled for developing community links. He also helped organize the first preservation neighborhood conference in 1976 to focus on the southern, predominantly African American, area of the city, which had large numbers of stately Victorian mansions. The Department of Community Affairs director, Frederick Williamson, brought to the city the nationally renowned African American preservationist Carl Westmorland to give the keynote speech at the conference. Out of this conference grew the Stop Wasting Abandoned Property (SWAP) organization, still active in preserving Providence's stock of Victorian housing.[39]

Cianci's search for allies led him to look downcity, the local vernacular for the area bounded roughly by Empire, Dorrance, Sabin, and Pine Streets. Working collaboratively, the mayor's and the Providence Foundation's staffs cast about for a project to establish a new policy direction for downtown during a burst of "saving downtown" efforts following the Allendale Insurance and state court threats to leave the city. The newly elected Cianci convened a meeting of representatives of the *Interface Plan*, the Providence Foundation, the Association of Downtown Merchants, and others to map out some projects that could be undertaken in the short term: "A new mayor, a new head of the Chamber of Commerce, a new concept for downtown . . . it was timing, timing, timing."[40]

The arts took center stage in these initial, project-based renaissance efforts. Romolo "Ron" Marsella, the new executive director of the Providence Foundation, serendipitously appreciated the importance of the arts.[41] Marsella was enamored by the *Interface Plan*, by the idea of rescuing Providence. "I fell in love with the plan, with the idea; it was a beautiful, colorful, pleasing response to a declining situation."[42] The restoration of the dilapidated Loews Theater using state and local funds and its reopening in 1978 as the Providence Performing Arts Center (PPAC, pronounced "P-PAC" in local vernacular) became a symbol of the concerted effort to save downcity.

The foundation and the mayor's staff put together more development projects using city bonds and low-interest loans from downtown banks, coordinated through the Chamber of Commerce, the foundation, the MOCD, led by chief city planner Martha Bailey, and the Providence Redevelopment Agency, then headed by Stanley Bernstein. Among the projects were the refurbished Providence Arcade (America's oldest shopping mall, 1828), using the Mayor's Office of Community Development money; the renovated Union Station, using federal Economic Development Administration grants and state historic preservation funds; and the restored Biltmore Hotel, the grande dame of hotels in Providence, using private money primarily from Textron, the *Providence Journal*, and the Outlet Company. Johnson and Wales University, a newcomer to the city, announced the renovation of the former Gladding's department store as classroom and library space. Although the federal role was limited, Congress had enacted the first federal tax credits for historic preservation in the form of accelerated depreciation of historic structures retrofitted for commercial use. It was "the first glimmer that something could be done downtown."[43]

A breakthrough renaissance project: The expanded and renovated Providence Performing Arts Center demonstrated to policy entrepreneurs in the late 1970s that public-private partnerships could work.

Courtesy of Gordon Rowley, Rhode Island College

Today Providence hosts both the oldest and newest down-town shopping malls in America: the country's first covered retail mall, the Arcade, opened its doors in 1828.

Courtesy of Providence Department of Planning and Development and Gordon Rowley, Rhode Island College (exterior)

While this flurry of activity was not enough to stop the relocation of the Allendale Group, three important lessons were learned during this period between 1975 and 1978. In the absence of large-scale infusions of federal funds, enough resources could be corralled from a mix of locally derived public and private funds to get things done.[44] As such, these small-scale successes were precursors to more ambitious public-private partnership projects that would emanate from the Providence Foundation and the MOCD in the late 1970s. The projects "didn't amount to a hill of beans in really making long-term improvement to the city, but . . . provided excitement and interest while you were building bridges with government personnel in their various levels."[45]

The second lesson was that without any preexisting relationships, human capital could be corralled in the effort to stave off the city's decline. A series of institutional and personal relationships that had not previously existed emerged from these small efforts, relationships that would generally endure over the next decade and forge a camaraderie built on professionalism, trust, and accountability.[46] A glimmer of hope for the future came when this informal "save downcity" coalition persuaded Governor J. Joseph Garrahy, a Mount Pleasant neighborhood resident, to build a new family court building in Providence, a decision that resulted in the 1978 opening of the expansive Garrahy Judicial Complex on Dorrance Street in downtown Providence.

The third lesson is that the Providence renaissance story is never too far from city-state politics and the individuals who are part of it. New "players" emerged in both the public and private realms. What might be called a renaissance generation of public and private actors surfaced who would stay active over the next decade and beyond to see projects to their conclusion. Their relentlessness would become a hallmark of the Providence renaissance.

"A Dash of This, a Pinch of That . . . Stir Gently": More Renaissance Plans

Interface, the Providence Foundation, and the flurry of small development activities were precursors to a much more ambitious agenda. The attempts to reverse the city's fortunes included more plans, organizations, partnerships, and individuals who became committed to change. These ingredients are summarized here so that as the story moves to individual projects, it should be clear that the Providence story is not about just building a single project but a commitment to continuously undertake a series of projects as opportunities to do so became available.

The Key Ingredient: Capital Center—The Ground Beneath the Renaissance

The Capital Center district is the foundation of the Providence renaissance. With its creation the Providence renaissance began to take on a conceptual and physical shape. The Capital Center plan was crafted in 1979 in response to a sudden and unforeseen opportunity to move the railroad tracks in the center of the city. This large tract facilitated urban planning on a much grander scale than previously envisioned or attempted at any time in the state's history. Chapter 5 is devoted to the tale of the railroad track relocation and the creation of the Capital Center district. A sizeable portion of the more than $1 billion of downtown development since 1980 has occurred in the Capital Center development zone, which continues to have parcels available for development.

Water, Water Everywhere: Moving Rivers and Roads

If Capital Center is the basis of the Providence renaissance, then water is its soul. Until the drawing and implementation of the *Memorial Boulevard/River Relocation Plan*, the old adage could be paraphrased, "water, water everywhere, but not a drop to see!" The Crawford Street Bridge, officially recognized at one time by the *Guinness Book of World Records* as the second-widest bridge in the world, covered long stretches of the rivers that ran through the heart of Capital Center. This river relocation plan moved the confluence of the Moshassuck and Woonasquatucket Rivers one hundred feet or more to the east and replaced the Crawford Street Bridge with a series of smaller, historically themed vehicular and pedestrian bridges with arches high enough to permit leisure craft to navigate the rivers. The public art "happening" known as WaterFire takes place along the rivers and newly created parks. Barriers to public access were removed, sight lines and vistas were improved, and an area for appropriate development was created from the Capital Center district all the way to the Old Harbor. Chapter 6 tells the story of how Providence rediscovered its rivers and waterfront. To this day efforts continue to focus on reconnecting the city with Narragansett Bay.

The Old Harbor Plan: New (Old) Kid on the Block

Water and its relationship to roads remain central to renaissance planning in Providence. Interstate I-195 is a 1960s-era highway that begins in downtown Providence at an intersection with I-95 and heads due east toward Cape Cod. That intersection is the second busiest in New England. Its curves, twists, and turns make it accident-prone. The varied New England weather as well as heavy use make its surface and bridges in constant need of repair. Moving the highway one-quarter of a mile south, just past the Fox Point Hurricane Barrier, at a cost of approximately $300 million is the latest and largest infrastructure project in the Providence renaissance since the 1980s. The result will be a more than forty-acre expanse of property for development along the Old Harbor in Providence. The I-195 relocation is contained in the Old Harbor plan (1992), as updated and incorporated into *Providence 2000: Comprehensive Plan of the City of Providence* in 1999. The relationship of this project to the city's future is addressed in chapter 12.

Downcity Plans: An Attempted Renaissance within a Renaissance

The term "Providence renaissance" tends to obfuscate the discrete nature of development activities in the urban core area. Plans to rescue a declining down-

The pre-renaissance Crawford Street Bridge, one of the world's widest, consisted of iron and concrete road decking that rendered the Providence River almost invisible (lower left). It was demolished in the 1990s to make way for the River Relocation project, which included several new vehicular and pedestrian bridges.

Courtesy of Rhode Island Department of Transportation

town core began with the 1960 plan, extended through *Interface Providence* (1974), and continued with the Westminster Street Pedestrian Plan (1983), the Carr, Lynch/Levine Providence Development Strategy (1986), the urban design and land use charettes hosted by the renowned Florida-based architect and planner Andres Duany (1993), and the Arts and Entertainment District Plan (1994) that grew out of those planning sessions. All of these plans received much less attention precisely because they focus on the old downcity rather than the higher-profile Capital Center and its associated projects, such as the Providence Place mall. The ongoing concerns with the future of downcity are addressed in chapter 12.

Renaissance Partners, People, Projects, and Purposes

In the American context an urban renaissance invariably requires a blending of the public interest with private capital accumulation. Simply put, the interests of government and the interests of private markets intersect as urban renaissance policy is pursued. The participation of civic boosters and nonpublic players is necessary for success. The lines between public and private players are increasingly blurred in this policy environment. In contemplating a new definition of urban regimes, Clarence Stone makes the point that "the division of labor between market and state is contingent and negotiable."[47]

The term "public-private partnership" was a new one in the 1970s, but the concept was embedded in actual urban revitalization practice across the nation. With the contraction in federal revenue sharing for economic development and social programs, city administrations looked to other, more localized mechanisms to leverage funds for downtown development projects. These could be formal chartered organizations with their own by-laws and tax status or informal conduits by which local government agencies funneled money to private firms wishing to develop projects downtown. Whatever the format selected, the goal was the same: to subsidize private capital investment in downtown locations in order to produce jobs and tax-paying enterprises. While there were and are many organizations that have this public-private nature and purpose within Providence, it is the Providence Foundation that was the key agency in the story of the Providence renaissance.

Stone's contention that the lines between public and private players are increasingly blurred in urban policy environments is bolstered by the remarkable extent to which key actors in the Providence renaissance drama were private, public, and sometimes both throughout the redevelopment history of the renaissance. This shifting constellation of players remained visibly involved in different aspects of discrete projects at separate times, sometimes sitting in different organizational seats. Some actors moved back and forth between the private and public sectors, while others came from the world of journalism. There were career city, state, and federal officials, the bureaucrats, as well as elected officials. There were private developers and other private nonprofit sector participants.

The glue that holds the actions of these and many other individuals together is a sense of professional and civic responsibility, perhaps obligation to the city. While certainly there were many individual motivations, time and again the leadership of these organizations and other observers claimed that "there has been very consistently a strongly held sense of civic identity among the elites [old money] and elected officials."[48]

An impressive list of projects, big and small, was undertaken and brought to fruition between 1980 and 2000 (see table 4.1). These economic development projects were designed to fit certain policy purposes or themes that have come to define the Providence renaissance. Those themes are return of retail, financial services, higher education, destination city, arts and entertainment, and historic Providence. These themes are not the product of a comprehensive public vision of thirty years ago, and certainly not that of a single individual. Project ideas that established or enhanced themes have emerged over time as one opportunity has replaced another and has found its advocates, audience, and funding.

The components of those themes are varied, and the various projects we discuss had different intentions. Certain projects did not provide lasting employment or necessarily improve the tax base of the city but were important invitations to those seeking a place to locate a business. These projects were not associated with any particular theme, were very costly, were usually federally

TABLE 4.1
COMPLETED RENAISSANCE PROJECTS, 1980–2000

Popular name	Date completed	Approximate cost	Primary financing
Capital Center	1981–1987	$169 million	Federal
(Railroad and river relocation; Providence Station; highway interchange; and Waterplace Park, below)			
Union Station (parcel 1)	1989	$80 million	Mixed private-public
Gateway Center	1989	$23 million	Private
Center Place	1990	$43 million	Private
Citizens Bank Tower	1990	$34 million	Private
Convention Center/Westin/garages	1994	$290 million	State
Waterplace Park	1994	(see above)	Federal
Providence Place/garage	1999	$465 million	Mixed private-public (land; sales tax rebates/abatements)
Courtyard by Marriott	2000	$16 million	Private-public (abatements)

financed, and were designed to lure private investment by providing infrastructure: roads, bridges, walkways, garages, utility conduits, and uncontaminated sites. During the Providence renaissance period such projects involved moving railroad tracks, constructing a highway interchange, assembling the land and parcels to create the Capital Center district, and paving and utility work.

Some projects held out the promise of a vibrant, exciting experience for those participating in economic development. The hope was that those who took part would establish businesses and create jobs, refurbish and reinvest in existing ventures, visit the city as tourists, maybe even buy a home and become part of the "happening," to resurrect a term from the 1960s. Most, if not all, of these projects required a substantial amount of public financial commitment.

A variety of themes are associated with these "happenings." Unquestionably, the most dramatic project was the uncovering of the Providence River, which resulted in the creation of a series of riverfront parks, walkways, and historic plaques from Waterplace Park, which reclaims a portion of the Great Salt Cove, down to the Old Harbor. This complete restructuring of the physical environment is responsible for the emergence of Providence as an art and entertainment venue and the rediscovery of Providence's history and has made it a destination. Specific examples include the nationally acclaimed WaterFire exhibit; the Convergence Art festival; the fledgling museum mile; the expanding presence of RISD into downtown; the television series *Providence*; the selection of Providence for Xtreme Games; and the too-numerous-to-mention well-regarded restaurants and art galleries. The historic Providence theme includes the large collection of eighteenth-, nineteenth-, and early-twentieth-century homes and office buildings throughout the city; the Revolutionary War–era sloop *Providence* sometimes berthed in the harbor; the Venetian gondola rides routinely offered on the Providence River; the two-acre Roger Williams National Memorial; the restored World War I memorial; and the new Korean War memorial. Trolley tours of eighteenth- and nineteenth-century East Side homes, including that of Providence native H. P. Lovecraft, are under way. Also included might be a stop at the Providence Athenaeum, where Edgar Allan Poe often whiled away hours.

Finally, some projects were intended to produce sustained tangible economic benefit: permanent jobs, enhanced tax yields, and improved land values. Thematically, these projects are varied but have contained some unexpected twists. Financing was mixed; there was significant private as well as public investment, often in the form of tax rebates and the like. Financial service was the expected result from the Capital Center project, although the Citizens Bank and the now former American Express Building are the sum total of financial services within Capital Center's fifteen parcels. A number of other projects have been incorporated into Capital Center, most notably the return of retail embodied in the Providence Place mall, and the goal of destination city embodied in the Rhode

Island Convention Center and Westin Hotel, the new Courtyard by Marriott, and the attempt to lure the New England Patriots to build a stadium in downtown Providence.

The higher education theme has surfaced in the old downcity of Providence. More than $21 million in acquisitions, restoration, and new construction of downtown buildings by Johnson and Wales University established that institution as a major property owner and source of private (but tax-exempt) investment in the old downtown. The state's $35-million renovation of the former Shepard's department store into the University of Rhode Island's College of Continuing Education (URI-CCE) has brought back foot traffic to two formerly deserted streets. Roger Williams University's urban campus, the result of its purchase and renovation of the Siegal block a few hundred feet away from URI-CCE, also contributed to an improved streetscape. Brown University has added dormitories and a conference center. RISD renovated the "What Cheer" Garage, a former underground Rhode Island Public Transit Authority bus repair center, into classroom and artist studio space and expanded its art museum.

Other similar projects have surfaced away from Capital Center. Arts and entertainment endeavors are less grandiose than those already mentioned, but they nonetheless represent important choices. Aggressive public sector financial support for Trinity Repertory Theater, one of several in Providence and one of the oldest community theaters in the nation, is an example. The recent gift by Citizens Bank of one of its oldest and most ornate branches in the central business district to Trinity is also significant. A hoped-for museum mile anchored by an ambitious Heritage Harbor Museum is making progress. This last project combines donated waterfront property, private philanthropy, and government assistance in a public-private, nonprofit, large-scale venture that will cost more than $250 million.

Summary

The Providence renaissance did not just appear but rather came out of several antecedent developments. The renaissance, however, was not the product of a comprehensive plan. Efforts to save College Hill property rekindled the old elites. The *Downtown Providence 1970* (1961) and *Interface Providence* (1974) plans envisioned a future for the entire Providence downtown but did not serve as blueprints for action. They stimulated debate in the public and private sectors about what to do downtown. *Interface* in particular brought together elements that would be crucial to later renaissance policy, including the stimulation of the Providence Foundation and the engagement of the federal delegation. The earliest renaissance activity was a reaction to a precipitous decline and the need to "do something" among public and private individuals who learned that even with the withdrawal of federal interest in urban renewal, enough state, local, and private resources could be corralled by those committed to changing the fortunes of the city. These efforts brought new individuals and organizations into the attempt to revive the city's fortunes.

Less comprehensive than moment-to-moment, the development projects took advantage of circumstances or opportunities that presented themselves as one set of plans or another began to unfold. There emerged different types of projects, built around certain themes. They were not seen or even planned that way; they just happened that way.

Moving Rails and Earth:
The Creation of Capital Center

5

The climate was favorable, the money was available, and the railroad was being upgraded. It all came together at exactly the right time.

Louis Thompson, Federal Railway Administration Regional Administrator, 1985

I would say that without the railroad relocation project, there would have been no Renaissance in Providence.

J. Joseph Garrahy, Governor, State of Rhode Island, 1977–85

■ When Sydney Hansen in the television drama *Providence* strolled through the city's downtown, it was through the Capital Center district, the setting that most observers refer to when they mention the Providence renaissance. Capital Center is about seventy acres of land created by moving railroad tracks, sidings, and walls. The idea was to provide Providence with the ability to compete for financial sector economic development. Improved transportation was the hook that brought piles of federal money to create this new district. The Northeast Corridor Improvement Project (NECIP) money created "a flurry of money-driven opportunities."[1] Quickly thereafter, federal highway funds became essential in the Providence renaissance story.

Moving the railroad tracks and constructing the Civic Center interchange were projects that initially created forty acres of virgin land in downtown Providence that stretched from the State House to Kennedy Plaza, the core of Capital Center. In 1978 the future Capital Center district was the "Chinese Wall," a deteriorating railroad viaduct and surrounding tracks, sidings, rail yards, service facilities, and buffer zones that quite literally carved a quarter-mile swathe through the historic downtown, cleaving it in half. Gaspee and Francis Streets provided limited vehicular access to the State House from the central business district, but there was no safe walkway over the tracks, so pedestrians were forced to navigate a half-mile circuitous walk around the periphery of the urban core. This was one reason the *Downtown Providence 1970* advocates wanted the railroad bits and pieces moved. In addition to the rail viaduct, a substantial portion of the area was a sea of dirt or blacktop parking lots, sometimes referred to as the "pork chop" for its shape. Two small, polluted, channeled, and barely visible rivers were within the forty acres.

This ugly patch of ground was surrounded by unrealized potential. To the

Just four years before the Capital Center plan was adopted, downtown Providence was a wasteland of disused railroad sidings and parking lots.

Courtesy of William D. Warner, Architects & Planners

east was College Hill, with its colonial and Federalist-era institutional and residential architecture undergoing substantial rescue and rehabilitation. To the south lay the old commercial core, with its nineteenth- and early-twentieth-century office buildings and streetscapes leading to the Providence Harbor. To the west was a government complex consisting of URI-CCE and the state offices for the Department of Education and, just beyond, the north-south stretch of I-95. The architectural jewel in Rhode Island's crown, the State House on Smith Hill, sat majestically to the north. The white Georgia marble State House was designed by the New York architectural firm McKim, Mead and White and constructed between 1895 and 1904. The Rhode Island State House dome is the fourth-largest marble-covered, self-supporting dome in the world. Only St. Peter's in the Vatican, the Minnesota State Capital in St. Paul, and the Taj Mahal in Agra, India, are larger.

Moving the rails, building the highway interchange, and creating Capital Center is the story of strenuous and dogged efforts of public- and private-sector individuals who saw an opportunity open, however briefly, to take a much-needed chance for the city. "It was one of those unique ideas that surfaced just exactly at the right time in the right way."[2] With the movement of the tracks, an opportunity presented itself to set a new and vigorous agenda for urban regeneration. The resulting Capital Center facilitated urban planning on a much grander scale than previously envisioned or attempted at any time in the state's history. Without Capital Center the Providence downtown would not have been

The Rhode Island State House.

Photograph by the authors

transformed, because there would have been no physical space to pursue the economic development themes of the Providence renaissance.

The basic idea of moving the tracks had been discussed many times among members of the business and government community. A consensus already existed in the public and private realms that moving the rails would clearly benefit the city and state if the opportunity presented itself. The resourcefulness, inventiveness, and creativity of federal, state, local, and private administrators would be needed to transform a decayed portion of Providence into the new heart of the city. The lesson is typical of the renaissance period: when an opportunity was there to be seized, and the resources could be corralled, and where an underlying consensus had been reached at some earlier time, and there was a person around whom the effort could be organized, a Rhode Island elite coalition would form and swing into action.

The Northeast Corridor Rail Project

The origin of the railroad relocation, Capital Center, and highway interchange project is rooted in events that caused a fortuitous change for Providence in federal transportation policy. The construction of the federal interstate system not only began the suburbanization of the United States and the ascendancy of cars and trucks as people and product movers but also spelled doom for the private passenger and freight rail system. Throughout the 1960s rail bankruptcies were commonplace. Into the 1970s the imperative to improve the rail system expanded beyond the concerns of a bankrupt system. "The need for such large scale efforts [to improve rail passenger service] is supported by mounting concern over environmental degradation brought about by competing modes of transportation, particularly the automobile, and by national concern with respect to energy conservation."[3]

The nation's concern with environmental issues and energy conservation played an important role in keeping rail transportation policy on the national agenda. The Clean Air Act and the creation of the Environmental Protection Agency (EPA) signaled the national concern over the need to reduce auto emissions. Conservation as a national energy strategy was thrust on the American public as a result of U.S. support for Israel during the 1973 Arab-Israeli War. The United States endured its first OPEC-led oil embargo in 1973–74. The embargo led to high prices and long lines at the gas pumps and various gasoline rationing programs for the first time since World War II.

Consequently, as cars and commuter air shuttles replaced passenger rail service as the dominant mode of passenger transportation along the Boston–Washington, D.C., corridor, environmental and conservation concerns helped keep passenger rail service on the policy table for the millions of East

Coast commuters. The federal response to the decline in rail passenger service, prior to the energy crisis, was the High Speed Ground Transportation (HSGT) Act of 1965. A principal patron of the HSGT Act was Senator Claiborne Pell, an ardent railroad booster ("I hate to fly," he remarked, "I'm scared of airplanes!")[4] In 1966 Senator Pell published *Megalopolis Unbound*, an influential book deploring the passenger rail crisis. He was instrumental in stewarding the HSGT Act through Congress with the support of President Lyndon Johnson.[5] Senator Pell was able to sell Johnson on the concept of a national rail passenger system by pointing out to the president that the likely routes ran across a huge collection of potential electoral votes: "That stirred up his enthusiasm a great deal."[6] Johnson needed only one look at the routes to reply, "Sold!"[7] Using an authorized $90 million in federal demonstration grant funds, the Pennsylvania Central Railroad built a Metroliner that on 16 January 1969 made the New York–Washington run in less than three hours.

The Metroliner's performance restored some popularity to commuter rail passenger service and kept alive congressional interest in saving railroads.[8] However, popularity did not mean that profits flowed to the private Pennsylvania Railroad, but the railroad's continued financial problems did not cool congressional railroading ardor. "For various members of Congress, the question no longer was whether to provide support for intercity-rail service, but rather 'In what form and through what institutional channels shall such Federal assistance be directed?'"[9] This prevailing attitude resulted in the Rail Passenger Service Act of 1970. The 1970 act created Amtrak, the national, initially for-profit railroad, which began operating in 1971 by taking over from the bankrupt freight rail systems the responsibility of operating intercity passenger service.[10]

Creating Amtrak did not solve the national rail crisis. By 1973 the Penn Central railroad was asking Congress for hundreds of millions of dollars in loan guarantees, precipitating the willingness of Congress and the president to consider a reform primarily focused on freight service. The Regional Rail Reorganization Act of 1973 authorized the federal acquisition of most of the right-of-way along the entire Northeast Corridor.[11] On 3 July 1974 the Federal Railway Administration (FRA) awarded a contract to Bechtel Corporation to assist the FRA in the development of detailed improvement plans leading to the establishment of better high-speed rail service in the Northeast Corridor.[12] Providence was one of the stops along this proposed high-speed right-of-way.

Moving the Rails in Providence

Not only was Providence a stop along the Northeast Corridor, but that stop was in the middle of the city. Two of the pre-renaissance plans, *Downtown Providence 1970* (1960) and *Interface Providence* (1974), recognized the impediment to new development presented by the railroad embankments that ran between the commercial and government centers of downtown. This alignment was the legacy of a much earlier track-moving venture. In the 1890s the city prevailed upon the railroads to bring the tracks closer to the city's commercial core. The result was the abandonment of existing switching yards at the bottom of Smith Hill; filling in what was left of the old cove park created in the 1840s; and channeling within pavement the Woonasquatucket River, which "ceased to be much of an element in the landscape."[13] To maintain street access from the city core to the now more attractive Smith Hill setting with its newly rising elegant State House, the tracks were elevated onto a railroad viaduct in front of the new Union Station, completed in 1898. The embankment was known in Providence as the "Chinese Wall." The tracks and viaduct were unsightly barriers between the commercial core and the State House and the older East Side. In the 1950s the New Haven and Penn Central Railroads proposed to move the tracks as part of a track improvement plan, but they failed to generate interest. The *Downtown Providence 1970* plan proposed realigning the railroad tracks to create numerous new land parcels. Government officials and business leaders at the state and local levels wanted to move the railroad tracks out of the vicinity of Kennedy Plaza in downtown Providence. However, it was a "good idea" whose time never seemed to come, primarily because the costs were so daunting.[14] By the time *Interface Providence* was published in 1974, the strong consensus among public and private officials was that the railroad tracks had to be moved north and east.[15]

So as the smaller, preservation-oriented, downcity projects in the old retail core got under way between 1976 and 1979, events were unfolding in Washington, D.C., that would have a profound effect on the city's development. NECIP was

By 1860 the Providence cove had been contained by walls to make way for the railroad.

Courtesy of Providence Department of Planning and Development

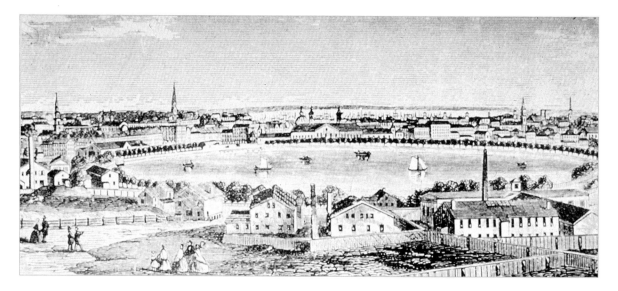

enacted in Title VII of the Railroad Revitalization and Regulatory Reform Act of 1976. That act established the goal of reduced rail travel times to three hours or less between Boston and New York and New York and Washington, D.C., by upgrading the rail infrastructure along the Northeast Corridor. Funds were available to improve the rail corridor through Providence as part of the original $1.6 billion appropriation that eventually would be increased to $2 billion. Included in that total was about $200 million for rehabilitation of historic railroad stations along the route, including Providence's Union Station.

Satisfying mutual interests is very much the story of this early era in renaissance making. The NECIP legislation guaranteed that the state could buy abandoned railroad property along the right-of-way for "net salvage value." The regional FRA preferred a new passenger station for Amtrak rather than rehabilitating Union Station and was prepared to abandon it and 7.2 acres of rail easements. Gerry Pieri, a contract employee hired by Joseph Arruda, the Rhode Island Department of Transportation (RIDOT) Assistant Director of Planning, pointed out that it would be possible for the state to buy Union Station and the accompanying acreage for $57,000, but it only had thirty days to exercise its option. Arruda felt that the purchase would provide the state with leverage in ne-

The Great Divide, ca. 1950: railroad platforms and abutments created what Providence natives called the "Chinese Wall" between the government/education center to the north and the commercial center to the south.

Courtesy of Rhode Island Department of Transportation

gotiations with Amtrak over passenger rail service and create an opportunity to link with a new East Bay rail system. The Act stated that Rhode Island had the right to have access to passenger rail service (the Boston MBTA service through Providence) without having to pay for those rights.

Agreements were reached and some preliminary work began in 1978 to plan to realign the railroad tracks going into and out of Providence. Work was begun refurbishing a railroad bridge over the barely visible course of the Woonasquatucket River. What was not on the FRA designer's drawing board yet was a major realignment of the tracks. The FRA incentives to cooperate were many, including a new station and a much-desired track alignment to accommodate its envisioned higher-speed train services for Amtrak. The state would retain passenger rail service rights plus the land and Union Station. In the background was Senator Pell, whose well-known advocacy for rail service weighed on the minds of FRA administrators. "Pell's name was like a hammer. Our staff could get anything done because of having him behind us."[16]

Ron Marsella sat in his downtown Providence office of the Providence Foundation in September 1978, staring at a copy of the *Downtown Providence 1970* master plan still pinned to his wall. That plan advocated the removal of the Chinese Wall. Marsella knew, as did many others, that the FRA had $15–$20 million of NECIP funds committed to track improvement and a station. Marsella was upset because a Providence Foundation effort to bridge the Chinese Wall by constructing an office building over the tracks with considerable assistance from the state, city, and Textron Corporation had fallen apart.[17]

The thirty-seven-year-old Marsella was busy helping along other city projects and was not to be stymied by this setback. Following a "eureka" moment, a series of phone calls took place: first to Rob Freeman on the staff of the Historical Preservation Commission; then to Robert Rowland, a state transportation engineer; and then to Stanley Bernstein, the head of the Providence Redevelopment Agency. Each was asked a simple question: What about moving the tracks if it did not cost more than our original plan? Each in his own way found Marsella's question humorous but all liked the idea. Martha Bailey, the first city planner in Providence, also thought there were possibilities.

These encouraging responses emboldened Marsella to make two pivotal phone calls. The first was to Steve Maguire, a private engineer acting as a consultant to RIDOT with whom he had worked closely for more than two years. Maguire was very familiar with the numbers involved in the attempt to bridge the Chinese Wall. Marsella wanted to make sure about the costs involved in moving the tracks and if NECIP money already allocated would be sufficient. Maguire was unequivocal: the available funds would be ample to relocate the tracks.[18]

The second call was to Joseph Arruda. Marsella suggested another look at the possibilities of removing the Chinese Wall, moving the railroad tracks about one-quarter of a mile northeast of Kennedy Plaza to a new location abutting the State House grounds, and building a new railroad station, in the process creating acres of developable land. Arruda's initial response was "It will never happen," even though he expressed a liking for the idea and told Marsella he would not oppose the plan if it emerged eventually.[19] These calls, within an hour of each other, suggested to Marsella that at the staff level of key planning and regulatory agencies there would be support. He then called Joseph Noonan, the president of the Providence Foundation and a local developer, who felt the risk was worth taking, just another in a long list of potential successes, albeit a much larger one than the effort to refurbish PPAC.[20]

Marsella solicited the help of Bruce Sundlun and in tandem they prevailed upon the 21st Century Providence Group, an offspring of the Chamber of Commerce, to provide $5,000 for a track-moving feasibility study by C. E. Maguire, a firm working on the NECIP for the FRA, that would estimate the potential costs of realigning the tracks and going *underground*, which would thus make the "pork chop" adjacent to I-95 and other former railroad properties open to development. The feasibility study money was contributed by G. William "Bill" Miller at Textron, Michael Metcalf at the *Providence Journal*, Terry Murray at Fleet Bank, Woody Woodbridge at Hospital Trust, and Bill Heisterly of Citizens Bank, all presidents or CEOs of their locally owned institutions.[21]

Marsella called Sundlun in late October 1978 to tell him that the costs of realigning the tracks could be borne by the FRA's already approved $15–$20 million available for improvements in the Northeast Rail Corridor in Providence, including the construction of a new railroad station. Marsella and Sundlun set about the task of mobilizing public- and private-sector elites behind the effort to reunify downtown. Arruda and Marsella dusted off the old *Downtown Providence 1970* plan and went to Sundlun's Outlet Company office to discuss further the idea of moving the railroad tracks. Sundlun at the time was the president of the Outlet Company and the chair of the Greater Providence Chamber of Commerce. Joe Arruda reiterated the long-held view that track relocation would present the opportunity for better state planning for a Federal Highway Administration (FHWA) I-95 Civic Center interchange project.[22] The railroad abutments and associated tracks prevented that roadway project from unfolding because the Chinese Wall effectively barred the addition of the eight-movement interchange necessary to accommodate the number of highways and city streets that came together at that geographic location.[23]

As Marsella and Arruda watched, Sundlun telephoned Senator Claiborne Pell, who happened to be in his Providence office that day and arranged a meeting with Marsella. Sundlun and Pell had been friends since the 1950s and he was the finance chair for Pell's re-election bid to the U.S. Senate. Sundlun suspected that his longtime friend would love the idea because Pell was "a railroad and train nut" and to a large extent an intellectual patron of the NECIP. In his quiet way Senator Pell would help "nudge along" the railroad relocation.[24] Marsella and Sundlun drove the three blocks to Pell's office on the same day that Marsella alerted him to the possibility of moving the tracks.

Not surprisingly, Pell was enthusiastic about the idea as long as the mayor and governor were. Sundlun called the governor, who invited them over that same day. The three men drove together to the State House, past the Chinese Wall, to Governor J. Joseph Garrahy's office. Garrahy cautiously climbed aboard the "move the tracks" train, particularly after being told that his chief transportation planner, Joe Arruda, was expressing great enthusiasm for the idea and that the trains "would not run across the lawns of the State House."[25] Garrahy also knew that Mayor Cianci would have to support the idea, but he would not speak to him: "Go see him yourself."[26] Garrahy and Cianci were not fond of each other, although Garrahy felt that Cianci was a "tireless advocate for the city and a good cheerleader."[27] Later that evening, Sundlun and Marsella met with Mayor Cianci to assess the extent of his interest. Cianci jumped aboard the train in typical Cianci style: "Hey, if the federal government's going to pay for it, let's do it."[28] In late October 1978, at the Providence Foundation annual dinner, the feasibility of the track realignment plan was announced.

Fortune was kind to this informal association of "track movers." Brock Adams, President Jimmy Carter's secretary of transportation, had scheduled a visit to Rhode Island to announce the results of a federal investigation into a rail mishap and some federal grants for rail and highway projects in the state. Pell decided to speak with Adams quietly about the track moving idea after years of persistent cajoling to *upgrade* tracks. He did so by telling Adams he'd be hearing more about a track-moving project eventually.[29]

As potential state and local participants in a railroad relocation plan were assembled, Marsella called Hanan Kibbet, the chief planner for the NECIP, and asked the basic question: Would the FRA planners be willing to consider yet another look at the problem of the Chinese Wall? There was some concern that FRA administrators would be skittish. The FRA at the outset of early NECIP planning already had discussed its more limited track upgrading plans with city and state officials, but the response was ambiguous at best.[30] When Marsella initially broached to Arruda the more radical idea to remove the Chinese Wall and go underground the RIDOT planner's reluctance was based on his feeling that "They [FRA] won't change their path at this point."[31] The FRA already had contracted with the New York office of Skidmore, Owings and Merrill (SOM) to draw plans for a track realignment, and time constraints might block the ability to perform what would be another required environmental impact statement (EIS).

Marsella was surprised at the open-door reaction he received. Louis Thompson, Kibbet's boss at the FRA, loved the plan. "Here is the first railroad plan that actually helps a city," was Thompson's reaction.[32] Thompson, who was eager to move the rail project along, asked SOM to redraw the plan. Some vaguely defined water feature was drawn and the idea of a "new cove" was mentioned in the Capital Center plan.[33] A newly constructed Providence Station was destined to become one of only two new stations built as part of NECIP.[34]

The FRA was sold on the plan, but to reallocate funds in the way now envisioned would require the approval of the federal Department of Transportation. Pell continued his quiet nudging of Adams to proceed with funding the new railroad relocation plan. The Providence Foundation contributed $5,000 so that SOM could build and take to Washington, D.C., a model of what the center of the city would look like after the tracks were relocated. When he saw the model Senator Pell commented in his reserved way, "Make no small plans."[35] Pell successfully lobbied the FRA administrators in Washington to consider redirection of the funding earmarked for renovation and upgrading of the Northeast Corridor tracks to support realigning the tracks and related allied infrastructure projects in Providence. On 28 June 1979 U.S. Transportation Secretary Brock Adams gave conditional approval for the track relocation by ordering a halt to the preliminary work that had begun until a full assessment of the proposed new use of federal funds was completed.[36]

To ensure FRA approval the state and city had to demonstrate the physical and fiscal feasibility of the proposal. To do so, the private owners of the property where the tracks then stood, and where they would be relocated to, needed to indicate their willingness to cooperate. The principal landowner was the Providence and Worcester Railroad (P&W) and Capital Properties. Rhode Island owned Union Station and seven adjoining acres, and Amtrak would build and own a new station under the plan that was emerging, but without the privately held land the project could not go forward.[37]

The P&W's roots reached back well into the nineteenth century, but it was now about to become centrally important to the twenty-first-century Providence renaissance.[38] The railroad had obtained charters in the 1840s to operate a railroad along the Blackstone Canal to Worcester, Massachusetts, which it did successfully for decades and then leased its assets to J. P. Morgan's New York, New Haven and Hartford Railroad in 1892 for one hundred years. The lease provided annual payments to P&W stockholders. Robert H. Eder, a young entrepreneur, decided to buy stock in the railroad that he came to know about only because he and Joseph R. DiStefano, a Providence lawyer, had gone out to view an old Shell Company terminal along the Seekonk River through which a railroad track belonging to the P&W ran. Eder got curious—"What the heck is this? What is the Providence and Worcester railroad?"—leading him to wage a successful proxy fight and take control of the railroad in 1966.[39]

Eder became president of the company in 1966. He had taken control (although in name only) from the New Haven Railroad, which was about to be taken over by the Penn Central. In 1965 Eder had hired DiStefano and directed him to clear titles and to keep the railroad from the Penn Central, itself on the brink of dissolution.[40] He was successful and by 1973 the railroad once again was an independent operating regional freight railway. Because of an element in the 1892 lease, property acquired throughout the life of the lease would revert to the P&W; this led to the acquisition of many parcels through tough negotiations with the Penn Central to avoid litigation.[41] At the time of these purchases and swaps there was no discussion of Capital Center.

By the time railroad relocation was being discussed, the P&W also owned portions of the railroad yards near the State House. By 1982 the railroad had acquired eighteen acres of land in Capital Center through the efforts of Capital Properties, the railroad's real estate parent company, created in 1980 with DiStefano as its president. Eder was the largest stockholder in both companies. As a result, Capital Properties held clear title to a significant portion of the land that made up Capital Center.[42]

The P&W did not want the land consumed by the railroad relocation plans. Taking the private land by eminent domain was possible because the outcome was a public benefit. However, in a decision to forgo the complications, delays, and expenses associated with the inevitable lawsuits, the public- and private-sector officials opted for a series of complex land swaps. Ron Marsella and Bruce Sundlun were the chief problem solvers in that sensitive process.[43] The state did own the air rights over Capital Center and could block private development in the future. By October 1982 Ron Marsella secured Capital Properties' signature to the Master Property Conveyance Contract, in which a series of property swaps—land readjustments—would ensure that all landowners with titles to property abutting the new track locations would benefit from the creation of a "Capital Center," a name coined by Marsella at a Providence Foundation executive board meeting in October 1978 to announce the planned track relocation project.[44]

Each property owner agreed to erase all previously drawn property boundaries. All profits from future sales would be apportioned among the real estate owners in proportion to the share of the total land they had contributed to the project.[45] In this way it was possible to avoid more conventional land condemnation and all of the expense associated with it. Each property owner's reward would come when the parcels were sold. No landowner opposition emerged, despite the potential for legal action.[46] The benefit to real estate interests was obvious: Capital Properties' costs associated with assembling its acreage and making its required contribution to the cost of Capital Center infrastructure improvements was about $6 million, with a much greater potential return.[47]

What was once the utopian possibility of a revitalized downtown now seemed within reach with these key officials at all levels of government in agreement and private property owners on board. Throughout the later months of 1979 meetings were held at the Providence Foundation under the sponsorship and willing leadership of Ron Marsella, meetings that were to form the basis of the Master Property Conveyance Agreement of 1982. A very "tight group" of railroad movers came together who had a real enthusiasm for the project and were professionals in the right place to make ideas become realities. This group included Marsella, Sundlun, Joe Arruda, Stan Bernstein (Providence Redevelopment Authority), Martha Bailey (DPD), Ken Orenstein (MOCD), and eventually Gordon Hoxie (FHWA) and Victor Bell (Rhode Island Department of Environmental Management). Pete Pointner, an architect from Chicago and an acquaintance of the local architect Bill Warner, was hired by the FRA to complete the required EIS for this new railroad relocation and Capital Center plan.

The importance of this contingent coalition is plain to see in the Capital Properties discussions with Amtrak over its original plan to come and repair the railroad viaducts' underpinnings. The P&W made clear that they did not want the quasi-public railroad coming onto the private railroad's land. DiStefano went to Senator Pell for assistance and soon Amtrak abandoned those plans "because they had to." Instead, the cooperation among the FRA, FHWA, and other public and private agencies that was the hallmark of this era in renaissance building came to the fore: "One of the best examples of cooperation among the three levels of government and the private sector you will ever see."[48]

There were potential stumbling blocks and some outright opposition to the ideas emanating from this group of civil servants and private sector participants. Bruce Sundlun found himself in the role of ensuring that any state-city political rivalries were subordinated to the greater need to accomplish something beneficial to the city.[49] The heated gubernatorial campaign between Garrahy and Cianci was under way, and while both men supported the Capital Center idea, ill-spoken words could derail the project. What might be termed a "railroad lobby" put up a vociferous opposition.[50] *Interface Providence* advocates and allied environmentalists still hoped for an intermodal transportation center near Union Station to reduce traffic in downtown Providence. Preservationists, worried about the future of the nineteenth-century Union Station, joined the fray as well.

As these little battles took place, "no wars erupted."[51] Capital Properties agreed to delay development of their parcels until the infrastructure was in place and to operate under strict zoning requirements.[52] Providence would get its first significant post–urban renewal federal infrastructure investment as soon as the FRA agreed to the proposal. The EIS process moved forward during the summer of 1980, when a second round of public hearings were held. The opposition this time met a well-scripted hearing at which speaker after speaker praised the plans as a necessary component of Providence and Rhode Island economic health. Senator Pell, the twenty-year veteran and now the senior U.S. senator from Rhode Island following the retirement of Senator John O. Pastore, was present and "that was enough."[53] It helped that Sundlun promised Antoinette Downing that Union Station would not be demolished and an alternative use would be sought for a refurbished station.[54]

Ron Marsella was taking no chances. He had become the classic policy entrepreneur. Between 1979 and 1981 he handled most of the conceptualization and planning logistics involving the railroad project. He was a consultant to the P&W and the Providence Redevelopment Agency and was under contract with RIDOT. He also was a consultant to the FRA and Capital Properties. His ability to bring together the varied interests was critical to getting the rails moved. On 27 January 1982 all parties signed a final cooperative agreement to move the tracks, put them underground, and build a new station.

Creating Capital Center: 1979–1982

If railroad relocation was an unforeseen opportunity ready to be seized, an "elegant engineering solution"[55] to a major development problem, then creating a

Physical and functional transformation: A dead zone that separated College Hill from the commercial core (ca. 1975) was transformed by the rail and river relocation projects with new riverwalks along the Moshassuck at One Citizens Plaza (ca. 1995).

Courtesy of Capital Center Commission (Before) and Thomas Payne, WaterFire Providence (After)

commission to oversee Capital Center came to be seen as a necessary corollary. In 1979 the Providence Foundation, the city, and the state established a task force that worked under a cooperative agreement to move the Capital Center project forward. This task force engaged the planners at Skidmore, Owings and Merrill, the firm suggested by the FRA, to draft a comprehensive plan to rationalize the parcels around the new railroad alignment. Marilyn Taylor was the principal Capital Center designer. On 1 May 1979 the firm presented a plan for Capital Center to the Providence Foundation, the City of Providence, and the State of Rhode Island. These drawings became a partial blueprint for a revitalized Providence. The renderings focused on land north of the old Union Station.

Creating a commission was the idea of Governor Garrahy as a way to mediate the interests of the city, state, and federal governments relative to use, design, architecture, and other matters. Governor Garrahy and Mayor Cianci were not known for having a close working relationship with each other, but both men came to support the idea of a commission. Businesses such as Textron, Outlet, Fleet, and Hospital Trust put pressure on the political actors "to do the right

thing," to find a solution to their differences over "control" of the Capital Center district.[56]

Many American city regimes have created formal public-private partnerships, often in the form of large-scale downtown development authorities.[57] These entities usually have sole discretion over what gets built, by and for whom, in carefully demarcated downtown development districts. Generally such a district's governing authority focuses on downtown viability within the overall metropolitan economy and carefully coordinates all initiatives toward those goals. Capital Center is as close as Providence came to a downtown development district. The Capital Center Commission (CCC) initially was incorporated in 1980 as a nonprofit corporation to consider the Capital Center plan within a more formal framework, but in 1981 the commission was converted by the General Assembly to the legislatively chartered body it became.[58] In the same year the Providence City Council formally adopted the Capital Center plan as required by the commission's enabling legislation, which formally established the city-state partnership envisioned in 1979.

The commission was a structure to smooth the entire process of moving the tracks, assembling the land, and managing the future of the resulting acreage. The Capital Center plan contained a provision for a commission, advocating that it was perhaps the best mechanism for ensuring the interests of all parties.[59] The commission's power rested in its ability to circumvent existing city-dominated entities and to create a single set of documents guiding decision making, land swaps, and transportation and building design issues. Unlike other projects that physically rebuilt Providence, establishing the CCC was central to the potential success of other projects in Capital Center, because it would alter and then manage the political relationship among the city, state, and federal agencies and private developers. The commission's central political purpose was to continually find common ground among the public and private signatories of the cooperative agreement that otherwise would be difficult to achieve if they acted separately.

Governor Garrahy envisioned control over the projects in the area as an executive agency responsibility, one deserving close and direct oversight by the governor. The commission's Capital Center Construction Project Management Team, the agency primarily responsible for the coordination of construction projects within Capital Center, was located in the governor's office. Its staff of about ten engineers and four managers were on loan from RIDOT and were responsible for overseeing construction of parks, streets, and bridges within the Capital Center district and eventually would oversee the river relocation project. The agency's being in the governor's office gave the team direct access to the governor and his policy office. That position symbolized its importance and allowed it to cut through red tape.[60] It also removed the necessity of the city planning agencies' and mayor's office's dealing directly with RIDOT, which city officials were loath to do.[61]

The structure of the commission was designed to keep forward momentum and minimize friction. Twelve commissioners—four each appointed by the governor, the mayor of Providence, and the Providence Foundation—formed the decision-making body. A thirteenth commissioner was the chair, who would be selected by majority vote of the appointing authorities—governor, mayor, and chairperson of the Providence Foundation.[62] An effort was made to ensure that two types of people were on the commission: people who represented an affected interest, and people in decision-making positions—top-level CEOs, executive directors, or high-ranking department- or cabinet-level individuals.[63] Nine of the original thirteen members were chief executives of principal businesses headquartered or located in Providence. Providence Foundation appointees were Bruce Sundlun (CEO of Outlet Communications), Louis Hampton (chairman of Providence Gas), Terrence Murray (president of Fleet Bank), and Harry Baird (partner at Peat, Marwick, and Mitchell). Governor Garrahy appointed Jacques Hopkins (partner at Hinckley, Allen, Tobin, and Silverstein) and J. Joseph Krause (vice president of Textron), and Mayor Cianci appointed Richard Oster (president of Cookson America), Stanley Blacher (owner of Blacher Brothers Inc.), and Herbert DeSimone (partner in DeSimone and Del Sesto). Antoinette Downing of the Providence Preservation Society, a mayoral appointee, represented preservationist interests; Robert J. Powell, who sat on the executive board of the local AFL-CIO, was appointed by Garrahy, as was Glen Kumekawa, professor of planning and policy at the University of Rhode Island. Retired Associate Supreme Court Justice Alfred Joslin was chosen as the first commission chair.

Of particular concern was that the separate private and public ownership of different land parcels be maintained. In this way the contentious interest over land taking was avoided and never turned into a barrier to development. Furthermore, the commission's enabling legislation required a mandatory public design review process for all public and private development in the Capital Center district. A high value was placed on maintaining distinctions between public open space, public streets, and private building lots and on sensitivity to the historic context of the district, which abuts two National Register historic districts (College Hill and downtown); a national memorial park (Roger Williams); and several individual National Register landmarks, such as the State House and the Masonic Temple/Veterans Memorial Auditorium complex. The CCC Design Review Committee (DRC) was established to foster this element of the legislation.

At the heart of the Capital Center agreement was the idea of a binding contract among the parties. Each agent, government or private, undertook its own set of priorities in concert with all other agents. This contract was important since each agent had to commit resources that could not be recommitted and had a right to see its own set of priorities fulfilled, but also had the duty to avoid negating the legitimate aspirations of all other parties.[64] The plan detailed the responsibilities of each party: The FRA was to move the tracks; the state and city were to demolish the viaduct, create a commission, make appropriate zoning changes, and undertake improvements. The private sector was to develop commercial office space; limit retail to support of the commercial activities; develop residential projects primarily on the northeast side; and ensure that use of the old Union Station complex be maximized.[65]

Not everyone favored the idea of Capital Center or a commission. Skepticism was most evident among those tied to the economic fortunes of the old downcity retail core. As a major property owner there, Joseph Paolino Sr., father of the city council president and eventual mayor Joseph Paolino Jr., expressed concern that even though Capital Center was created as an urban financial district, allowing retail in Capital Center would kill any chance of bringing retail back to life in downcity. Foot traffic would be drained from downcity, which in turn would dry up the businesses that occupied much of the Paolino interests.[66]

Preservationists had doubts that were not to be calmed until the EIS was completed and indicated that the acreage in Capital Center would reduce development pressure and the need to tear down historic buildings.[67] Preservationist concerns also were allayed somewhat by Capital Center's being made subject to the National Historic Preservation Act and consequently brought under the regulatory oversight of the National Park Service and of the Rhode Island Historical Preservation and Heritage Commission (RIHPHC). The RIHPHC opted to approve the Capital Center Commission's design review process, which was the responsibility of the DRC, rather than a project-by-project review.[68] Nevertheless, historic preservation was beginning to flex more of its muscles, which were first tested in the saving of College Hill properties and the ongoing preservation efforts in downcity. "One thing people tend to forget is that Rhode Island has more historic buildings per acre than any other state in the country."[69]

The design and development criteria for Capital Center developed by October 1980 were essentially the same ones presented by SOM in 1979. They were stated as four objectives that made clear that the new district was not to concentrate on retail and was to reconcile three different contexts: "the city as historical and cultural center"; "the city as the symbol and center of government power"; and "the city as economic engine." Major retail projects were specifically prohibited from the district.[70] The design criteria squarely focused on commercial office space. The Capital Center plan and its design and development regulations detailed land use, open space, street and parking requirements, parks (including a "river park"), and paths for pedestrian movement and service vehicles through the office development parcels.[71] Architectural requirements were not as fully detailed in legislation or the commission's own regulations, because the CCC was reluctant to impose too much conformity on a plan expected to unfold over a twenty-year period.

The first objective was to create marketable land for a new office-based commercial sector, one in which available development parcels would be large enough to attract major new tenants to the city without the problems of land assembly that so frequently send prospective urban developers to the suburbs. The intention was not to compete with the historic business district but to support it: to attract development without destroying the "old" downtown and without razing historic structures to create new development sites. This intent was linked to the second objective, which was to enhance access through the project area and downtown Providence by integrating the relocation of the railroad and the construction of the Civic Center interchange and Memorial Boulevard. The retail and financial districts lacked any direct access to Capital Center; their only connection was a few tenuous lanes that threaded beneath dark and aged railroad bridges.

The Capital Center plan also considered the human scale of the area. The third objective was to provide functional and aesthetically appealing public open spaces, to attract residents and employers to the Capital Center district while at the same time establishing an infrastructure and amenities to which private investors would respond in kind. However, in any urban area, open spaces are successful only when they are carefully planned and integrated into a land use package that leverages private investment. Capital Center was to be a dense urban district where contiguous structures defined a diversity of open spaces, not a suburban setting where buildings sat discretely on large, unused, landscaped sites.

The fourth objective of the district was to create the visual and physical links between the "old" and "new" downtown, which would strengthen the economic base of both areas. This last objective has proven to be the most difficult to reach. The most visible symbol of the objective is the skybridge linking the Providence Place mall with the Westin Hotel/Convention Center, which in themselves are supposed to act as catalysts for both the new and old downtown revitalizations.

Developing design criteria and regulations to implement these policy objectives is at the heart of the commission's power. On 15 September 1983, after a series of public hearings, the commission adopted the Capital Center Project Development Plan and Design Regulations, the enforcement mechanism, overseen by the DRC. Subsequent battles over design issues and development regulations for individual projects, such as the Providence Place mall and the Masonic Temple restoration, demonstrate the political importance this type of structure takes on: to mediate disputes and to wield enough power to make decisions that can move projects along or hold them up.[72]

In January 1982 a cooperative design and construction agreement was signed by representatives of the FRA, Amtrak, Conrail, the State of Rhode Island, the City of Providence, and Capital Properties. The FRA money was secured and physical design work on the track realignment began. The FRA agreed to move the tracks 600–850 feet to the north and to construct a new Providence Station on Gaspee Street, just below the State House. The state turned over Union Station and the seven acres of rail easements that they had bought from Amtrak to Capital Center. SOM did the design and construction work. A construction management design team was created by executive order in 1982 by Governor Garrahy. Wendell Flanders, the former director of RIDOT, was selected as design team director. "I saw this as a tremendous challenge, to see the potential of what could be done in revitalizing our capital city. This intrigued me to no end: the potential that was there. I just looked at it as a once in a lifetime opportunity."[73] The City of Providence formally created the Capital Center district by ordinance on 15 June 1982.

Once the master conveyance agreement was completed in 1982, moving the dirt and tracks that would yield the parcels of developable land that would be Capital Center began on 16 February 1983. The track relocation (1984–86), the new Providence railroad station and its garage (1986–87), and assembling the acres of land in the Capital Center district (1981–87) cost $58 million in mostly federal funds by the time the project was completed in the fall of 1987.

Moving Rails and Earth: Creating a Renaissance Possibility

The railroad moving, highway building, and land-creating projects are the core elements of the Providence renaissance. The motives, catalysts, constraints, tools, and expected benefits dovetailed in a way that created a policy domino effect: moving rails helped build an interchange and in the end created land—lots of it. At an opportune moment the right people with the right ideas were in place at the right time for policy to move forward.

Same Goal, Different Motives

The public policy–related local motivation for moving the tracks was to create a spatially unified downtown, long thought to be a solution to downtown ills. Prime private motivation was to retain ownership of acres of now developable land in the center of the city, because all parties saw the opportunity to accomplish their goals without condemnation procedures. By breaking the railroad logjam the highway interchange became possible, an opportunity long coveted by FHWA administrators. As the next chapter details, the signature project of the Providence renaissance, moving rivers, could be contemplated once the idea of Capital Center and the highway interchange started to become a reality.

These differing motivations were mutually reenforcing: a condition that smoothed the way to completing the project without endless debate over the "why" of the project. Opposition was not related to the benefit of the project, but to the how: "don't destroy Union Station"; "make sure that the intermodal transportation idea is not lost"; "don't kill any chance at downtown retail." These objections, however, were motivated by a positive vision of Providence: to improve historic preservation, relieve congestion, and rescue retail. In other words, the opposition to railroad relocation was rooted not in concern over private aggrandizement, but in concern over what change would mean to the livability of the city. Ultimately, each of these objections would be met in a way that enhanced the story of Providence and did not sink the city into policy paralysis. The Capital Center project presented the single opportunity to do something for the city, for the public sector to engage in economic development, and for private interests to use valuable land.

Multiple Catalysts Overcame Financial Constraints

Simply put, without federal money none of these projects would have happened, because the major constraint was the cost of the project. The money for the railroad project became available because of events over which the city and state had little control. The catalytic factors that were killing the U.S. railroad system became the seed for the Providence renaissance, once the federal government decided that passenger rail service was important enough to try to rescue. The nation's rising concern over pollution and congestion and the unfortunate Arab-Israeli War, which produced a widespread energy crisis, further nudged the renaissance along by acting in part as impetus for developing an improved Northeast Corridor. These events beyond the state's control kept rails on the national agenda at a time when the state had perhaps the most authoritative voice on rails and cities sitting in the U.S. Senate, Claiborne Pell.

Once the federal policy piece and its accompanying funds were in place, except for the actual physical difficulty of moving railroad tracks and building a railroad station, the sudden availability of federal funds made this project a "go." Within the state the idea of moving the tracks was well understood by decision makers and had been thoroughly vetted. The existence of the idea in the urban renewal–based comprehensive plan *Downtown Providence 1970* kept the idea alive, as did the notion that rails would play a role in the intermodal system advocated in *Interface Providence*, which was sensitive to the congestion and energy concerns of the times.

The availability of federal money was critical but so was the ability of local elites to mobilize quickly when an opportunity presented itself. The idea had been there for some time; it was still there when money became available and the right people were willing to act in a timely fashion. Rhode Island was fortunate indeed to have Senator Pell, whose lifelong policy interest in railroads put him in a position to urge changes in federal policy. (The National Corridor Initiative, in recognition of his accomplishments, bestows the Claiborne Pell Award for outstanding service to passenger rails on individuals who continue to do work to improve the rail system in the United States.) His ability to persuade presidents, legislators, and bureaucrats that passenger service was worth preserving was an important catalyst for the Providence rebirth.

Rail moving needed an advocate, not so much for the idea, but to ensure that multiple interests had someone to turn to for answers and someone who could doggedly pursue the idea. That person was Ron Marsella. As the policy entrepreneur for this project, Marsella inserted himself into multiple organizations in order to move the idea forward. His presence in the Providence Foundation and his multiple roles within downcity placed him at the center of this project. The coalition that formed largely as the result of Marsella's coordinating efforts was rooted in the 1970s arts alliance that had formed around PPAC, and other smaller local projects were critical to larger projects.

The professional career bureaucrats also acted as catalysts for these projects. Administrators at the federal, state, and local levels used their discretion to interpret statutes and regulations to move the project along. The informal meetings of the public sector railroad movers and highway builders showed that a convergence of ideas, money, and people was present that enabled them to solve some very big problems.[74] "Providence was uniquely fortunate in having a group of people who could organize all the people involved, could reach more or less a unified picture of what they wanted, and could mobilize the various resources at the state, and at the city and at the private level . . . and pull the whole thing together."[75]

Even more remarkable was the absence of political interference from either the mayor or the governors. Participants in the process almost uniformly make the point that the politicians acted as enablers, but then allowed the private- and public-sector interests to undertake activities without constantly regarding political considerations, even as contentious mayoral and gubernatorial campaigns took place. There were no community activists concerned with ripping down affordable housing or breaking up ethnic enclaves. Building I-95 had done that more than a decade beforehand.

The Creation of New Organizations as Administrative Mechanisms

The vehicle for much of the communication, elite and otherwise, was the Providence Foundation, an organization founded not to move railroads or build highways but to secure funding for a design grant and to help rebuild the downcity core. These same policy makers and private partners had worked together on smaller development projects in Providence, such as the PPAC. This effort produced a trust among individuals who previously did not know each other. Moving the railroad tracks taught these same individuals that the state, city, and federal governments and local private partners could put together a fairly unified effort to accomplish a much larger-scale development project to benefit the capital city.

The CCC became an administrative tool to smooth opposition and to ensure that specific interests were represented in the development of the new district. A series of cooperative agreements and in particular the property conveyance mechanisms were crucial. Allowing interests to retain ownership and to potentially profit from the creation of the district eased concerns about land taking and condemnation.

Well-understood Outcomes

The expected outcomes were well understood, could be easily identified, and spanned a wide spectrum of potential private and public benefits: land, economic development opportunity, better traffic movement, cleaner air, less fuel consumption, and so on. The visible outcome of spatially unified, potentially developable land did result. About $170 million in public, primarily federal, funds would be spent on Capital Center and the river relocation project. The FHWA contributed about $135 million, the FRA over $30 million, and the balance came from the State of Rhode Island and the City of Providence.[76] The resulting acreage within the district is divided into parcels, initially eleven, then fifteen, as it is today.

The large parcels are testament to the notion prevalent at the time that insurance companies required an acre per floor.[77] The technological changes that were to hit the financial industry were not anticipated. About twenty-eight of the seventy-seven acres that eventually would be created (once river relocation plans hit the policy agenda) are publicly owned, and the rest are in the private hands of Capital Properties. Development projects are negotiated and agreed to by the CCC on a parcel-by-parcel basis.

Development has occurred fitfully. The public infrastructure projects, including the new I-95 interchange, Memorial Boulevard, train station, and realigned tracks, were completed by 1994. Private investment in Capital Center approximates $600 million, the lion's share being about $500 million for the Providence Place mall (1999); Gateway Center ($23 million) on parcel 8 in 1989; Citizens Bank ($30 million) on parcel 3 in 1990; the historic rehabilitation for commercial use of the old Union Station by a Ron Marsella–led consortium; CenterPlace (1990) on parcel 5 (Harvard Management Company and Barry Libert, a Boston developer); a garage (Capital Properties); and the Courtyard by Marriott (2000). The Rhode Island Convention Center and Westin Hotel represent further public investment (1994).

RAILROAD RELOCATION
PROJECT
(CAPITAL CENTER PROJECT)

STATUS OF PARCELS
MAY 2003

1-12	**Development Parcels**
1	Old Railroad Station: *renovated and occupied*
1A	New Hotel Completed 2000
1B	Development Site: *on hold*
2	Hotel and Condominiums: *in planning phase*
3	New Bank Headquarters and Office Building: *occupied*
3 E&W	Office Building: *on hold*
4 E&W	Office Building: *on hold*
5	Apartments: *occupied*
6	Development Site: *in planning phase*
7	Relocated Railroad Station
8	New Office Building: *occupied*
9	Office and Retail Building: *2004*
10	Providence Place Mall: *completed Fall 1999*
11	Convention Center and Hotel: *completed Fall 1994*
12	Development Parcel: *on hold*

RIVER RELOCATION PROJECT

A   Relocated Woonasquatucket River with
     riverwalks and new bridges
B   Relocated Moshassuck River with
     riverwalks
C   Relocated confluence
D   Exposed river walls with uncovered river
     and new bridges
E   Auto-free riverwalk
F   Waterplace Park
G   New Parcel
H   Memorial Boulevard Extension
J   Pedestrian Concourse
K   Boat Landings
L   Relocated World War I Monument

▪ RIVERS AS RELOCATED

▪ ▪ ▪ ORIGINAL RIVER LOCATION

RIVER RELOCATION PLAN

0 20 50 100   200   300

WILLIAM D
WARNER
ARCHITECTS
&PLANNERS

URBAN DESIGN
LANDSCAPE
ARCHITECTURE

LOCUST VALLEY FARM
595 TEN ROD ROAD
EXETER, RI 02822
TEL 401.295 8851

Status of parcels in the Capital Center district after the completion of the railroad and river relocation projects, 2003.
Courtesy of William D. Warner, Architects & Planners

Decision makers felt the excitement generated by Capital Center projects. Even before a mall was on the table, the link between the railroads and the eventual Providence Place mall was made early on by Mayor Joseph Paolino Jr. He envisioned the entrance to the train station as the entrance to an eventual mall after visiting Copley Place in Boston. In 1986 he even tried to get Governor Edward DiPrete to halt the development of Providence Station until a new potential mall design was drawn.[78]

Conclusion

A number of policy lessons are derived from these early Providence renaissance projects. Policy is not necessarily a rational, linear process. When opportunity knocks, be ready to grab it. Federal funding can be crucial to the success of a project, and having a delegation in tune with the goal of local development helps immensely. Varied motivations to pursue a project enhance coalition building and bring a greater will to overcoming obstacles. Policy entrepreneurs help keep these varied interests in line. Bureaucrats are important because they control resources.

This tale also emphasizes the presence of a committed elite willing to create the tools and structures needed to move projects along by discussing ideas and overcoming opposition. These projects were driven by the availability of resources that became accessible for policy reasons at the national level, but quickly allowed state and local policy makers to achieve their own ends. Those mobilized elites presented a unified, cohesive front crucial to leveraging the massive amounts of federal aid needed to spur private development. The goal of railroad relocation was to produce a large parcel of undeveloped land in downtown Providence, which it accomplished. Of course, the federal government expected benefits, as well, including reduced travel time, more rail passengers with Providence as their destination, less pollution, less automobile congestion, and improved safety and comfort for rail passengers.

An unanticipated outcome, however, is what occurred next: a complete rethinking about what downtown Providence could be. It is not an overstatement to argue that, without the relocation of the downtown section of the Northeast Corridor railroad tracks, there would be no Renaissance City today. According to a retail market analysis of the Providence Place mall in 1995, the realigned railroad tracks (and river channels) made possible significant private investment opportunities in the "new" downtown. "Providence Place [mall] will derive support from a number of built-in sources. . . . The creation of Capital Center has involved massive infrastructure improvements [which will lead to] the creation of upwards of two million square feet of office space and an unspecified number of residential units."[79]

In 1982 the possibility of gondolas plying downtown Providence waterways

Before and after: Downtown land parcels, railroads, rivers, highways, and local streets were reconfigured by massive infrastructure improvement projects carried out in the 1980s and early 1990s.

Courtesy of Rhode Island Department of Transportation

with dreamy-eyed Hollywood actors and actresses gazing at a moonlit sky had not yet made it onto urban planning drawing boards. In fact, in 1983 it was more likely that concrete decking would forever cover what remained of Providence's still feeble link to its waterfront past.

6

Roads and Rivers

People love the water.

James Rouse

Once you started looking at the downtown area, you could see that it was basically a bunch of neighborhoods separated by highways and water.

Bill Warner, architect

In Providence, Rhode Island, WaterFire was crucial in bringing people to the downtown waterfront . . . filling the beautiful but previously empty spaces with people.

Urban Age, Winter 1999

■ On 19 March 1981 three Rhode Island architects sat, as they usually did on Thursday after work, in the Blue Point Oyster Bar on Providence's South Main Street. The mood was somewhat downbeat that evening as they pondered the future of the city's downtown. William Warner, Irving Haynes, Friedrich St. Florian, and Warner's wife, Peggy, a former set designer for Trinity Repertory Theater, reflected on the Capital Center plan adopted by the Providence City Council a few months earlier. They felt an opportunity had been missed and were upset that the attempts by the local American Institute of Architects (AIA) Design Task Force to influence the Capital Center plan had been rebuffed.[1] The task force members were told by Capital Center principals, including Ron Marsella, now a private consultant and developer, that the plans for Capital Center were "too far along" to be changed.[2]

The Capital Center plan at that point reflected the simple fact that the federal money available for planning had dried up, and that the Capital Center plan as it currently stood was sufficient to meet the real estate development needs of the principal property owners within the district. Numerous development parcels covering many acres now existed, but the architects at the Blue Point felt that Capital Center planning simply did not address the confounding transportation problems of the city. Motorists still had to cope with the congestion at

"Suicide Circle," and pedestrians still walked at their own risk anywhere near the Crawford Street Bridge and Memorial Square. The Capital Center plan did include a four-acre water park, but funding, design, and implementation matters involving the rivers flowing through Providence were ignored. On a white napkin Warner and his two colleagues began to doodle: "Just ideas, just sketches, nothing serious" in a "visceral reaction" to the "closed" design process of Capital Center.[3]

Their "doodles" have become part of the lore of the Providence renaissance. While not a detailed blueprint for the design of a river project, these sketches did contain in them the idea to reestablish a relationship between Providence and its long-abandoned rivers and waterfront. Warner and his colleagues' musings eventually were to change the practice of urban planning in Providence and substantially raise the cost of preparing for the renaissance to come. As one participant put it years later, with the coming of river relocation and a true, urban water park Providence "found its front door, again."[4]

Bill Warner, a Connecticut-born, MIT-educated, established architect and urban planner, became a policy entrepreneur by putting on the public agenda an idea that contained the heart and arteries of the Providence renaissance: creating Waterplace Park (and three other parks) and reclaiming the Moshassuck, Woonasquatucket, and Providence Rivers. The artistic soul of the Providence renaissance, Barnaby Evans's WaterFire, came to be as a result. To create these projects Warner had to find a solution to the more mundane but important traf-

The infamous Suicide Circle traffic intersection, ca. 1978, provided a triangle-shaped glimpse of water (foreground) through the extensive decking over the Providence River.

Courtesy of Providence Foundation, Inc.

fic flow problem created by Capital Center and the planned new highway interchange.

Warner's genius is often associated with his urban design idea of moving the rivers and reconnecting Providence to its waterways. From a policy perspective, though, his genius was being able to plant an idea and then marshal the political and physical resources in less than two years to make it become a reality. Warner consistently came to be regarded as a consummate "political architect" who was "doggedly determined . . . he got about 90 percent of what he wanted."[5]

In a December 1982 speech before the Greater Providence Chamber of Commerce, James Rouse, the nationally known urban planner and designer of Baltimore's Inner Harbor and Boston's Quincy Marketplace, came to Providence to participate in the annual conference sponsored by Brown University and the *Providence Journal*. That year the theme was "Who Will Save the American City?" Rouse told his audience to uncover the buried rivers and reestablish roots as a maritime city: "People love the water," he told the crowd.[6] Later in the day he urged those who felt that the Capital Center plan was a missed opportunity to get going and tackle the issue. Rouse's speech confirmed what many locals like William Warner and his friends at the Blue Point Restaurant already recognized: water would be a critical element in redefining Providence and making it an appealing place to be.

Providence and Its Rivers

The historical development of Providence was linked inextricably to its waterways. Rivers were clearly on the policy agenda in Providence in 1764 when the profits from a city lottery were used to build a drawbridge at the river end of College Street. The bridge enabled livestock and tradesmen to reach Market Square by a direct route rather than having to cross one half mile downstream. The choice of a drawbridge at that location allowed the large square-riggers of the China and triangle trades to get farther up the river to discharge their cargoes.[7] Without these trade routes Providence certainly would not have grown as quickly as it did during the eighteenth and early nineteenth centuries. A natural deep-water harbor at the head of Narragansett Bay, linked to navigable river mouths, meant easy access to wharves, piers, warehouses, and mercantile exchanges where the bounty from international trade could be transshipped.

In the mid-nineteenth century rail began to supplant water as the principal commercial transportation mode. The city fathers transformed the sprawling, flood-prone salt pond that sat at the confluence of the Moshassuck and Woonsquatucket Rivers into the Providence cove basin. By creating an artificial, circular cove with sturdy brick walls, the rivers' tendency to flood was constrained and railroad companies such as the Providence and Worcester, the New

Haven, and the New York and New England could bring eight more lines into the downtown.

Water, in the form of steam, was an important source of manufacturing energy. By 1900 the steam technology that powered manufacturing and railroads enabled the number of factories in Providence to grow to 1,200; those factories employed some 26,000 workers (one-quarter of the city's population) and produced goods that filled to capacity three hundred trains per day.[8] Companies such as Nicholson File, Brown and Sharpe, and others were arrayed along the banks of the two rivers. In the mid-1890s the city filled in the cove basin to construct a railroad station, lay tracks, and create freight yards over the two rivers. "Land interests had triumphed over water interests."[9] By the dawn of the twentieth century the Moshassuck and Woonasquatucket were little more than sewers, and the cove a giant septic tank.

The last insult to the Providence waterfront was averted by an accident of location. Today, traveling west from Massachusetts into Rhode Island and Providence on I-195, a motorist will loop slightly north through the city and then loop slightly south to link with the north-south I-95. That loop was made necessary in the 1950s because the Manchester Street power station and the Narragansett Electric coal yards and electrification facility blocked the straight route across the Providence River. The thwarted *Master Plan for Thorofares* of 1946 had proposed to fill in the Providence River.[10] So highway planners in the early 1950s had to create the link of I-95 and I-195 as it is today, rather than along a filled-in riverbed, saving for the unforeseen future the ability to create WaterFire on the Providence River.

For nearly eight decades water languished. Railroads declined, highways were built, industry and jobs left, and urban blues set in. Both the front (water) and back (railroad) doors of Providence were closed. As he relentlessly pursued his dream of a Providence riverfront, Warner reminded the city in 1985 that "Providence had an active waterfront for 300 years ending in the 1930s when the last night boat to New York stopped service, and was dealt the final blow when the great hurricane of 1938 destroyed many of the remaining wharves. Except for the Port of Providence, well south of downtown, the waterfront for the last 50 years has been abandoned and the amenity of its rivers forgotten."[11] The back door was reopened by railroad relocation. Warner would do his best to reopen the front door to Providence by reintroducing the rivers as a vital part of a vibrant Providence.

Blending Roads and Rivers

The decision to move the rails and create Capital Center opened the policy window to a rethinking of the relationship of Providence to its water. When the architects and planners for SOM finished with the design of Capital Center, a one-hundred-foot-wide trench of water—the Woonasquatucket—flowed past, through, or under what would be the newly aligned railroad tracks and train station within the boundaries of Capital Center. The Capital Center plans did recognize the possibility of utilizing the rivers and creating a water park. The 1979 plan called for a "stepped river pool" and a widened Woonasquatucket framed by pedestrian paths.[12] The open space guidelines in the plan adopted in 1980 contained a "Waterplace" formed by an expansion of the river channel or by the creation of ancillary water elements.[13] Drawings showed little more than a short stretch of river labeled "Waterplace."

Capital Center also failed to address the increased volume of traffic that was expected to materialize from the new highway interchange. This design omission was simply a matter of money. By 1979 federal money for Capital Center planning and design was exhausted. Everyone simply stopped drawing when the federal spigot was turned off, so access to Capital Center and from Capital Center to downtown went unaddressed. The significant traffic congestion and poor vehicle circulation to the south and east of the Capital Center project area were left untouched, as well. Thus the locally notorious "Suicide Circle" that surrounded the Paul Philippe Cret–designed World War I monument in Memorial Square remained to challenge motorists' skills.[14] "The Skidmore, Owings, and Merrill plan merely dumped all the traffic coming from the proposed new I-95 highway interchange into Memorial Square. That was not a solution . . . it would have made matters worse," recalled Warner.[15]

The lack of further road planning was not a hindrance to the Capital Center developers. Throughout 1982–83 Capital Center parcels were laid out and preparations for actual earth moving, track relocating, tunnel building, interchange constructing, and train station assembling took place. The time needed to accomplish those tasks afforded an opportunity for Warner and other concerned individuals to try to address the traffic congestion that everyone could see was coming. The Capital Center design's failure to address the water and traffic issues left three interconnected subplots to be unraveled: How to extend Memorial Boulevard? What to do about the rivers? Could the Providence waterfront again be part of the city's future? Underlying these three questions was the central concern: how would any of these projects be financed—including the Highway Interchange, which was still on the drawing board in 1982?

Another Policy Dream Becomes Reality:
Building the Highway Interchange

With the likelihood of railroad relocation taking place on a much grander scale than previously contemplated, including a plan to knock down the Chinese Wall, the FHWA's moribund agenda of improving the flow of traffic into and out of Providence stood to be a prime beneficiary. Moving the tracks opened up the option of building the long-awaited eight-movement interchange to relieve traffic congestion in Providence and to create a continuity of links among the highways that came together in Providence.[16] For a number of years the state contemplated an interchange in Providence that would not have addressed the traffic problem created by the various on/off ramps from I-95 into downtown Providence, but the federal urban systems highway funds available to Rhode Island up to that time had been inadequate to finance such an interchange without seriously jeopardizing other transportation projects in the state.[17] Although a lesser version of an interchange was conceivable, J. Norm Chopey, the chief special projects and bridge engineer at RIDOT, kept prevailing upon Joe Arruda not to sign off on any plans that did not contain an eight-movement interchange.[18]

Their patience and foresight were rewarded when railroad relocation reached the policy table. The physical space requirements would be met by moving the rails but the financing challenge remained daunting. As had been true of rail policy, changes in federal highway policy became critical to the coming of the Providence renaissance. Rhode Island was well equipped to take advantage of changes in policy in Washington because of the presence of Senator John Chafee within the congressional delegation. The Republican Chafee, a former Rhode Island governor who was first elected to the Senate in 1976, was, along with Senator Pell, able to secure for Rhode Island highway money "way out of proportion to the size of the state."[19] It is also of no small significance that in Rhode Island the First and Second Congressional Districts share borders in Providence; the entire delegation thus benefited in some way from the flow of federal funds into Providence.[20]

The transportation policy decision embodied in the 1981 Federal Interstate Highway Act to move states away from new highway construction and to permit federal transportation funds for alternative uses was fortuitous. From his seat on the U.S. Senate's Environmental and Public Works Committee (the committee with jurisdiction over FHWA funds), Chafee helped construct different ways to use federal transportation dollars. Chafee was in the Republican caucus at just the right time: the first Republican Senate majority in decades had control of that body.

Using his position, Chafee was able to secure changes in federal law that would help the Providence renaissance immeasurably. The first such change was to get the word "rural" dropped from the federal Interstate Transfer funds legislation. Formerly restricted to projects that met the definition of "rural" these funds could now be used to complete urban projects. Suddenly $120 million in previously unavailable funds were potentially available for the Capital Center interchange.[21]

That change in legislation would not have been important except for the cancellation by Governor Garrahy in 1983 of a planned I-84 highway to link

Foreground: As part of the railroad relocation and Capital Center projects, the new Civic Center interchange provides direct access to downtown Providence from I-95 and Routes 6 and 10. Background: Capital Center has driven revitalization in abutting neighborhoods, including the rehabilitated Foundry Building, which provides upscale office space to public- and private-sector clients.

Photograph by the authors

Hartford, Connecticut, and Providence. This project, for which considerable federal highway funds were already earmarked, had been popular among Rhode Island road builders, an important part of Garrahy's political base, and among local Chambers of Commerce. Beginning in the late 1970s, however, there arose considerable public skepticism over the environmental impact of that roadway on the Scituate Reservoir, the main source of water for many of Rhode Island's communities. The costs associated with containing the proposed roadway's runoff—collecting "every drop of rain" in what euphemistically were called "mosquito ponds"—kept escalating.[22] Garrahy's own Department of Environmental Management director, Ed Wood, had raised doubts about the project and its impact on the Scituate Reservoir. The federal Environmental Protection Agency was hostile toward the project for the same reason and convinced Governor Garrahy that the roadway should be shelved.[23] His decision later caused uncertainty when Ed Wood was appointed director of RIDOT.[24]

The cancellation of I-84 (and of I-895 across Narragansett Bay) made those funds available under the Interstate Transfer fund for urban systems. The Capital Center interchange project became "one of the easiest projects we ever built," according to Gordon Hoxie.[25] The interchange from I-95 and a boulevard to connect the interchange with the north end of the existing Providence River

decking were suddenly "a go." The FHWA was already motivated to move the interchange project forward, so that this highway project, which policy makers and bureaucrats in Rhode Island and Providence knew had to be undertaken, was no longer stymied.

By 1983 the importance of the meetings among the participants in the Providence Foundation planning discussions was particularly evident in the story of the interchange. The FHWA modus operandi was to respond to state plans for the use of federal formula dollars allocated to the state by Congress. The FHWA was "to stay attuned to the state DOT processes and respond to their plans" with FHWA design and engineering suggestions.[26] With RIDOT's director, Wendell Flanders (and eventually Ed Wood), in on the Providence Foundation discussions concerning Capital Center, along with the federal regional highway administrator, Gordon Hoxie, it was possible for the two bureaucracies to anticipate what one or the other was thinking and doing. The Providence interchange was particularly challenging because it had to be built for a relatively cramped, non-suburban downtown.

Timeliness was important, too, because much of the process was driven by the deadlines established by the FRA as it sought to complete its NECIP project. Therefore, the state was under significant pressure to determine that it wanted the interchange completed. Plans that reflected Capital Center and the railroad relocation were folded into the EIS process that Pete Pointner was completing for FRA.[27] By the early summer of 1979 the U.S. Department of Transportation conditionally approved the track relocation. The EIS was completed in near record time: less than a year. No significant environmental impact was found in the area extending down to the Crawford Street Bridge.

Building an interchange as a result of moving the rails also created the necessity to address an expected increased flow of traffic to downtown. The development prompted the realization that traffic could not just be dumped from the new interchange into downtown.[28] Memorial Boulevard was planned to ease traffic flow. Planning for the boulevard from the new interchange to the Crawford Street Bridge was integral to the interchange project. The need to confront the traffic problem led to a rediscovery of the rivers as an urban asset.

Planning "As You Go": Linking Capital Center with the Rivers

In early 1982 Ed Wood was wrapping up his time as director of the Rhode Island Department of Environmental Management (DEM) before taking on his new assignment as the director of RIDOT. Wood was taking over from Wendell Flanders, whom Governor Garrahy appointed as the chief planner for the Capital Center project management team. Wood's phone rang and his former assistant at DEM, soon to be its head, Robert Bendick, asked Wood to meet with Bill Warner to look over some drawings.[29] Warner had met with Bendick on occasion to vent his continued frustration over the failure of Capital Center plans to address the river issue and that of the area south of Capital Center where I-195 cut off access to the Providence waterfront.[30] Bendick was a former Woonsocket, Rhode Island, city planner with whom Warner had teamed to prepare a master plan for the Blackstone River Valley. He shared Warner's enthusiasm for thinking on a grander scale. Wood thought very highly of Bendick because of his acknowledged expertise in urban design issues. He actually made it a condition of his own move to RIDOT that Bendick become the DEM director.[31] Garrahy acceded to the request because Garrahy himself felt that it was important to develop an administration built on the ability to delegate responsibilities to individuals with close working relationships.[32]

Warner's ideas fascinated Wood and provided a way for the new RIDOT director to mollify his own reluctant feelings about taking that post. Wood knew that he "was not going to be satisfied paving roads," and Warner's plans met his desire to "do something that would make a difference."[33] The meeting with Wood focused on Bendick's idea to apply to the NEA for a feasibility study of the Providence waterfront.[34] The core of the plan was to remove the Crawford Street Bridge and to replace it with smaller bridges, thereby opening up parts of the long-covered Woonasquatucket and Moshassuck Rivers to view again. NEA funds would provide an infusion of resources to jump-start planning. Wood was hopeful that state funds might be available as well. Encouraged about the prospect of federal and state support, Warner completed an application in the fall of 1982 for NEA funding.[35] Wood also suggested the creation of a waterfront design review committee made up of as wide a range as possible of private and public agencies that could have interest in such a plan.

Providence city planners were more ambivalent about the idea. When Warner and Bendick in February 1983 asked Sam Shamoon, the associate director of planning for the City of Providence, for the city's support for the NEA application, there was such "hemming and hawing" that both men left without approval having been given. Instead, they walked across the street to Ken Orenstein's office at the Providence Foundation and elicited his support.[36] In 1980 Orenstein, who previously had worked for the city, had taken over from Ron Marsella as director of the foundation. Warner and Bendick were well aware of the foundation's track record with obtaining NEA grants for the *Interface* project.

Orenstein almost immediately pledged the support of the foundation as a local sponsor of the NEA application, much as it had done for the *Interface* project in 1974.[37] The Providence Foundation, the incubator for Capital Center, could now join with Bendick and Warner to confront the traffic dilemma posed by its Capital Center project and develop a plan for the Providence waterfront up to Capital Center and Memorial Square. If all went well, the planning process would begin in the spring of 1983.

The state's transportation planning bureaucracy's cooperation was needed as well. Wood held a general meeting with the RIDOT planners and engineers about Warner's basic ideas; he weathered their initial cynical desire "to throw up their hands" in disbelief. "I can't believe we're trying this" was the general sentiment—"at a time when we had the Jamestown Bridge to build."[38] Initially even Joe Arruda thought it could be a disaster. However, Arruda, in a subsequent meeting with Wood, expressed enthusiasm and a willingness to work on that type of road and river project as long as an answer to a basic question could be found: "Where was the money going to come from?"[39] Arruda asked Wood to meet with J. Norm Chopey, whose portfolio included the Jamestown Bridge and the new effort to relocate the rails and build the Civic Center interchange. Chopey thought Warner's ideas were feasible, assuming that the timing of everything could be accommodated, including moving tracks and utilities.

February 1983 may have been the most critical month of the entire Providence renaissance story. Momentum on Capital Center, track relocation, and the highway interchange was moving forward. Actual Capital Center construction began 16 February 1983, after years of planning and discussion. Solutions had been found for resolving the nettlesome problems that confronted that project. Just ten days earlier, on 6 February, Warner's efforts at planting the seed for waterfront development bore fruit. Governor Garrahy and Mayor Cianci found a way to bury their political hatchet long enough to announce a new Bill Warner study of Providence waterfront revitalization to be supported by funds raised through the Providence Foundation and provided by the NEA.[40] The focus of this study would be on the Providence River south of Memorial Square toward the hurricane barrier that had been constructed in the 1950s to prevent the type of devastating damage to downtown caused by hurricanes Carol (1954) and Diane (1955). As Providence waterfront plans emerged, Ed Wood kept a very receptive Governor Garrahy apprised of the emerging river development plans, and city policy director William Collins would do the same for Cianci.[41]

Cianci was narrowly re-elected in 1982 following his embarrassing gubernatorial loss in 1980. The popular Garrahy had swept virtually every community in the state. Cianci also was coping with a disastrous 1981 budget year, so he was looking for a way to revitalize his administration. Cianci was intrigued by the focus on the rivers, although like others he wondered whether the project could actually be accomplished. The city stood ready to commit $25,000 of community development funds, even as his own staff voiced some doubts.[42] Cianci stated, "Times have changed, but there is no reason why we should have to give up our birthright, which is access to the water."[43] Garrahy articulated a Providence renaissance mantra: "The Capital Center project has demonstrated how the state can be an effective partner in the economic development of the city. . . . Redevelopment of the city's waterfront can strengthen both the city and the state economies by making Providence and Rhode Island a more attractive place to live, visit and do business."[44]

The public swirl was matched by the city's planning efforts to solve the obvious traffic problem posed by the looming Capital Center/interchange bottleneck at Memorial Square. Sam Shamoon completed a Providence Planning Department memorandum outlining an auto-restrictive alternative to ease the traffic problem and submitted it to the city Design Subcommittee for Memorial Square Traffic Alternatives.[45] Essentially the plans called for some form of "decking" the rivers by widening roads, finishing the job that started more than one hundred years earlier, eliminating parking, and in various other ways reducing the volume of traffic in the area. Monday, 22 February 1983, was the date for review of these alternative plans. Shamoon gave Ken Orenstein a copy of the city alternatives.

Ken Orenstein was aghast that "they were just going to pave the rivers."[46] While his fear may have been a bit exaggerated, it brought into sharp contrast the need to get on with development within Capital Center and the burgeoning idea to focus on new waterfront development. Orenstein, hoping to forestall what he viewed as a grave mistake by the city, showed the plans to Warner on Sunday, 21 February 1983, at Warner's Exeter, Rhode Island, home. He urged Warner to do something, anything, to stop the plans from going forward. That day Warner and his wife, Peggy, sketched out a number of schematics to satisfy Warner's urge "to do something" about what he called the "sausage links of river left behind" by the Capital Center planners: to use the rivers rather than losing them forever, as the city plan suggested.[47] The time had come to actually do something with the nearly two-year-old napkin doodles.

Warner's focus that Sunday was not on the Providence waterfront but on the traffic flow within the downtown area from the I-95 interchange to Capital Center. His long-held view that a series of bridges would improve traffic flow at Memorial Boulevard and beautify the area now would be given a public hearing; it was his chance to have an impact on Capital Center planning, something he

An early concept drawing by William D. Warner for new road and riverwalks along the uncovered Providence River, 1982.

Courtesy of William D. Warner, Architects & Planners

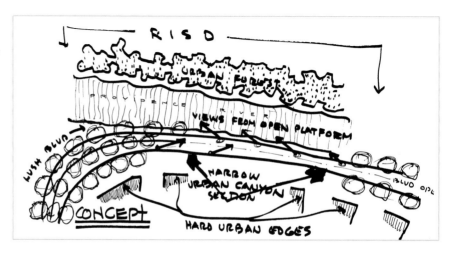

had wanted to do for quite some time. Adding bridges and extending Memorial Boulevard south toward the waterfront were at the core of his plan, not moving rivers. Warner gave his sketches to Orenstein in time for the Memorial Square subcommittee meeting the next day.

While plans were under way to put bulldozers, cranes, and trucks in position to move earth, demolish embankments, dig tunnels, and relocate tracks to create Capital Center, Orenstein presented Warner's sketches at the 22 February 1983 Memorial Square Design Subcommittee meeting. RIDOT's Ed Wood and DEM's Bob Bendick supported the Warner sketches at the meeting because they disliked more decking. City planners were skeptical; at least one engineer threatened to leave the meeting unless the Warner plan was "put back in [Orenstein's] briefcase."[48] Some committee members considered the plan too outlandish and costly.

However, Ron Marsella thought the idea had merit. The next day he invited Warner to present his ideas to the Capital Center Commission. Marsella and Joseph DiStefano, the president of Capital Properties, were concerned about the impact any new set of plans would have on the development of the parcels within Capital Center. DiStefano suggested to Warner that he must have been "smoking funny cigarettes" when he saw Warner's plans.[49] DiStefano believed, with some justification, that a river project would stall development within Capital Center. He did not want their real estate consumed by a river project. Nevertheless, Marsella suggested that Warner's already announced waterfront study made the link among the rivers flowing through Capital Center, Memorial Boulevard, and the waterfront to the south.[50]

The Waterfront Study: Memorial Boulevard and River Relocation

Marsella's suggestion further opened the window for Warner, who began to refine his ideas. Moving the confluence of the Moshassuck and Woonasquatucket Rivers crept onto the drawing board. During the spring of 1983 Warner continued to work on the waterfront study and the idea to link Capital Center with the waterfront. Funding for Warner's work came from a mix of public and private sources. Orenstein and the Providence Foundation board chair, Louis Hampton, president of Providence Gas Company, kept their vow to work for private donors. The Rhode Island–based Champlin Foundation pledged $23,000.[51] Michael Metcalf, partial owner of the *Providence Journal*, got on board "big time."[52] After entreaties by Warner and Ken Orenstein, approximately twenty Providence corporations, including Narragansett Electric and Amica Insurance, contributed a total of about $50,000 to the waterfront study.

Senator Pell continued his invaluable contribution in the unfolding Providence renaissance. Pell "warmly received" and "quietly moved the Warner NEA application along" within the NEA.[53] Just as he had been able to do with the *In-*

terface study, the senator's "gentle touch" produced a $27,500 NEA grant for the waterfront study that was announced on 18 May 1983. Warner was selected as director and designer of the project, the Providence Foundation acted as the fiduciary agent, and Bendick's DEM was to act in an oversight capacity. In addition to the NEA funds, the city put up its previously announced $25,000 in federal community development funds, and the state contributed funds through the RIHPHC. The RIHPHC also developed a history of the Providence waterfront for public consumption.

The city's funds were available despite the skepticism evinced by Cianci's policy staff, partly because they had not seen Warner's drawings before a meeting in Cianci's office with Ken Orenstein, Bill Warner, and Ed Wood on 24 May 1983. That happened to be the day Cianci learned of his indictment for assault that would lead to his conviction and subsequent resignation on 25 April 1984. Cianci was a bit taken aback by both events. However, after what some describe as a "Buddy moment" of intense vocal wondering about how the boulevard/waterfront design got so far down the road without his involvement, told his staff that he supported the project.[54]

Cianci's decision to get behind the project and not become an obstacle is very characteristic of his approach throughout the renaissance era. In addition to his invaluable boosterism, the mayor's primary contribution in the eyes of many who were designing and implementing the projects was to know when not to say "no" and then to get out of the way.[55] "If you had some knuckle-brain as mayor, these projects would not have happened," Joseph Paolino Jr. remarked.[56] Because of Cianci's legal distractions, some credit Cianci's policy aide William Collins as acting as de facto mayor on the river projects.[57]

By 1 July 1983 Warner had $125,000 to continue his efforts to integrate Memorial Boulevard and the rivers from Capital Center past the Providence River and up the eastern shore of the Seekonk River. Those sketches drawn two years earlier over drinks at the Blue Point were moving toward reality. Wood, Warner, and others took seriously the federal grant requirement for an open design process. By July 1983 a twenty-member Waterfront Study Design Review Committee made up of representatives of the state and city governments, the Providence Foundation, the Providence Preservation Society, the Capital Center Commission, and a variety of other private interests was established to meet the open process requirement. The Providence Foundation encouraged the Rhode Island Committee for the Humanities to hold a series of public workshops to involve citizens in the planning process. The idea was to build support among those agencies that could implement the project, provide the conceptual input necessary for such a large undertaking, and anticipate opposition.

Warner worked quickly—actually, he had never stopped working on his plans. So by 6 July 1983 he had drawn schematic-level design proposals for an integrated waterfront plan. He had listened to Marsella's general suggestion to tie together a series of development efforts, including Capital Center, development along South Main Street, Kennedy Plaza, and East Side urban renewal, using the waterfront plan.[58] The plan extended the geographic boundaries of Capital Center downriver, recast some of the infrastructure and design proposals of the Capital Center plan, and placed emphasis on the use of bridges to expose the rivers and to relieve traffic with a new road alignment.

Warner believed that the unaddressed problems of traffic congestion and decked rivers could be solved simultaneously. After all, the 1979 Capital Center plan did have a solution for the very troublesome railroad tracks: move the station and tracks a quarter of a mile north and bury the tracks in a tunnel. The problem of accessing downtown from I-95 was handled nicely in the plan by a new Civic Center interchange, creating on and off ramps right in the heart of downtown. How difficult could it possibly be to further improve traffic flow and open up Providence's waterfront?

Warner was able to present his schematic drawings for the Memorial Boulevard extension to the Design Review Committee of the full Waterfront Study Committee at their 6 July 1983 meeting. It was the first official discussion focus-

The course of the river channels after the relocation proposed in Warner's Providence waterfront study, 1984.

Courtesy of William D. Warner, Architects & Planners

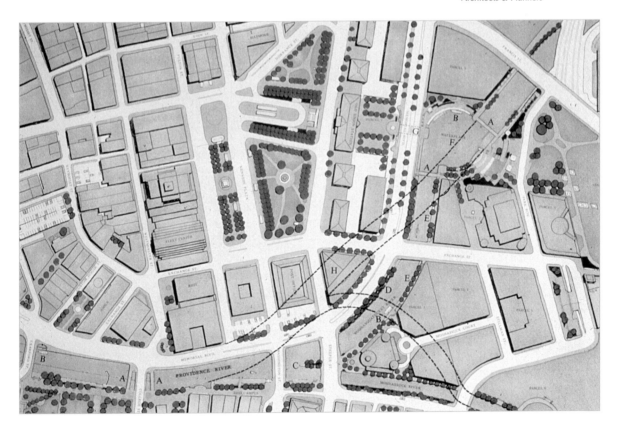

ing on the possibility of moving the confluence of the three rivers (Woonas-quatucket, Moshassuck, and Providence) about one hundred yards, permitting an extension of Memorial Boulevard (then called Washington Row) between the post office and the river's new location and doing away with several streets in the process. The rivers could then be uncovered. The committee was stunned. At one point Ken Orenstein, an enthusiastic supporter of the waterfront study, jokingly questioned the "sanity" of Bill Warner.[59]

Reaction to Warner's idea generally was favorable among elites and the public, although representatives of Capital Properties remained skeptical. The FRA also expressed some concern about delays in track moving, and RIDOT recognized the delay that a new EIS process would entail. Marilyn Taylor, SOM's own award-winning architect for Capital Center design work, was asked about the possibility of linking the Capital Center and waterfront plans, with Memorial Square being the focal point, to which she responded positively.[60] On 28 July 1983 the Capital Center Commission discussed the idea without endorsing any particular plan.

Cianci's support had changed the city planning department's attitude to-

Warner's sketch of the proposed confluence of the Woonasquatucket and Moshassuck Rivers, Providence waterfront study, 1984.

Courtesy of William D. Warner, Architects & Planners

ward the project. The Waterfront Study Committee urged the city to amend its own Memorial Boulevard design drawn by the city's design consultant, Wilbur Smith and Associates, to reflect Warner's proposals. Joseph Arruda also pointed out that if the Memorial Boulevard extension could be classified as an urban connector highway, it might be eligible for 85 percent federal funding.[61] On 30 September 1983 Mayor Cianci's office announced public workshops that would focus on the waterfront plans. Among the ideas raised were the removal of the Crawford Street Bridge; rerouting I-195 ramps; a waterfront campus for RISD; a marina; a river road; and building dams and locks to eliminate low tide odors. River relocation was not mentioned.

Over the course of the projects strong efforts were made to identify and include in the planning process as many concerned groups—stakeholders—as possible. The long list includes Save the Bay, the leading environmental advocacy group in the state, the Providence Preservation Society, the League of Women Voters, the Chamber of Commerce, the Providence Intown Churches Association, the South Main Street Merchants Association, and many neighborhood groups. The intent was to develop an extensive outreach network and communication avenues that in the long run would avoid conflicts and develop support.[62]

Warner and his staff, however, continued to develop several river-moving schemes, essentially channeling the Woonasquatucket out from under the post office and moving the confluence of both rivers one hundred yards to the east. Memorial Boulevard could then be extended and the decking removed from the rivers. Providence River Park, Memorial Park, and Waterplace Park could be created, boat traffic could return to the river, and traffic circulation would be improved considerably.[63] By 9 November 1983 the planning pieces were in place for a waterfront revival from Capital Center to Narragansett Bay. After more tweaking, in February 1984 a joint city-state press release proclaimed the completed plans for a river relocation project and presented diagrams showing the relocated rivers.

Financing the Memorial Boulevard/River Relocation Project: If It Walks Like a Duck . . .

What has become known as the Memorial Boulevard/River Relocation project was not a linear process. Even as Warner was drawing plans for river relocation, Ed Wood pressed ahead as if sheer determination could make the project become reality. In October 1983 Wood and Arruda announced that they wanted to begin the Memorial Boulevard extension project by conducting an EIS, which was required in order to receive federal highway funds. Pete Pointner, who by now was a very familiar face in Providence as a result of his work on the Capital Center/railroad relocation EIS, was contracted to conduct the Memorial Boulevard extension assessment. Pointner, Bill Warner, and Wilbur Smith

1980 SITE CONDITIONS
Elevated railroad tracks known as the Chinese Wall and parking lots separate downtown from the State House.

1981 CAPITAL CENTER PLAN
Relocated the railroad tracks to beneath an extension of the State House lawn, provided a downtown interchange at I-95, constructed a new railroad station above the tracks, and transformed parking lots ringing the south end of the State House lawn into development parcels.

1984 RIVER RELOCATION PLAN
(From the Providence waterfront study)
Capital Center did not address the decking covering the rivers or the traffic congestion at the north end of the decking where the boulevard abruptly ended at Memorial Square, nor did it provide funding for the design and implementation of the four-acre Waterplace Park. The Waterplace Park and River Relocation projects addressed all of these issues.

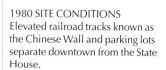

Warner took the Capital Center plan of 1981 toward a more rational solution in his creative approach to the downtown's traffic congestion, land use, and aesthetic problems in the 1984 Providence waterfront study.
Courtesy of William D. Warner, Architects & Planners

Associates, traffic consultants to Providence, began working on an assessment of five Warner alternatives to ease Memorial Boulevard's traffic congestion. Warner applied the brakes to the waterfront study in order to link it to the EIS process.[64] Only one of his alternatives did not include moving the rivers, but none included Waterplace Park. In December 1983 Ed Wood, with the backing of Cianci and Collins, prevailed upon the City Plan Commission to approve the entire revamped river relocation plan and Memorial Boulevard extension.

Good ideas involving major infrastructure challenges required millions of dollars that neither the state nor city had available, but Ed Wood soon understood that the federal government's continuing transformation of federal highway policy would once again prove invaluable to Providence and the state. Again Senator Chafee helped secure the needed federal assistance, thus ensuring that Washington, D.C., would bear a large portion of the cost of the Memorial Boulevard/River Relocation projects. He was instrumental in building "reprogramming" into federal transportation policy, a concept that allowed highway funds to be used for broader infrastructure, urban design, and beautification projects, including bridges, pedestrian walkways along the rivers, tunnels, lighting, and other public amenities not normally funded by the federal government for transportation projects.[65]

The federal highway Interstate Substitution Program contained in it the possibility of using previously earmarked highway funds for other uses (at an 85–15 percent federal-to-state split), so the unused federal highway funds from the cancellation of the I-84 and I-895 projects became available for other road projects.[66] The resulting, fortuitous policy impact of Garrahy's decision to cancel these projects was that the FHWA had nearly $600 million in unused federal interstate highway funds for Rhode Island projects. These funds could be accessed through the Interstate Substitution Program when states chose to withdraw from federal highway projects such as the I-84 roadway. The generous 85 percent federal funding would make the Memorial Boulevard/River Relocation project affordable.[67] In essence, the killing of the Providence-Hartford project was the step necessary for a complete transformation of the physical appearance of downtown Providence. In addition, the road and river projects, and other state road projects, helped mollify the pique of the Rhode Island road builders associations.[68]

When Ed Wood had taken over as RIDOT director, the former journalist and DEM director freely admitted his need to learn his new job quickly. As was true with railroad relocation, the availability of federal funds would prove critical to the next phase of the Providence renaissance. Millions were needed for the new idea to become a reality. Ed Wood's optimism about finding the money was to be tested.[69] He had asked his staff to meet with communities around the state to set priorities among the very large list of projects in the state's Transportation Improvement Program—there just was not enough money to undertake them all. Suddenly, because of the road cancellations and the redefinition of federal Urban Systems Funds and the Interstate Substitution Program within a very short time, nearly $600 million of federal funds became available. Not only would the big and little projects get done, but RIDOT would now be funded adequately enough to hire the staff necessary to help plan, design, oversee, and participate in the building of Providence renaissance road projects.[70] Once this reality set in, both Ed Wood and Wendell Flanders, the chief engineer of the Capital Center Commission, knew the Memorial Boulevard/River Relocation projects could go forward. "The dream was sold on the merits of the dream itself, plus the fact that we had the money," recalled James Capaldi.[71]

Throughout the latter part of 1983 and into 1984 elements of the Capital Center project, including a Maguire and Associates study related to replacing the I-195 bridge through Providence, were put on hold. Joe Arruda wanted "the piece in the middle" (Memorial Boulevard/River Relocation), resolved following a completed EIS before moving ahead with that highway project. The I-195 relocation would not be revisited until the early 1990s.[72] A meeting was held with the entire congressional delegation to assure them that the FRA plans for track moving and a new rail station would not be delayed and that the EIS for the rivers project would be the same as that for the railroad project; the Capital Center

The heavily congested Memorial Square, known as Suicide Circle, prior to the implementation of the Capital Center and river relocation plans, ca. 1976.

Courtesy of Capital Center Commission

Commission's support for the river project was noted as well.[73]

Despite senatorial blessing, it still took administrators to figure out how to define the Memorial Boulevard extension project. It was a river project unless someone could convince the FHWA otherwise. The challenge was to convince the FHWA that Warner's ideas were *not* a river relocation project but an extension of Memorial Boulevard. Robert Bendick was simultaneously engaged in selling the project locally as a riverfront park designed to attract people to the city. The two efforts needed to strike a tricky balance.

It fell to Wood and Arruda to lobby the FHWA administrators in Washington to approve federal money for this project. Wood and Arruda were important go-betweens and helped persuade Gordon Hoxie, still the regional FHWA administrator, to assist these local projects. "Thank God we had Joe [Arruda] and Ed [Wood]" was the general sentiment held by those closely involved in this project.[74] Both men attended transportation planner conferences, where Wood "learned the buzzwords/jargon that federal highway transportation planners valued, in this case 'safety' and 'easing congestion.'"[75]

That the planned Memorial Boulevard extension and resulting bridge and river work met the basic requirements for federal funding was a crucial point. To strengthen their position Wood and Arruda decided to make the "safety" and "congestion" points visually. As part of the federal EIS related to the Memorial Boulevard portion of the waterfront study, Wood invited the FHWA director, Ray A. Barnhart, to Providence to view Suicide Circle congestion both from a state helicopter and on the ground. Barnhart had a reputation as a professional and wary administrator who had to be convinced by strong evidence of the merits of the projects presented to him.[76] Local bureaucratic lore has the federal administrator being driven into Suicide Circle at rush hour, when a near mishap, complete with shouts and gestures, seemed to be a decisive moment.

Cooperation between federal and state administrators remained a consistent theme in Providence renaissance making. "Continuity of players does make a difference. People grew to know other people over the years," according to Capaldi.[77] Wood had created a capital development committee that came to oversee many of the discussions concerning highways and rivers. In a series of meetings among Warner, Ed Wood, Joe Arruda, and Gordon Hoxie, they discussed the possibilities for Rhode Island's unused highway project funds.

Gordon Hoxie was willing to take up the remarkable effort of the federal government to use its money to rebuild rather than tear up downtown Providence. Hoxie "was ready to be persuaded."[78] This mix of funds became a large element in bringing about the Memorial Boulevard/River Relocation project.[79] Funding for the Memorial Boulevard extension project, labeled river relocation by 1984, was predominantly federal, although a great deal of "coordination of purpose and hand holding" occurred, as this project stretched the definition of a road-related project.[80] In the end the FHWA would contribute approximately $135 million to the Providence renaissance, of which $60 million was for river relocation, $6 million for Waterplace Park, and the balance for the interchanges. However, by August 1984 not a penny of federal money was yet committed to the project, because the EIS and public participation phases of the proposal were yet to be completed.

Final Approvals

The excitement shared by local architects, planners, administrators, politicians, and the general community was not universal. Opposition to the river relocation project came from Capital Properties. Joseph DiStefano objected, "This river relocation is going to stop me in my tracks and I don't want it to happen."[81] To relocate the rivers, land would have to be condemned, a clear departure from the earlier Capital Center agreement, which avoided public taking of land. Ron Marsella and Joe DiStefano were correct. The waterfront recommendations, if adopted, would change a portion of the Capital Center district, for which development discussions were already under way. Both the Woonasquatucket and Moshassuck Rivers would have to be moved, making some dry land wet but also creating new parcels. These moves would change land that had been painstakingly assembled through the Capital Center negotiation process.

This opposition arose during the public participation phase of the waterfront study. The public nature of the project was emphasized throughout the second half of 1984, as the Providence Foundation and the Rhode Island Committee for the Humanities began a series of bimonthly public hearings in keeping with the NEA grant requirements for an open planning process. The openness of the process was not bothersome to Warner because he and members of the Waterfront Study Committee did not want to repeat what they felt was the relatively closed process leading to the Capital Center design.[82] Successive groups and the public at large were invited to comment on what really were seven Warner proposals to address the traffic flow problem and integrate the riverfront with Capital Center. Joe DiStefano, virtually anytime there was a public discussion of the project, raised his objections. His view of the river relocation project was that "this plan is just so many feet of blue sky."[83]

Nevertheless, the EIS process was completed when on 22 June 1984 federal highway administrator Gordon Hoxie gave his approval of the EIS for the Memorial Boulevard extension project. The project, including land condemnation, was likely now to receive federal highway funds. A waterfront study public workshop and exhibit was held at the Providence Preservation Society in the Arcade on 12 July 1984 and remained open for public review and comment until August 1984. It drew almost two thousand visitors.[84] The exhibit featured plans for four waterfront areas: Capital Center; Old Harbor; Fox and India Points; and the Seekonk River. Included in these areas were a Providence River Park, Waterplace Park, Memorial Park, and improved access to the Providence River via boat landings. On 8 August 1984, following a period of public comment, the EIS-preferred Alternative "E" for river relocation was recommended to the FHWA by RIDOT: the plan would guide the moving of rivers and roads and create eleven acres of parks and a mile and a half of pedestrian walkways.

DiStefano was still unhappy, convinced that the announced dates for undertaking the project were not realistic and that there would be further delays that would affect ongoing Capital Center development negotiations. DiStefano was also chair of the Democratic State Committee and as such had developed a good relationship with Governor Garrahy. Garrahy was enthusiastic about the river relocation plan but was also concerned over the issues raised by DiStefano.[85]

Bruce Sundlun once again was willing to take on the role of conciliator. Sundlun, too, had endorsed the river relocation plan earlier, but he also felt that DiStefano's concerns were legitimate. Sundlun called Ed Wood to his office on 8 August and, with DiStefano present, said to Wood, "Joe and I have done a deal. . . . Look me in the eye and tell me these dates are right. If things get screwed up I will buy these two pieces of property from you [DiStefano]."[86] Sundlun would sell the property back to DiStefano for the same price after the rivers were moved and the property improved as a result. Sundlun had already spoken with Michael Metcalf at the *Providence Journal* as well as local financial and business institutions to guarantee the millions necessary to buy the property.[87]

Wood was correct in his time estimates. On 8 November 1984 FHWA approved the EIS for river relocation and on 13 November city, state, and federal funding for river relocation was announced. DiStefano continued to raise objections, refused Sundlun's offer, and sued the state in late 1984 for $5 million in damages while dropping his constant barrage of criticism. His political experience as a state senator led him to see the "handwriting on the wall—in retrospect they were right and I was wrong about the rivers."[88] Opposition by Capital Properties did not end until Mayor Joseph Paolino developed a plan to fund the city share of river relocation by using land swaps with the state and making Capital Properties whole again.[89] The city received the new parcel (Parcel 12) that would be created by the relocated river and the state controlled Parcel 9, which it gained from Capital Properties through a condemnation proceeding. Capital Properties, through the Capital Center Commission, allowed the state to take the land, but the company reserved the right to dispute the value of the compensation the city paid it for its loss. Years later, Capital Properties successfully challenged the amount of the award.[90]

In February 1985 Warner and C. E. Maguire, the engineers for Capital Center, began the design and engineering for the Memorial Boulevard/River Relocation project. In August 1985 the Capital Center Commission amended their design and development criteria to incorporate Warner's planned relocation of the Woonasquatucket and Moshassuck Rivers. The Open Space Plan contained the circular Waterplace Park, "envisioned as the major public square within the Capital Center project," extensive river walks, and a new parcel of land.[91]

Meanwhile, Capital Center continued to evolve. By 4 December 1986 the cranes had started to dismantle the "Chinese Wall." In March 1987 the Providence River/Memorial Boulevard Extension Project Comprehensive Agreement was signed between RIDOT and DEM, establishing a collaborative relationship among the RIHPHC, the Army Corps of Engineers, and the CCC to oversee and complete the project. Groundbreaking for river relocation occurred 12 April 1988.

Capital Center met the river-moving project when Ron Marsella and Henry Collins in 1987 announced plans for a twelve-story Citizens Bank Tower development on parcel 3, the first private development within Capital Center and the first class-A office space to be built in Providence in more than a decade. Marsella had left the Capital Center Commission in 1983. The development group in which he was then a partner, Bay Head Group, had in 1986 been awarded the rights to develop the old Union Station; at the same time the group was discussing with George Grayboise, president of Citizens Bank, the possibility of the bank's moving into Capital Center. Marsella and Collins's company had obtained exclusive rights to develop that property from Capital Properties. The river relocation plan put the office tower partly on land and partly in the relocated river; Marsella naturally opposed the plan.[92]

A solution was found: the additional cost of moving the bank would be funded through the use of federal and state financing, and the tower would be situated at the confluence of the newly relocated rivers. Citizens Bank decided not to occupy the building until the river project was completed, prompting in part a resolution of the still outstanding legal roadblocks that Capital Properties was pursuing. In perhaps the most remarkable engineering feat of the Providence renaissance, realigning the Moshassuck and Woonasquatucket Rivers proceeded even as the Citizens Bank Tower was being built.

Creating Waterplace Park

Throughout the process Bob Bendick and Bill Warner never gave up on the idea of an urban river park system. Just slightly to the north and east of Capital Center was the small Roger Williams National Memorial, another pet project of

The new confluence of the Moshassuck and Woonasquatucket Rivers and the foundations of One Citizens Plaza (a bank headquarters) were built simultaneously in 1990, where Suicide Circle once stood.

Courtesy of Capital Center Commission

Senator Pell, which had quietly been completed in 1981.[93] The Williams Memorial is the northernmost of Providence's river parks, which now include the Providence River Park; Memorial Park; and the Renaissance City signature, Waterplace Park. In March 1984, as the public phase of the river relocation project was heating up and still no federal funding having been approved, Bendick authorized Warner's firm to undertake a Waterplace Park feasibility study. The Waterplace Feasibility Committee was formed to review plans for a park between March 1984 and October 1985.

Bendick saw the park system as a feather in the cap of the barely ten-year-old DEM, and Warner worked hard to overcome any design issues. By 22 April 1985 Warner's plans had developed to the point that Bendick could recommend to the newly elected Republican governor, Edward DiPrete, that he approve the Waterplace Feasibility Plan, which DiPrete did on that same day. Once again, federal funds played a critical role in the creation of a renaissance project. Joe Arruda discovered the possibility of getting federal funding for pedestrian walkways through the Independent Walkways program.[94] Several studies were done that showed that river walks would be in demand.[95] In October 1985 Gordon Hoxie determined that the plans for walkways, bridges, a pedestrian crossing, and a concourse under Memorial Boulevard now contained in the Capital Cen-

Above left: As construction of the riverwalks, roads, and bridges progressed, the new Moshassuck/Woonasquatucket confluence and One Citizens Plaza were substantially completed in 1991.

Courtesy of Capital Center Commission

Above right: The Woonasquatucket flows gracefully through its new channel toward the relocated confluence and One Citizens Plaza.

Photograph by the authors

ter plan constituted an independent walkway system, making it eligible for nearly 100 percent federal funding.[96]

Gordon Hoxie's role in supporting renaissance efforts from Capital Center forward is evidence of the importance of bureaucratic discretion in advancing public policy. His staying attuned to state planning efforts and becoming an active participant in the discussions from almost the beginning were important to the constantly evolving Providence renaissance "plan." His knowledge of the appropriate state uses of federal funds and his willingness to use his discretion were critically important. If Hoxie had been a "tough-ass, show-me, drop-dead bureaucrat," much of the funding for these infrastructure projects would not have been available.[97] Hoxie himself had to stave off some quizzical looks from federal auditors, particularly in the case of the amenity money that would be used for the pedestrian tunnel from Kennedy Plaza to Waterplace and for lights, handrails, and ornamental features along the bridges.[98] Federal matching requirements made it imperative that the state pick up the tab for any pieces not covered

Before and after: Once the road decking over the rivers (a) was removed, the downtown area was vastly improved. The riverwalks and public open spaces, vehicular and pedestrian bridges, and landscaping and street furniture created a more harmonious and more functional urban fabric, both to the north (b) and to the south (c).

Courtesy of Rhode Island Department of Transportation (a) and Thomas Payne, WaterFire Providence (b and c)

a

b

by federal funds. Bendick announced in October 1985 that DEM would allocate funds and formed yet another committee to help coordinate an increasingly complicated design effort.

The initial idea for some "water feature" in the 1979 plans for Capital Center had grown by 1985 to a park system relinking Providence to its rivers and entailed more concern over its integration into the overall rejuvenation of a new downtown. At the urging of J. Norman Chopey, the RIDOT special projects engineer,

c

the River Relocation Coordination Committee was authorized to review the final design phase from November 1985 on to ensure that no design "clashes" existed among the plans for Capital Center, Memorial Boulevard/River Relocation, and Waterplace. This committee was the last of the waterfront-related committees designed to include as many interests as possible in the policy process. Public- and private-sector representation on the three committees, Waterfront Study, Capital Center Park, and River Relocation Coordination, recog-

Before and after: Waterplace
Park and the riverwalks along
the Woonasquatucket were
built, quite literally, from the
rubble of the past.

Courtesy of Rhode Island Department of Transportation (Before) and
Thomas Payne, WaterFire Providence (After)

nized the community-wide stake in the success of this project. On 7 July 1987 the
Capital Center Commission approved the design phase of DEM's portion of the
project, clearing the way for Waterplace to be incorporated into a combined project design process.[99]

Warner's design gave prominence to a "historic Providence" theme. Waterplace Park is bounded on the south by Memorial Boulevard, on the west by
Providence Place, on the north by the State House, and on the east by an undeveloped parcel. A 240-foot-diameter cove basin, a "memory piece," is the heart of
the design and constitutes a historic pastiche of the long-since-filled Providence
Great Salt Cove.[100] The tidal cove is fed by waters ebbing and flowing through
the Providence River from the upper reaches of Narragansett Bay and by the
Woonasquatucket River. Surrounding this central pool is a series of walkways
and arched roadway and pedestrian bridges constructed high enough to allow
some boat passage underneath and connected to a network of river walks, arterial streets and adjacent transportation, and tourism and business hubs. A series
of graffiti-proof panels on a pedestrian concourse are placed strategically to tell
the story of Providence's development from Roger Williams's village through

today. The design of the multitiered amphitheater was produced during a one-day workshop that included local architects and RISD faculty and featured William Whyte, who made the suggestion that grass rather than concrete would make the amphitheater a better performance venue.[101]

Work began on Waterplace Park on 12 September 1991, after the lead agency, DEM, signed an interagency cooperative agreement with the Capital Center Commission in August 1991. As construction took place a number of issues arose that required the same type of cooperation and adjustments that had been characteristic of the renaissance infrastructure projects since 1979, such as the need for a harbor master and rubbish disposal, and the broad question of the responsibility for the park. None of these issues posed major obstacles; they produced little battles, not wars. Nearly a decade and a half of renaissance making had taught various parties that policy cooperation was important to seeing projects to a successful conclusion.

Necessary to creating Waterplace was a high level of intergovernmental cooperation. That cooperation was evident even after the park formally opened on 14 July 1994. Federal and state money built the park, but the city would end up owning it. A cooperative agreement between the city and state, which required the city to accept all responsibility for the operation of the park and to ensure police protection, governed the first phase of the transfer. In return, the city was granted the right to enter into agreements with all vendors, including restaurant owners for the pavilion area. This latter responsibility was key, because a restaurant war had broken out in Providence over the degree to which an upscale restaurant would hurt existing eateries or, conversely, the harm that might be visited on the park by fast-food venues. The need for a restaurant that would be sufficiently profitable and open daily, year-round, was an important consideration.

The gourmands prevailed, a decision primarily driven by the need for revenue to support park maintenance and cleaning. Phase 2 of the city-state agreement authorized the Rhode Island State Properties Committee to transfer ownership of Waterplace Park from the state to the city on 11 July 1995. This transfer was prompted by the need for the restaurant to have a liquor license. State parks prohibited the sale and serving of alcoholic beverages, but city parks did not. Income generated through vendors, including the restaurant, and special events and programs was dedicated exclusively to the maintenance and management of the area. Consequently, gondola vendors, kayaking outfitters, water taxis and water tours, and Xtreme Games and Gravity Games operators pay fees to the city for their permission to operate. An upscale waterfront restaurant opened in 1997.

In November 1995 the 542 pieces of the World War I monument were reunited at the two-acre Memorial Park, after seven years in storage and some controversy.[102] In a testament to the adages that "nothing good ever comes easy" and "all politics is local," Italian social groups battled World War II veterans' organizations over the new site for the monument, where a statue of the Italian explorer Verrazzano was prominently featured. The veterans' organizations felt that locating the towering monument near the Verrazzano statue would be an insult to American soldiers who fought against Italian soldiers during World War II. Mayor Vincent Cianci, himself of Italian heritage, persuaded both groups that no insult was intended and that the design of the park would lend a proper memorial to both, and objections were dropped.

On 19 July 1996 Governor Lincoln Almond and Mayor Vincent Cianci dedicated the Providence River Waterfront and Memorial Park with a reassembled World War I monument. Like the monument, Providence and its waterfront were reunited after a century or more of being "in storage." The river relocation project won the 1995 Presidential Federal Design Achievement Award. The U.S. Department of Transportation recognized the efforts associated with creating Waterplace and river relocation by granting one of its eleven Transportation Honor Awards for Design in 2001. However, more than awards, Capital Center project construction chief engineer Wendell Flanders caught what policy makers intended: "The success [of Waterplace] is measured by seeing people use it, by seeing people back in downtown Providence."[103]

Symbolic Rebirth of Providence: WaterFire

The signature experience of the Providence renaissance is WaterFire, the public art event that draws tens of thousands of people to Providence when the fires are lit. Its coming contains the basic facets of the Providence renaissance story: a good, somewhat unplanned and outlandish idea; a talented professional

By the late 1990s gondolas and trolleys provided alternative modes of transportation for tourists arriving in the Renaissance City.

Photographs by the authors

and advocate; a concern over where the money would come from; and some good luck. Its theme—rebirth—unites the old Providence through its rivers to a new downtown.

The originator of WaterFire is Barnaby Evans, a West Coast native who came to pursue a bachelor's degree in biology and environmental science at Brown University. He remained in Providence after graduation, pursuing his interest in public art and photography and creating in 1988 a nonprofit organization called Visual Arts of Rhode Island. In the small community that Providence is, he became known in local art circles and was asked to serve on the board of the city's First Night organization as that board sought a diverse representation of artistic interests. He remained on the board until 1992.

When Waterplace Park opened in July 1994, Evans felt it was well designed but wondered what it would take to get people to use it. He realized that people rarely visited the park, certainly not the outcome hoped for. The opportunity for Evans to bring people into Providence began just before New Year's Eve, 1994, the tenth anniversary of the First Night celebrations in Providence. The board of directors of First Night wanted to do something to celebrate that milestone as the city welcomed the new year. The First Night organizers called a meeting and invited local artists to present ideas on how to best mark that tenth anniversary. Evans had been ruminating about an idea to link fire and water as symbols of life and rebirth; he was developing a proposal to memorialize victims of a recent helicopter crash in the Pacific near Seattle and thinking about how to respond to the Providence Jewish Community Center's call for a proposal for a Holocaust memorial. Evans's thinking ranged from fountains to eternal flames.

The First Night board liked the basic concept of using Waterplace during First Night when Evans made a suggestion along those lines, and they gave him about $3,000 to do something celebratory. His basic idea was to create a civic ritual involving the rivers and fire as a way of getting people to visit Waterplace on New Year's Eve. He wanted to celebrate the historical context of Providence and what he felt were the "romance of the ruins" and "Lovecraftian" feel of the city.[104] His vision evolved into lighting eleven fires in the circular basin that commemorates the Great Salt Cove, bringing together themes of history, community, and rebirth.

The first WaterFire was lit on 31 December 1994 after Evans overcame the considerable skepticism expressed by the relevant permit-granting bureaucracies. As so often was the case in the Providence renaissance story, these agencies used discretion to permit a good idea to go forward. The absence of any regulations governing the type of activity that Evans proposed provided the opportunity for the bureaucrats to "not deny permission" without expressly approving the activity.[105]

Evans was unsure if anyone would see his artwork because the cove basin site required people to walk away from Kennedy Plaza and other First Night venues. His objective was to make people feel safe while walking, to make them feel they were out for a nighttime stroll in the city along with many others. People did go to Waterplace that evening to watch volunteers in boats ignite wood placed in eleven fixed braziers as music played for forty-five minutes, then turned off for forty-five minutes, and then on again throughout the evening. Though people generally liked the experience, Evans felt that this WaterFire was a failure because there were too few braziers and so it lacked the scale necessary to achieve his objective.[106]

Consequently, WaterFire was not exhibited again for another year and a half and then only by a reluctant Barnaby Evans. In June 1996 the National Sculpture Conference and the Convergence Art Festival were scheduled to occur simultaneously in Providence over four nights. Organizers for Convergence asked Evans to consider staging WaterFire then. Evans thought they "were crazy," that the 1994 First Night event was a one-time thing. However, their persistent contention that "it's a good thing to do for the city" won the day. At a chance meeting at the College Hill Bookstore on Thayer Street, Evans talked about the idea with Buff Chace, a developer and the scion of one of the old families of Providence. Chace eventually wrote a generous check to help sponsor the next WaterFire.

This second WaterFire was an unqualified popular and critical success. For four nights thirty-six floating braziers on the Woonasquatucket, all the way to RISD, were lit as music played continuously. Volunteers did most of the work and equipment was donated, but the scope of the activity was much greater than in 1994. Since 1996 WaterFire has grown in size, frequency, and theme. WaterFire is now WaterFire Providence, Inc. The event has become more "populist" and more allied with tourist activities, in addition to its role as a social ritual. "It is very important that this is something a five-year-old or ninety-five-year-old can enjoy; whether you get an art student or a troubled teen from the mall, they all belong."[107] It remains a volunteer activity—a gift—a rekindling of the flames of community. It is also much more expensive to stage, requiring significant sponsorship from corporations, individuals, and the government, which seem willing to do so.

Thinking Differently about the Future of Providence

The river and parks projects were infrastructure projects that created a paradigm shift in Providence. Without moving the rivers and creating Waterplace, the Renaissance City would not look or feel as it does today. In many ways these large projects set Providence apart from other urban economic development endeavors. The *Providence Business News* quoted the senior vice president of a major mall developer, the Taubman Companies, who claimed in 1995 that "the key is to develop the malls that are going to be 'destination malls' in [their] markets, that

Throughout the late spring, summer, and fall, WaterFires are staged as frequently as funds allow. Barnaby Evans's award-winning installation draws tens of thousands of residents and visitors to this civic spectacle.

Photograph by the authors (above); courtesy of Providence Department of Planning and Development (opposite)

is, malls that capture a larger regional market share by providing attractive settings and linkages to other activities in addition to providing quality retail opportunities."[108] No one who has seen it can doubt the aesthetic appeal of the rivers and park clearly visible from Providence Place mall.

Professionals Wanting to Make a Difference

No one had to move rivers or create the WaterFire exhibits or even improve the traffic circulation. There was no legal imperative to do anything, or even a profit motive. The projects were driven by aesthetics, design, and, to some extent, function: opening the waterfront and improving traffic flow. Those most driven by development concerns, Capital Properties in particular, actually opposed the projects, although inevitably they stood to benefit from property improvements. Downcity businesses would not directly feel any benefit, although developers and others with real estate interests hoped that something positive would arise.

The motivations to succeed were rooted in individuals willing to use their professions to create something very different from the Providence that existed. The goal was a different way of thinking about the city, as institutions and individuals succeeded in their particular vision of what Providence ought to be. Bill Warner was motivated to create a signature piece of urban architecture and is the person most associated with this project. But in many ways the bureaucrats and the administrators, including Ed Wood, Ken Orenstein, Gordon Hoxie, Bill Collins, Joe Arruda, and others, drove this process forward by wanting to make a difference.

Others were motivated in different, more tangible, ways. The state planners at DEM and RIDOT got a new park and a much improved transportation system. The FHWA witnessed an almost complete urban transport system come into being. Trains, cars, water vehicles, and pedestrian walkways were now situated in a locale where a decade before Suicide Circle limited the traffic and pedestrian flow. Senators Chafee and Pell got to see the capital city benefit directly from federal largesse. The mayors, Paolino and Cianci, and governors, Garrahy and DiPrete, who were somewhat sidelined as these projects evolved, saw the beginning of the transformation of the city from a smudge to a showcase.

While traffic circulation was the stated rationale for the Memorial Boulevard/River Relocation project, the collaborating state and city agencies, mindful of the ingredients necessary for a successful urban space, required the designers of the park to provide maximum accessibility for pedestrians and small pleasure boats. The design was geared to stimulate tourism activities by providing an indoor destination (the restaurant), the amphitheater, and picnic and gathering/resting places. Because one of the purposes of the park was to stimulate private investment on adjacent parcels, the design incorporated numerous pedestrian access points to link the park to surrounding developed and undeveloped spaces. The park also was to serve as a major pedestrian connector between the State House and Kennedy Plaza.

Policy Entrepreneurs Joining Forces: Right Time, Right Place, Right Idea

Two major constraints dominated this phase of renaissance making: the loftiness, some said outrageousness, of the ideas, and the more mundane matter of cost. Perhaps in no other renaissance project is there more focus on the discussion of what Providence was to become than in these water-related discourses. Capital Center was an office park. However, it was clear, according to Bill Collins, that "Warner recognized that anyone could build an office park, but he wanted an office park that integrated elegance and other elements that had never existed, including granite stones from the old riverbeds."[109] Warner's real contribution to the renaissance was forcing public and private policy makers to decide that Providence was not going to be just a smudge with an office park.

While Bill Warner undoubtedly was a driving force behind the new Providence waterfront, these three projects were pushed forward by a succession of individuals in a variety of public positions who were willing to use their authority and discretion to put their institutions behind the project. The Providence Foundation continued in its role as a catalyst by securing backing, both financial and political. Appointed and career bureaucrats showed a willingness to accept the challenge of Warner's ideas. Far from being red tape–laden, unimaginative, and hidebound, as so often the stereotype goes, administrators, engineers, and planners at critical junctures themselves became catalysts, not conservers.

Willingness to accept an idea was not enough to overcome the inevitable cost constraints. As was true of the Capital Center and railroad projects, no moving of rivers or creating of water parks would have happened without federal financial assistance. For that reason the position of the Rhode Island senators was fortuitous and enabled millions of federal dollars to flow into Providence. The change in federal policy that provided more state discretion in the use of federal transportation dollars permitted the defining of a river-moving project as a highway project, an indispensable part of the Providence renaissance.

Cooperation and Committees as Policy Tools

The goal of these projects was to reacquaint the community of Providence with its waterfront. Perhaps the principal tool used to move these projects forward was the experience various participants had in policy cooperation. The seemingly endless use of committees at many points in the design process made sure that the process was open enough to allow various interests and institutions and the public to have their say without creating policy paralysis. With the notable exception of the Capital Center primary interest, there was little public opposition to these ideas. Constraints that emerged from professional design disagreements were overcome by the combination of compelling vision, federal money, and the determination of individuals to see the project completed. The cooperative agreements signed at different times were symbolic of the coming together of committed organizations to complete the project with the greater interests of the city in mind rather than the particular interests of individuals and organizations.

From Napkin to Reality

The immediate outcomes of these water-related projects were quite visible, even more so than in Capital Center: the confluence of two rivers was moved;

Suicide Circle was eliminated, along with the Crawford Street Bridge, and a better traffic flow was created by an extended Memorial Boulevard along the Providence River; three riverside parks and pedestrian walkways appeared; and changes were made to the Capital Center District Plan in 1985 to reconfigure parcels to reflect the new river alignments. This was quite an outcome from a sketch on a napkin! As Bill Warner says, "We all wanted a better place than what was initally being proposed."[110]

The success of moving water as a public investment can be measured by its use and, more important, by the degree to which it achieves its purpose of attracting people and development. People undoubtedly have been attracted. The developers of parcels surrounding Capital Center, including the developers of the Providence Place mall, have cited Waterplace Park either in their planning applications or in subsequent press releases as one of the key reasons for locating in the new downtown. Rouse's statement about people loving water has a ring of truth in the Providence case.

Attracting tens of thousands to the downtown waterways during the "season," the rivers and their parks, most notably Waterplace, have become an outdoor gathering place for the people of Providence and from many places beyond. The spectacular public "happening" of WaterFire, with its burning braziers floating in the rivers from Waterplace Park to the old Providence harbor, lit in the evening by shrouded figures in darkened vessels as atmospheric music serenades the thousands of spectators who walk the riverbanks, is symbolic of the Providence renaissance. Gondolas ply the waterways. Outdoor Shakespeare productions performed by Trinity Repertory Theater players are a regular feature in Waterplace Park. Undeveloped land near the park has been the venue for productions of both the Xtreme and Gravity Games. Scenes of the television show *Providence* were filmed along the riverbanks and on the park's bridges.

Conclusion

Important lessons learned by moving railroads were reinforced when relocating the rivers and constructing Waterplace, and a few new ones were learned, as well. Of all the renaissance projects, river relocation comes closest to being a planning-based effort. But it was planning on the run, as plans often shifted to involve many elements. For example, plans for the highway interchange that were long on the drawing table at this point could be dusted off and updated and the process begun for what would become one of the last major downtown FHWA interchange projects in New England. As railroad relocation had been, building an interchange was a long-held policy goal.

The story of moving rivers is a tale of individual determination to see a project through to its finish as much as it is a narrative about planning and design. Warner's idea of moving rivers became possible only because a number of key individuals shared a common vision of the finished product: the right people were in the right place at the right time and were able to take advantage of this idea, outlandish as it seemed, once it was proposed.

Mobilized elites presented a unified, cohesive front, which was crucial to leveraging the massive amounts of federal aid needed to spur private development. The continuing availability of a large pot of federal money helped immensely. Further aid came from a fortuitous change in federal highway policy, which allowed for highway reprogramming that came to include a river-moving project. Federal money for the highway interchange became available because of the failure of the state to achieve consensus over other highway projects. Predicting that rivers and boulevards would be built because of popular opposition to unrelated highway projects would be a challenge for even the most talented public policy prognosticator.

As was true in the case of the railroad project, elites played an important role, but the nature of these elites and their forums was different. Appointed and career civil servants used their positions to develop an aesthetic soul for the city, not just land for development. Their goal was both amorphous and tangible: amorphous because they were trying to create something beautiful, and tangible because there was function. The continual use of coordinating committees helped keep the project in the eye of the public and anticipate stumbling blocks that might arise from various interests. In the end each of the actors in this story helped bring the most ambitious project of them all to a successful conclusion: a reunification of the city with its water.

The river relocation and Waterplace have created a special, authentic sense of place. Since their unveiling, the rivers and their allied beautification projects have become vital to much of the new economic activity in the central city. They are a distinct destination for tourists, convention goers, weekend visitors, and downtown office workers. These projects provide extensive, aesthetically pleasing public amenities that may enhance the extent and pace of economic development in the new downtown and place some of the locus of new development activity squarely on the waterfront. The river and park projects emphasize "historic Providence" and "destination city" development themes, in contrast to the idea that Providence would be a financial services center.

In the nineteenth century Providence turned its back on its waterfront in favor of its railroads. Then the railroad economy collapsed. It is the great irony of the Providence renaissance that both its railroads and waterfront, two long-since-forgotten economic engines of Providence, have become so vitally important to the hopes of Providence—a "back to the future" theme. The Providence Preservation Society puts it this way: the city's renaissance has "rediscovered the rivers that flow through the city center and exploits them to glue the city back together."[111]

a

This sequence of aerial photographs shows how post–World War II downtown Providence was unrecognizable by the turn of the twenty-first century: contrasted with the chaos of the declining industrial city of 1952 (a) and the fading commercial core of 1981 (b) is the Renaissance City of 2000 (c).

Courtesy of Rhode Island Department of Transportation (a and b) and Pillsbury Associates (c).

b

C

The Providence Place Mall: Coming on the Agenda

7

You can't have a great city without a great marketplace.

James Rouse, 1977

■ James Rouse's comment from a 1977 Providence meeting referred to the medieval marketplace as the crossroads for society, where the public met to transact business and the city took its own civic pulse.[1] The saga of the Providence Place mall is not just about the attempted economic revitalization of the city. The rivers and waterfront redevelopment symbolize the reclaiming of the city's history, but building Providence Place is the story of the city's and the state's attempt to reestablish its capital as the state's urban center, a crossroads for the twenty-first century.

Urban mall building is risky business. More potential hazards await the unwary developer and public policy maker than are encountered by intrepid computer adventure gamers. The Providence Place mall, the largest public-private effort in Rhode Island's history at a cost of approximately $500 million, was built after more than a decade of effort. Numerous twists and turns challenged those who as an article of faith believed that a mall was necessary for a renaissance to occur in the city.

Stripped to its essentials, Providence Place mall is a regional shopping and entertainment venue. It occupies about twelve acres of land between the Rhode Island State House to the north and the Convention Center/Westin Hotel complex to the south. Its frontage on the east is along Francis Street opposite Waterplace Park. The park's walkway extends to the mall itself. I-95 runs along the west side of the mall; an access ramp leads directly into the mall's four-thousand-space parking garage.

Providence Place was a private development idea, but its scale and its role in achieving a public policy outcome, a revitalized urban retail center, inevitably involved obtaining significant public support. Building the mall signaled a shift in thinking about Capital Center, from a financial services venue to a destination "tourist bubble," an idea that would be furthered by the building of the Rhode Island Convention Center. The public-private nature of the mall featured adroit and very public deal making, as all parties learned to cope with economic and political circumstances that threatened to unravel the concept.

Unlike the rails and rivers projects, this large undertaking had no policy window suddenly open. No external factor created an opportunity to build the mall. Instead, in incremental fashion the idea crept onto the public agenda as an extension of the perceived change in the climate in Providence. External factors almost killed the mall entirely. There were elites lined up both for and against the idea. A high level of financial and political risk existed for all involved, including the Rhode Island taxpayer. The mall got caught in brutal statewide election politics; interinstitutional battles between the legislative and executive branches in Rhode Island; the rivalry between the state and its capital city leadership; and an uncertain economy that created skittish private lenders. It certainly was not a project that was planned and carried out under a shroud of secrecy.

What this story has in common with the previous ones was the sheer perseverance of individuals over a fifteen-year period to see the project through to completion. The constraints were legion and required endless renegotiations of every conceivable element as multiple actors and institutions coped with crisis after crisis. For more than a decade public policy makers and their private partners struggled and succeeded in building enough of a consensus that the project could go forward and found ways to overcome state and local politics, land use, building design, and retailer and financial obstacles. In the end, Providence had its jewel in the crown.

Mall Building: Evolution, Characteristics, Roadblocks

Retail, retail, retail: shopping has played a large role in city economics for a long time. Cyrus Butler built the first arcade (mall) in the United States in 1828 in Providence. Still there, between Westminster and Weybosset Streets, the Arcade was restored as part of the early flurry of development efforts in the 1970s. The idea then, as it is now, was to provide shoppers shelter from the elements and a pleasant interior. "By turn of the century the heart of most big cities was a popular retail district in which department stores, specialty shops, restaurants and entertainment all complemented each other."[2] By the 1960s suburban shopping centers burgeoned throughout the United States and then swelled in the 1970s and 1980s. What was good for the suburbs became deadly for the cities. While retail sales grew nationally, the downtown share shrank dramatically as retailers followed the population to the suburbs.

Throughout the 1970s and 1980s cities began to look somewhat more inviting as virgin suburban land shrank and land use and environmental regulation and opposition to overdevelopment increased. Suburbia was no longer willing to bond itself for these projects. Urban shopping malls, such as Copley Place in Boston, became more commonplace. More than one hundred new compact, mixed-use downtown retail centers opened between 1970 and 1988, aimed squarely at middle-level markets. Faneuil Hall in Boston represents a festival mall of the sort that typically opened in renovated historic areas. Still, national developers such as Melvin Simon chose to stay with suburbia: "The biggest thing we don't have is patience to wait five or six years and then have the whole project go out to bid. We've been fortunate enough—or unfortunate enough—to be kept busy in conventional shopping centers."[3]

The public-private partnership has characterized mall development since 1970. Between 1970 and 1985 significant amounts of public money were invested in urban mall development.[4] At the same time, city policy makers and bureaucrats began operating like developers. Mall development fit into a larger scheme of post–urban renewal through historic rehabilitation and removal of eyesores. Public policy maker attention focused on feasible retail projects. Typically, a city would supply a developer with a site at below market cost ready for building, as well as supporting facilities such as streets, sidewalks, parks, and plazas. The public would own a parking garage. Direct public financing through tax-exempt bonds or leasing arrangements was common. A city might agree to act as a financial broker and raise money from a variety of federal and state sources, private foundations, and businesses. Deals would have to be both politically defensible and profitable for the developer.[5]

Three types of roadblocks accompany most urban malls as they are developed. New and costly ramps, roads, and intersections constitute the first mall roadblock. Vehicular access to the mall from highways is an obvious concern of developers and retailers. Public safety officials fret over traffic spilling onto surrounding side streets. The second roadblock occurs when developers insist that the public build garages to supply sufficient safe parking close to the stores, since they lack the acres of flat surface parking the suburbs offer. Garages elicit contentious public debate over how much public investment should be made in a project.[6]

The third potential roadblock is an absence of department store anchors. The perceived risky nature of urban projects forces mall developers to obtain anchor stores to attract financing and, ultimately, shoppers. Potential lenders measure the financial strength of a project by the major retailers anchoring the mall. These anchor stores usually have considerable influence over the likelihood of a project coming to fruition. Paradoxically, many department stores had left cities for the suburbs in the first place.

However, today's malls are designed to be the center of community activity, not just places to go and shop till you drop.[7] Movie theaters, restaurants, video arcades, government and community services, police stations (or security zones), post offices, motor vehicle registries, banks, pharmacies, art galleries, and even schools are located inside malls. Consequently, malls serve the private purposes of developers, retailers, and consumers yet contain the elements of public gathering places inside a private venue.

Providence Place is very much designed to be a center of community activity. The mall has 1.35 million square feet of retail space occupied by 150 retail stores and anchored by Lord and Taylor, Filene's, and Nordstrom. About 2,500 people work in Providence Place. A seven-hundred-seat food court, with a variety of fast-food venues that feature American and ethnic cuisines, is located in a third-level "wintergarden," a high-ceilinged, glassed area that links the "Cityside" of the mall (the south) to its "Stateside" (the north) and provides a spectacular view of sunsets to the west and of Capital Center to the east. Above this area is a sixteen-screen stadium-seating Hoyts cinema complex and an IMAX theater. There are also several full-service restaurants, ranging from the Napa Valley Grille to Joe's American Bar and Grill. Dave and Buster's supplies arcade fun and food. There was at one time a public high school located in the mall whose curriculum emphasized retail. The mall is linked physically by a skybridge walkway to the Westin Hotel/Rhode Island Convention Center complex. The Friedrich St. Florian–designed skybridge is the symbolic link between the old and new retail centers of the city.

Building Providence Place forced private developers and public policy makers to cope with the typical mall roadblocks and others generated by the local mall-building climate. Over the fifteen years of development effort the following core issues had to be addressed:

•   A compressed, highly visible site within Capital Center devoted to retailing when Capital Center regulations forbade major retailing;

•   Continued downcity property owner and retailer opposition;

•   A disastrous economy marked by a national and regional recession and a state economic crisis;

•   A very public state–city–private interest disagreement over parking garage financing;

•   An equally passionate private developer–state disagreement over the financing of the mall itself;

- The lack of direct federal financial assistance for the mall project;
- Securing prominent anchor stores;
- Numerous gubernatorial election campaigns during which virtually every candidate (including the successful one) pledged to kill the mall;
- Local political opposition to tax treaties negotiated by the state; and
- Architectural design controversies concerning the mall's proximity to the State House.

Each of these potential "mall-killer" issues appeared over the course of three discernable phases that marked the development of Providence Place. In the first (1985–90) the idea for a mall-like project was placed on the public agenda as a mixed-use project at various times; it contained retail, hotel, and convention center components. Transitions characterized the second phase (1990–93), when policy makers and developers confronted the greatest economic challenge to the mall, which forced significant changes in purpose, design, and ownership. From 1994 to 1997 considerable political conflict erupted over the mall before ground was broken in March 1997.

Building Providence Place: The Beginning (1985–1990)

Early Catalysts

The old downcity of Providence has undergone continuous decline since the mid-1960s. All of the major department stores—Gladding's, Shepard's, Peerless, the Outlet—that had collectively served as the high-end shopping nexus for the state were closed by 1983. The *Providence Development Strategy* (1986) resulted in the closing of the old downtown's main shopping thoroughfare, Westminster Street, to traffic and repaving it as a pedestrian shopping zone. The goal was to create a welcoming atmosphere for daytime office workers and weekend visitors. Sidewalk cafés, public benches, shade trees, outdoor sculpture, and high-end clothing and gift shops were envisioned, with the goal of returning retail to the central business district. The result was a multimillion-dollar failure, as business continued to drop precipitously.[8]

Mayor Joseph Paolino Jr., who had risen from city council president to mayor when Buddy Cianci was forced to resign in April 1984, remained politically committed to a refurbished, retail-focused downcity with Capital Center, now under construction, becoming the financial services area of the city.[9] Searching around for more good ideas to rescue downcity, Mayor Paolino's newly reconstituted Providence Planning Department commissioned two Boston-based consulting firms, Carr, Lynch Associates and Melvin F. Levine and Associates, to prepare development scenarios for the area. The resulting *Providence Development Strategy* suggested a shift of emphasis for downcity from retail to residential de-

a

b

a. The pedestrianization of
Westminster Street in the
mid-1980s was an attempt to
resurrect retail activity in the
traditional heart of downcity.
b. A lonely shopper on a Saturday afternoon in 1987
demonstrates how this effort
failed.

Courtesy of Providence Department
of Planning and Development

velopment and themed tourist attractions in order to generate a demand for
goods and services. Paolino also realized that Capital Center was going to be a
catalyst for development. John Ryan, president of a local real estate company,
tried to interest Paolino almost immediately after he took office in an idea for
building a Copley Place–style mall that incorporated Union Station.

During 1985, as this soul-searching about the retail future of Providence was
under way, a developer from Greenwich, Connecticut, Alexius Conroy, drove
through downtown Providence on behalf of the national developer Nathan
Landow and drove away with a vision for a mall, not the office building that was
on Landow's mind.[10] Two years earlier J. Daniel Lugosch III, an executive of
Pyramid Corporation, also began watching the physical changes in Providence
as he worked on the six-year venture to build the Emerald Square Mall in nearby
Attleboro, Massachusetts. What they both saw and realized was that by the
mid-1980s the Boston-Providence retail markets were overlapping.[11] The region
bounded by Providence, Boston and Worcester, Massachusetts, and New Lon-

don, Connecticut, contained nearly three million people, one of the most densely populated areas in the United States. Providence by the mid-1980s, as Bill Collins noted, "was not only a city, but a part of a much larger metropolitan area. The suburbanization of Boston was beginning to have an impact on the much larger region and Providence was feeling the effects."[12] Times were good in Rhode Island. Real estate values were at levels never seen before in the state, personal incomes were up, and unemployment was down.

Providence was beginning to percolate. The possibility of a revitalized downcity was in the political and business wind. Capital Center was five years along. Rails and rivers were in the process of being moved. Retail in Providence was just about dead, but there were plans: to renovate the Outlet department store building; to build a convention center; and to convert Union Station to offices. The American Telephone Building next to the Civic Center in LaSalle Square was completed. The Carr, Lynch Associates and Melvin F. Levine and Associates report (1986) commissioned by the Providence Planning and Development Department regarding the prospects of downcity revitalization was published.

In incremental fashion the idea of a major retail mall crept onto the agenda, pushed forward by a number of catalysts. Along with a good economy, the general boom of the Boston metropolitan area, and the prospects for a revitalized Providence, ideas for feasible projects were emerging, and political opposition to locating the mall outside downcity, while still in evidence, was shrinking. The possibilities were not lost on local and national developers.

In June 1986 Antonio Guerra, who had purchased the abandoned Brown and Sharpe manufacturing company property just west of I-95, outside the Capital Center district, proposed turning the factory buildings into a $120-million complex complete with two hundred stores, office space, and a glassed atrium. "The Foundry," as the project was known, would require two publicly financed parking garages and incorporate a three-hundred-room Sheraton Hotel with a "water view" of the less than pristine Woonasquatucket River.[13] Guerra insisted that state or city tax-exempt bonds and a tax stabilization treaty were needed for the project to work.[14] He also proposed building a convention center across the river from the hotel, just as the city and state were considering one, as well.

Guerra's plans did not materialize. Financing was a problem because of the scale of the project. Substantial skepticism arose from downcity concerns unwilling to see their already precarious properties further marginalized by pulling what remained of Providence retail trade away from the immediate downcity area. However, in a fledgling way the development rationale for Providence Place was contained in this Foundry plan: a large retailing venue outside the traditional downcity core, near I-95 and a river, requiring private and public investment, and almost within the Capital Center district. The Foundry eventually became lofts and office space, after a brief period of consideration in 1997 as the location for the New England Patriots' stadium.

At about the same time in 1986 Alexius Conroy, president of Cadillac Fairview Shopping Centers Ltd., a large, nationwide developer, and former vice president of the real estate division of Macy's, commissioned a market survey that indicated the viability and profitability of a mall venture in Providence.[15] In April 1987 Conroy publicly announced a plan for a $300-million mall that would have three department stores, movie theaters, a luxury hotel, and a 4,500-space parking garage. The public policy makers in the mayor's office in city hall were receptive.

The prospect for a mall was strengthened because the political winds had shifted away from downcity retailers. In his January 1987 inaugural speech Paolino reversed a long-held city policy stance that opposed any mall outside downcity. Paolino's earlier objection to a mall located away from the traditional downcity area was rooted in an effort to protect the Outlet, the last remaining department store, and the failing Westminster Street Pedestrian Mall. The Capital Center Commission's development guidelines specifically forbade major retailing within Capital Center, restricting retail trade to those offering financial services within the district. Thus the prime motivation for those restrictive guidelines was removed when the Outlet closed its doors in 1982 and it became clear that the Westminster Street Mall plan was doomed. Mayor Paolino remarked at his inauguration: "Why should the popularity of shopping malls be limited to the suburbs when we can bring the convenience of a retail mall into the heart of downtown? . . . Now major retail is not in downtown any longer. . . . Westminster Mall will never be anywhere near in a competitive position to the [suburban] malls, and because of that we have to rethink and redirect our plans."[16] It was a difficult admission to make, because the Paolino family held significant real estate holdings in downcity Providence. It was difficult to "do anything without him [Joseph R. Paolino Sr.]."[17] However, from a policy standpoint, it was less risky to encourage retailing somewhere near downcity than it was to preside over the complete collapse of retailing in the city.

Providence was in a position to take advantage of the national trend away from suburban mall building and toward urban ventures. Conroy discussed with Bruce Sundlun the possibility of bringing Melvin Simon and Associates of Indianapolis, the second-largest suburban shopping center developer in the nation, to participate in the development of a "Providence Place" mall.[18] When Simon visited the city he was impressed with the number of students he saw in the daytime.[19] Sundlun also suggested that Nathan Landow and Company of Bethesda, Maryland, the developer of high-rise luxury apartments in Washington, D.C., might be interested in the hotel part of the project. Ironically, as early as 1984 Landow wanted to build an office building in Providence, but Conroy discouraged him after Landow had sent him to scope out Providence for the office building idea.[20]

By 1987 a number of catalysts were in place to impel the type of retail project embodied in the Conroy idea. Developers could see the possibility of private financial success, and the need to do something to bring retailing back into the city was clear. The city and state economies were in good shape, and the idea of building retail malls in cities was a national trend. Local opposition, at least for the moment, was muted when the city political leadership, who were likely to oppose the idea, endorsed it instead. Still, there was skepticism even by such Providence renewal advocates as Ron Marsella: "How practical it all is, is going to be somewhat dependent on the reaction of those potential developers to the strength of the retail market in Rhode Island and Providence in particular."[21]

Mall Building Constraints: History, Architecture, Place

The clarity of the desired outcome stands in sharp contrast to the tortuous road necessary to get there. There was a general consensus that something had to be done to rescue retailing if the city's revitalization was to come to fruition. This first period in the history of the mall was a time when the ability of mall advocates to overcome obstacles would be tested and made clear just how difficult it would be to get a mall built. Public debate in this first phase focused primarily on three specific concerns. Could a site be assembled for a retail project within Capital Center? If so, who would have jurisdiction over the project? Could a large-scale mall fit into the overall historical and architectural context of Providence? More traditional roadblock issues, parking garages and financing, were also present but would surface more prominently later.

Almost immediately the geographic sensitivity of a Capital Center site was questioned. The Conroy-Simon-Landow plan called for a mall on approximately fourteen acres on the east side of I-95, made up of seven state-owned acres just outside the Capital Center district boundary occupied by the University of Rhode Island College of Continuing Education (URI-CCE), and two Capital Center parcels: parcel 10, a 4.5-acre tract owned by Amtrak, and parcel 9, a 2-acre city-owned parcel. Governor Edward DiPrete publicly stated his concern that a mall there would overshadow the State House. He also was wary of the amount of public financing that might be required and the need to relocate the Rhode Island Department of Elementary and Secondary Education, offices of the Rhode Island DEM, and URI-CCE. DiPrete's support was crucial because without the state land the project was "dead in the water."[22] In April 1987, after considerable discussion, the governor gave his general support to the project without endorsing any particular design or financing plan.

The mall in this early stage was "of" but not "in" Capital Center. The idea for the mall clearly was aided by the existence of Capital Center, but physically the site occupied by URI-CCE and the state offices was not within the district. Throughout the mall's development history the Capital Center Commission, specifically its Design Review Committee (DRC), acted as the administrative mechanism to oversee the design of the project and as a forum to air public concerns over the various impacts of a mall on Providence. The somewhat byzantine relationship among the city, state, and CCC is evident in the deliberations during 1987 over the fate of parcel 9, within the district, and that of the URI-CCE site, just outside the original district.

Even though the CCC had development jurisdiction over land within its boundaries, control of the district land still remained within the hands of its owners. The hotel portion of the project was slated for parcel 9. Mayor Paolino would not sell the city-owned parcel 9 to the state for a previously agreed-upon $2.5 million until he was certain about the fate of the mall. The $2.5 million was part of the city's share for the river relocation project, which was in full swing.[23] The state, once it acquired ownership of parcel 9, would give it to the CCC in exchange for land the state needed to relocate the rivers. Paolino was also concerned over the fate of new land, which would be created once the rivers were actually moved and become parcel 12.[24]

The state owned the seven acres at URI-CCE that were not included in the Capital Center district; therefore, the mall portion of the project would not be subject to development and design guidelines of the DRC. Design was a critical issue throughout the process of building the mall and one that was central to preservationist support for the project. Since the College Hill rescue of the 1950s, historic preservation remained a powerful urban policy concern in Providence. The preservationists' battle flags were flying high because of the proximity of the project to the State House and the potential for a large, drab or garish building as costs of the project inevitably escalated and aesthetics became victim to cost cutting: "I don't think there's any argument that the State House has got to be our premiere building in the city," said Wendy Nicholas of the Providence Preservation Society.[25] In 1986 the developers had withdrawn a design that raised the ire of the revered figure of Providence preservation, Antoinette Downing.

Conroy did sign a contract agreeing to submit to CCC jurisdiction, but a number of commissioners expressed reservations about that arrangement. "If it's a matter of contract and there's a breach, you'd have a breach of contract action only," Sundlun remarked. "The Capital Center Commission, on the other hand, could bring an injunction to halt the entire project if need be."[26] The obvious dilemma was that if the state parcel was incorporated into Capital Center, then for the mall to be built, the DRC had to amend the district's guidelines, which prohibited major retail development, an obvious poison pill regulation for the mall.

The general will to see a mall built is evident in the resolution of this significant constraint. The CCC was predisposed to advance the mall because by 1988 Capital Center itself was not yet attracting private sector development at a significant rate. The market for downtown financial space had changed, as had the financial climate regionally. Though the Citizens Bank project was still under development, there was nothing else on the horizon. The state's executive and legislative leadership already had invested in the idea of a Providence renaissance effort through the railroad and river projects. To further the potential for a mall project, in 1988 the state legislature authorized the transfer of the URI-CCE site to the Rhode Island Port Authority.[27] In September 1988 Conroy and his developers and investors, now known as the Providence Place Group (PPG), obtained a twelve-month option to buy Amtrak's 4.5 acres within Capital Center for $13.2 million. In October PPG secured a fifteen-month option from the Port Authority for the seven acres of state land for an $18-million sale price, with a possible second fifteen-month option period to secure financing and approvals. URI-CCE would have to move. Conroy insisted that the investment was a good one: "Providence is in the midst of a Renaissance, and that's perceived by the market outside the state."[28]

Still, the only way to achieve the twin objectives of returning retail to the city and protecting the historical and architectural preeminence of the State House was to incorporate the state parcels in the Capital Center district and for the commission to drop the district's retail prohibition. The city's political leadership endorsed the idea, and in March 1989 the Providence City Council voted to incorporate the state's seven acres in Capital Center. During May and June the CCC held hearings regarding the incorporation and voted in September 1989 to bring the parcel within its jurisdiction and to eliminate the ban on large-scale retailing within Capital Center. Paolino was pleased by this achievement: "I do believe in keeping [the developers'] feet to the fire, but I don't feel that they should have roadblocks in front of them."[29]

By 1989 the land for a mall had been assembled, more or less, but there were still plenty of cautionary flags in the wind. Could financing be obtained? Who would be the anchors? Who would build and own a garage? However, the debate over achieving an acceptable design was the dominant, very public concern that overshadowed questions of finance, stores, and garages. By the time the mall was constructed, the architectural and preservationist concerns over the actual design were well vetted.

The plans for developing a mall would continue to have to pass the muster of a strong preservationist community passionate about design within the historical and architectural context of Providence. The preservationist interests had gathered their strength ever since the urban renewal fights two decades earlier, so that by the time the mall idea came on the public's agenda, preservationists had institutions such as the Providence Preservation Society and the Rhode Island

Historical Preservation and Heritage Commission and individuals such as Wendy Nicholas, Frederick Williamson, and Antoinette Downing committed to the preservation of a "historic" Providence. In 1984 the entire downcity of Providence had been placed on the National Register of Historic Places after a decade of struggle by the RIHPHC to overcome local fears (including those of the PPS) concerning restrictive regulations and their impact on property owners.[30] The RIHPHC were well prepared to do battle over projects that they deemed harmful to the city's historic character.

Wendy Nicholas, the executive director of the PPS, did not oppose Providence Place but pointedly stated, "It comes very close to putting a shopping mall on the State House lawn."[31] Frederick Williamson, the director of the state's preservation office, stated plainly that he would oppose Providence Place unless there were specific guidelines for the project. In his capacity as the state historic preservation officer, and under his authority granted by the National Historic Preservation Act and agreements with the FRA and the FHWA, the two primary sources of funding for Capital Center projects, Williamson could veto any changes in commission rules that threatened historic properties. Williamson's doubts about the mall were clear: "The architecture frequently used for such buildings involves large volumes of interior space with little exterior articulation in the form of frequent entrances, storefronts, window fenestration and variations in mass. . . . Such buildings could be a visual intrusion on surrounding historic properties and therefore constitute an adverse effect."[32]

Very much aware of these concerns, the CCC published new design guidelines in June 1989 in response to the developer's mall proposals. Marilyn Taylor of SOM, acting as Capital Center's planning and design consultant, developed guidelines that reflected the commission's concern about the overall visual impact of a large mall. The developer's plan to deck over the Woonasquatucket River was dismissed as unacceptable for the obvious reason that millions were being spent uncovering rivers as a centerpiece of a Providence rebirth. The commission required a bridge over the river for the project to go forward. Conroy's mall project manager, John Casson, argued that the bridge requirement would force the developers to move the planned hotel from the Amtrak parcel to the seven-acre URI-CCE site, thereby subjecting it to the eighty-foot height restriction that protected the State House's preeminence and thus making the project less economically viable. A planned Capital Properties garage was permitted under the guidelines, but only if a three-story townhouse was built to shield Gaspee Street from the garage. Capital Properties' Joe DiStefano argued vociferously that the townhouse "shield" for the garage was too costly and not feasible.

The policy objective of getting the mall built could not be achieved by adopting the guidelines as proposed, given the swift and negative reaction of the mall's developers and Capital Properties. The CCC voted to hold the design guidelines in abeyance, a suggestion made by Mayor Paolino, who was concerned that the rules would scuttle the project: "If they [the developers] don't make it, I don't want them [Conroy's staff] to say that we are anti-development."[33] To pass design guidelines for a project that was still questionable would have put a policy in effect that would have had no realistic use. As a practical matter, Conroy had not yet bought the site and in his still unsuccessful negotiations with prospective tenants he was using the design first unveiled in April 1987. Nevertheless, it was clear to Conroy that the proposed design would not be approved.

The Mall Idea Is Planted

Despite the constraints that emerged between 1985 and 1990, there were significant accomplishments. Just planting the idea of bringing large-scale retailing back to the city was crucial. The physical site of the mall was identified, more or less, and the process of assembling the parcels showed that it would take city–state–private interest cooperation for a project to be successful. The fact that design was more important early on than financing and other traditional mall roadblocks signaled the necessity of addressing the historic preservation community's concerns if a mall was to be built. The DRC became the vehicle for waging mall design wars and began to strengthen its muscle for later, very public battles. The mall's place in the larger context of a revitalized city and the policy objective of reclaiming the city's water heritage came to the fore.

As events unfolded, the CCC's decision not to impose new development guidelines just yet proved a wise one, as 1990 turned out to be a difficult year for the project. Conroy's prime residential property developer, Landow and Company, withdrew from the project on 10 January 1990. Melvin Simon followed suit a week later. Both cited the lengthiness of the development process and the need to reallocate sources as the economy began to change. Despite all the discussion to that date, no firm commitment by anyone for anything had been secured.

While public debate over financing the mall was not at the center of controversy yet, by 1990 the seeds were planted for future funding battles. The developers did not hide the fact that considerable public assistance would be needed to build a 4,500-space garage. The city's ability to perform infrastructure work such as roads, traffic lights, sidewalks, and other typical city contributions to mall development had not been considered yet. How much new revenue the city would derive was just beginning to be a consideration. In 1987 Mayor Paolino indicated a willingness to create a special tax district for the mall, with the idea that the parcels in the district were tax exempt. Neither Amtrak nor URI-CCE paid property taxes to the city. Alternatively, property taxes could be levied on Providence Place and be earmarked for repaying bonds that the city would issue to assist the developers.[34]

Difficulties to come were augured in January 1990 by the state's realization that it did not have clear title to the URI-CCE land. It seemed that history was conspiring against the mall. The URI-CCE acres were acquired by state condemnation at the turn of the nineteenth century in order to fill in the cove and move the railroad tracks. That condemnation created a defect in the title to the URI-CCE acres: Rhode Island law required that before the state could sell condemned land, it had to offer it to the descendents of the original owners. The legislature did change the statute governing property condemnations, but it was an inauspicious way to enter 1990.

Renaissance Troubles: Providence Place, the Rhode Island Convention Center/ Westin Hotel, 1990–1994

8

Boy, we need those jobs . . . this is a great thing.

Jack Cronin, Rhode Island Building Trades Association, at the 1997
signing of the Providence Mall Tax treaty

■ "What a revoltin' development this is!" Chester A. Riley, the 1950s sitcom character, a suburban, "head of household," blue-collar worker, would say as he faced yet another escalating crisis that consumed his family. That phrase summed up the feelings of many northeastern political leaders as they struggled to cope with a sudden rise of red ink in public budgets as a national and regional recession set in during the early 1990s. Rhode Island was not immune to these economic trends and in 1991 would experience a calamitous collapse of its credit union system. In perhaps the greatest irony of the entire Providence renaissance, while the economy slowed the mall, it acted as the principal catalyst to bring the Rhode Island Convention Center and Westin Hotel complex to fruition, the second element of a potential tourist bubble that mall planning began.

The Rhode Island Budget and Credit Union Crisis: 1989–1994[1]

Rhode Island was a victim of its own success in raising revenues and expanding services during the 1980s. A sudden early- to mid-decade boom economy flooded the state's treasury with new revenue. Governor DiPrete and the state legislature showed no inclination to restrain their largesse between 1985 and 1989. State spending outpaced revenues by considerable margins during those years. Rhode Island also reduced its tax effort in the 1980s by enacting a series of income tax rate reductions.

Underlying the apparently healthy 1980s economy were troubling signs that the boom really was a "blip." Single-family housing permit applications, a consistently cited indicator of the robustness of the state's overall economic health, declined precipitously after the 1986 peak. Yet state spending continued to grow and tax rates continued to be reduced. Also ominous were a rise in the prime lending rate and, subsequently, mortgage rates. Housing prices skyrocketed through 1988, shutting buyers out of the market. The end of good times came suddenly in fiscal year 1989–90, when revenues collapsed as people began to lose jobs and state income and sales tax revenues declined. For the next five budget cycles tough choices would face the state. In 1990–91 the state confronted a $200-million revenue shortfall on a total budget of about $1.5 billion.

Bruce Sundlun, successful in his third try to unseat Governor Ed DiPrete, was welcomed to office in January 1991 by a national recession, a regional real estate bust, and an imploding state budget. However, these issues paled in comparison to one other event: the collapse of the private credit union insurance system in the state. The Sundlun "take-charge" style that would be evident throughout his four years as governor went on very public display the day after his January 1991 inauguration, when he ordered the doors of all the privately insured credit unions in Rhode Island shut.

The statewide banking crisis was precipitated by the financial demise of the state's private credit union insurance agency, the Rhode Island Share and Deposit Indemnity Corporation (RISDIC). Rampant speculation by RISDIC-member credit unions and small banks during the mid- to late 1980s led to loan portfolios that proved seriously overextended in large-scale residential development projects.

Wholesale defaults on speculative real estate development loans brought insolvency to several of the credit unions. RISDIC did not have the assets to cover the depositor losses, so when Sundlun closed all the RISDIC-insured institutions, he froze the personal and business accounts held by them. It would take twelve years to clear the backlog of debt accumulated by these small banks and for the state to make accounts whole through the efforts of a newly created special state agency, the Depositor Economic Protection Corporation (DEPCO). State borrowing for the credit union bailout (and eventually for the Convention Center) doubled the state's debt service to 8 percent within a year.

As the local banks were failing, the real estate boom market of 1984–88, with one of the largest annual percentage increases in Rhode Island property prices of the twentieth century, went bust. Statewide property values, even in the prestige housing markets of East Greenwich, Providence's East Side, Newport, and Barrington, decreased between 1990 and 1994. New housing starts and construction industry employment declined precipitously, while aggregate unemployment peaked at levels not seen since the early 1980s.[2] The public's view of Rhode Island's state government was at its worst in decades, with barely 16 percent of the population believing that state government could make the right decision most of the time.[3] It is against this background that the mall inched ahead and the idea of the Rhode Island Convention Center went careening forward.

Providence Place: Transitions (1990–1993)

The mall's forward motion was slowed considerably between 1990 and 1993 as Rhode Island weathered its economic crisis, but important mall-related transitions did occur. The emphasis of the questions regarding the mall shifted somewhat from site and design to site, design, financing, and anchor stores. The financial relationship of the state and city concerning the mall came into sharper focus. New political leadership appeared when Bruce Sundlun, after nearly two decades of participation in private efforts to rebuild Providence, won the governorship. Mayor Vincent "Buddy" Cianci returned to his familiar perch in city hall after his legal hiatus by winning a very narrow re-election victory in a three-way race. Sundlun appointed former Providence mayor Joseph Paolino as his director of economic development.[4]

New mall developers for Providence Place appeared, as well.[5] An increasingly troubled regional economy made lenders nervous about large retail projects. To help the mall's prospects, in early 1990 Alexius Conroy invited Pyramid Corporation president Robert Congell to become the senior general partner in the mall venture, with Conroy becoming a limited 10 percent partner. Pyramid was a well-established mall development company located in Syracuse, New York. Congell suggested to Sundlun that Pyramid would have an interest in developing a large mall in Providence.[6] J. Daniel Lugosch III, who had supervised the construction of the Emerald Square Mall in nearby Attleboro, Massachusetts, in the 1980s, became the mall's project director and eventual managing partner.

Pyramid took a number of steps to keep the project moving forward, even though a substantial outflow of retail dollars from Rhode Island occurred, primarily to the malls in Massachusetts, including Emerald Square. John Sasso, former aide to Massachusetts governor Michael Dukakis and an associate of Mayor Paolino, was hired to obtain permits and approvals for the mall. Sasso had the appropriate "style" to get projects through the state permitting process and other public arenas. Paolino called him a great "flack catcher. . . . He did a great job."[7] Pyramid was aware of the CCC Design Review Committee's concerns, so they commissioned the architect Adrian Smith of the ever-present SOM to revisit the mall's design.[8] The CCC terminated its long-term (since 1982) relationship with its own SOM design consultant, Marilyn Taylor, in April 1990. Taylor's potential conflict of interest was obvious. She had developed the original, still un-adopted design guidelines for Capital Center that would apply to Providence Place.[9] By June, Smith had drawn a new mall design that included a hotel, office tower, and two garages and introduced the ideas of a domed roof and a vaulted arch over the Woonasquatucket River, and railroad tracks.

By late 1990 there were still grounds for optimism that a mall would be built, on the basis of favorable politics and a new, invigorated development team. The policy window for a mall had not closed, but the economy forced participants to struggle to keep it open. The basic components that supported building the mall—land availability, the intersection of five highways, and a large percentage of household incomes of more than $50,000 in a thirty-mile radius—remained in place. Although Pyramid canceled a number of planned projects in the Northeast, it did not abandon the Providence undertaking.[10] The idea that this mall was to be an upscale venture unlike any mall in Rhode Island or the bordering communities was squarely in the minds of developers. Pyramid announced in April 1990 that the Pyramid-owned retailer Bonwit-Teller would be a mall anchor, and in July Macy's agreed to open its first store in Rhode Island in the proposed mall.

The nature of the mall project also changed in one important aspect in 1990. By December the economy had forced the developers to abandon the hotel component because hotel financing had virtually disappeared. In 1991 a new 11.5-acre footprint was developed, which incorporated the Amtrak and URI-CCE sites but not parcel 9, the land once slated for a hotel. In 1992 Pyramid acquired two extensions on options to buy the Amtrak- and state-owned sites from the Rhode Island Port Authority (RIPA), because without them the project was dead. John Sasso declared at the time that Pyramid was "more optimistic" than ever "that Providence Place will be a reality."[11] Economic Development Director Paolino felt the extensions were warranted because Pyramid had "invested a great deal of money in this project."[12] In August 1993 RIPA agreed to buy the Amtrak land; the agreement was contingent on its ability to sell the land to Pyramid for mall development, and in February 1994 RIPA voted to execute a sales agreement between itself and Pyramid.[13]

Throughout the 1990–93 period more public and detailed discussions about the nature and extent of the public-private partnership took place. The developers began to put the onus on public officials to make the project happen. As Sasso put it, "Without the leadership of the governor and mayor, Providence Place just cannot happen."[14] Pyramid officials were clear that partnership meant direct public investment in the project, specifically for the garage: "We have said from day one that some sort of public-private partnership will be necessary."[15]

Federal financing had played a critical role in the development of Capital Center and in moving the rivers. The year 1990 marked the first time that federal money became a serious consideration for the mall project.[16] In May of that year, Pyramid proposed to the city and state a $290 million mall financing plan: $20 million in federal highway money for ramps and a garage; an additional tax increment financing (TIF) plan involving $100 million in sales and property tax revenues to be used to pay principal and interest on private bonds; and $170 million in private leases. This package formed the broad outline for discussions of mall financing for the next few years. Mall financing became an issue in the 1990 gubernatorial campaign, with both DiPrete and Sundlun opposing the use of state funds for mall purposes.[17] However, Sundlun enthusiastically supported the idea of using federal highway money for ramps and the garage, a stance he would aggressively pursue once elected.[18]

When Cianci resumed his duties as mayor in 1991, he became immediately invested in making Providence Place a reality. He took the position that the mall was a project for Providence, not just the state, and that the city had concerns that had to be addressed. Cianci indicated a strong preference for direct city financing rather than TIF. Jobs generated by Providence Place would have to be offered to Providence residents first. He wanted an assurance that URI-CCE would remain in downtown Providence.[19] The abandoned Shepard's department store building was mentioned as a possible location. By 1993 Cianci was making city financial support for the project contingent on a new state plan for financing public education.

The traditional mall roadblocks of finances and a garage shared the policy stage with the necessity of attracting a secure, upscale anchor. Both of the announced anchors, Bonwit-Teller and Macy's, were in receivership by 1992, leaving the mall proposal anchorless. Because mall financing is so dependent on viable retailers, at the end of 1993 Pyramid's Robert Congell organized an expedition to Seattle to discuss the possibility of Nordstrom coming to Providence. Mayor Cianci, Governor Sundlun, Joseph Paolino, Sundlun's director of administration, Harry Bird, and Cianci policy aid William Collins went to Seattle to attempt a long-shot sales pitch to the Nordstrom family about bringing their highly regarded name to Providence.[20]

The stakes were reasonably high at this juncture in the mall's story, as it now was seven years since the original Conroy proposal and Rhode Island still was in the depths of its financial woes. The mall idea needed a psychological as well as a tangible boost. The possibility of locating a Nordstrom store in an urban mall near Boston was feasible because Nordstrom effectively was blocked from the Boston market because of the number of existing upscale retailers already there. In 1992 a federal census redefinition of the southern New England region brought some suburban towns south of Boston within the economic orb of Providence. A much larger potential geographic market for Nordstrom, made up of households with a median income of $45,000, was now within the Providence population sphere. Nordstrom also knew that the Rhode Island sales tax exempted clothes, a significant advantage over Massachusetts, which has a luxury tax on high-end clothes.

The sales tax issue produced a dramatic moment. To address Rhode Island's revenue concerns, Governor Sundlun had proposed extending the state's sales tax to include clothes. At the Nordstrom headquarters meeting the question regarding the sales tax on clothing arose. Governor Sundlun began what might be characterized as a stump speech on the need for a broadened sales tax in the state. However, before he could warm to the task, Mayor Cianci gently poked Sundlun under the table. Sundlun took the physical cue: before Sundlun got a chance to make his point, Cianci made plain to the Nordstrom family that "there is no sales tax on clothing in Rhode Island!"[21]

The delegation left Seattle without a commitment but with strong interest and consequently hope as a new year began. The trip would eventually yield an important dividend: Nordstrom's eventual signing on as a mall store. Still, the state's economy and fiscal crisis continued to be a serious roadblock in moving the project forward at anything more than a snail's pace; the commitment of public funds to the project was unlikely in the economic environment engulfing the state. No shovel was put in the dirt; permits were not issued (eventually there would be more than forty needed); financing was not obtained and remained a critical concern; no formal design rules were issued, although much discussion of them took place; and there was still the problem of finding a home for URI, whose president announced in 1992 that any URI move could not add debt to the university. However, the idea was not dead: anchor stores were being discussed and Nordstrom seemed interested in Providence; a financial plan had been floated; a design change to accommodate some preservationist and river enthusiast concerns were in evidence; and land had been transferred.

As city and state leadership worked to get the private sector to commit to bringing retail back to the city, much of the state's energy between 1990 and 1993 was poured into a different project, one that was impelled more quickly by the very economic crisis that was slowing private and public investment in the mall. During 1991–93 the state decided to build the Convention Center and Westin Hotel next to the proposed site of the mall. The controversy engendered by the decision to build the Convention Center eventually had a serious impact on discussions over the willingness of the public to finance the mall.

Convention Center and Westin Hotel

Historical Background

Building a convention center in Providence was not a new idea in Rhode Island. In 1958 Governor Dennis Roberts submitted to the legislature a plan for revitalizing downtown Providence that included a convention center.[22] It was felt that such a facility would have a positive impact on the state's Rust Belt economy.

While that plan did not go forward, it represents the state's growing concern over the need to do something to revitalize its capital city.

When the Providence Planning Commission published *Downtown Providence 1970*, the plan included a civic and convention center. For the reasons detailed in chapter 4, that plan was not implemented, but the idea of building some facility to be the focal point of city recreational life remained alive. In 1963 the Providence Redevelopment Agency, the municipal authority with the power of condemnation and eminent domain, published *The Weybosset Hill Renewal Project*, which addressed the reuse of land at the western end of Sabin Street and LaSalle Square, including "a civic, sport and amusement center." When the Providence Civic Center became a reality in 1973, the convention and exhibition spaces detailed in the *Weybosset Hill Renewal Project* were excluded for cost reasons.

The convention center idea did not wither; instead, it reappeared as a state initiative. In 1969 the Rhode Island Economic Development Council (RIEDC) commissioned a convention center feasibility study, which turned attention away from Providence and toward its eighteenth-century rival, Newport. With a robust tourist industry anchored by the summer "cottages" of the Vanderbilts and their industrialist friends, the America's Cup yacht races, and its impressively intact colonial architecture, Newport seemed the obvious choice to become the center of the state's convention activities. Making much of the fact that there are very few genuine tourism magnets in the rest of the state, E.B.S. Management Consultants told their clients at the RIEDC, "only in Newport do the tourist attractions and hotel accommodations offer sufficient inducement for a convention center."[23] Indeed, Newport was the only location considered by the state until the 1980s.

As the railroads were being moved, Capital Center was laid out, the highway interchange moved off the drawing board, and a link between Providence and its water became a goal, the idea of a convention center located in Providence came back onto the policy agenda. In 1985 Mayor Paolino and Governor DiPrete publicly backed a downtown convention center as the logical follow-up to the infrastructure projects in Capital Center. Paolino's and DiPrete's agreement grew out of a favorable recommendation from a study by the consulting firm Laventhol and Horwath, commissioned by the Providence Foundation in 1981.[24] The consultants' analysis encouraged the foundation once again to act as a catalyst for a publicly funded downtown capital project.

A Catalyst for Downcity

When city council president Paolino assumed the mayor's office in 1984, it took very little persuading to get him to back a convention facility in Providence because, as noted earlier, his real estate family had more than a passing interest in the fortunes of downtown. A study commissioned by Paolino and released in

1986, *The Downtown Providence Development Strategy*, known as the Carr, Lynch/ Levine Associates study, urged an "around-the-clock" presence in the historic downtown core of the city as well as a much greater focus on financial and business services and travel and tourism attractions, thus anticipating shifts that were about to take place in the regional economy.[25] The report noted profound changes already under way in the downtown economy and proposed maritime-themed events, a festival marketplace, luxury shops, hotels, and condominiums on the empty upper floors of failing stores as the means to attract the middle and upper middle classes back to the central city. A convention center located at the crucial nexus of the "old" and "new" downtowns would provide an important link, according to the report, between the federally funded developments in Capital Center and the stagnant historic commercial core south and west of Kennedy Plaza.

Paolino and his chief city planners, director Arthur Markos and assistant planning director Thomas Moses, convened a task force in the spring of 1985 to examine ways of reinvigorating the old downtown, the traditional commercial core, using the ideas in the Carr, Lynch/Levine study. Simultaneously, Paolino and DiPrete brought together a separate city-state Convention Center Task Force to examine the feasibility of constructing a "world-class" convention center. That task force explored all aspects of building a major convention facility, including site selection, design, and financing, and it solicited proposals from national convention center developers.

Consultants are present at just about every turn in the story of the Providence renaissance. In the case of the Convention Center, consultants were important because they changed the entire direction of convention center thinking in the state and city. In 1986 Economics Research Associates (ERA) and Howard, Needles, Tammen and Bergendoff (HNTB) were selected as consultants to the city-state task force studying the feasibility and impact of the convention center idea to help determine potential sites and to evaluate two proposals that came forward as a result of a national solicitation by the task force for convention center ideas. The first proposal was for a 45,000-square-foot exhibition space with a three- to four-hundred-room hotel and parking for two thousand cars, to be located on West Exchange Street. The second was a proposed 60,000-square-foot Woonasquatucket Convention Center on the twelve-acre site occupied by the Providence Produce Market on the banks of the Woonasquatucket River, abutting I-95.

When the consulting team reported to the Convention Center Task Force in April 1987, they advocated for a completely new concept and design, which would require a much larger parcel of land and a significantly bigger building.[26] ERA/HNTB identified West Exchange Street as the preferred site for a potential 365,000 square feet of exhibition and meeting space, on land parcels occupied by the Bonanza Bus Terminal, the State Department of Employment Security, and the studios of Rhode Island's state-owned public television station, Channel 36. The task force advised the mayor and governor that a market existed to support a large-scale convention center and recommended that the state and city create a new Convention Center Authority and staff to work on developing a convention center as soon as possible. Suggesting that tax revenues generated by convention-goers would be "sufficient to cover 154% of its estimated annual cost," the consultants argued that a number of "intangible" benefits would also accrue to the city and state because the center would:

- Reinforce and strengthen the downtown business climate and urban fabric;
- Enhance the city and state marketing stance by improving their capacity to accommodate larger and more frequent conventions;
- Attract a broader segment of business categories and increase visitor exposure to Providence and the state as a whole; and
- Appeal to area residents by providing a unique venue for large events, either in conjunction with or in lieu of the existing adjacent Civic Center.[27]

In sum, the Convention Center would become a significant project by emphasizing that Providence could be a "destination city."

The Convention Center Authority

In the spring 1987 legislative session, with the state awash in revenues and in the midst of a spending spree, the General Assembly created the Rhode Island Convention Center Authority to develop a publicly supported facility in Providence. The enabling legislation acknowledged that the private sector could not afford the construction costs associated with such a large-scale building but pointed out that a convention center would enhance the public welfare and economic development in Rhode Island. The General Assembly gave the Convention Center Authority a clear mission: "To construct, manage, and operate a convention center and to acquire land by purchase or other means . . . vested with all powers, authority, rights, privileges and titles that may be necessary to enable it to accomplish those purposes."[28] The Authority was granted the power to issue bonds.

The legislation ensured that the Convention Center was a state-city partnership that would need broad support from the political and business leadership around the state and in the city. The Authority's enabling legislation reflected that need by granting to the mayor of Providence and to the governor the power to appoint four members each to the Convention Center Authority and to reach agreement on a ninth.[29] The original list of members included some key figures in Providence politics, business, and higher education, among them

Richard Oster, Authority chairman and CEO of Cookson America; Louis Fazzano, the vice chair and a successful local entrepreneur; Thomas Moses, treasurer and the director of the City Department of Planning and Development; Thomas DiLuglio, a former lieutenant governor; Robert Reichley, vice president for community and government relations at Brown University; and Joseph Mollicone, the president of the Heritage Loan and Investment Company.[30] The Convention Center Authority began operations on 27 August 1987 and met at least monthly until the center opened its doors in December 1993.[31]

The Authority became a catalyst to build the Convention Center. It never doubted that the benefits associated with a convention center would justify the significant outlay of public capital. In their monthly reports the Authority expected substantial economic benefits, including new tax revenues for the state and spending in Providence's downtown by convention-goers. Multipliers—hotel, meal, and sales taxes from the areas surrounding the center—were predicted to have a significant impact.

The importance of creating a Convention Center Authority was driven home by the 7 October 1987 announcement by Downing Corporation of Providence and their partners, Finard, Inc., of Massachusetts, that they wanted to build a hotel, parking garage, and offices adjoining the Convention Center, a facility that did not yet exist. It is a measure of the intense interest surrounding the convention center project at this time that a tentative proposal for an ancillary multifunction structure, including a hotel, was made within weeks of the Authority's creation. Obviously, that particular proposal was premature but foreshadowed the strong regional interest in Providence as a destination city.

Financing a Convention Center

The Convention Center initally was planned in a period of prosperity as a venture paid for by the public. What appeared to be a cast-in-stone deal between the city and state to use high-rated municipal bonds and state revenue bonds made the project attractive to both international and national private lenders.[32] Memoranda from the Authority's biweekly meetings during the fall of 1988 indicated that about $100 million in tax-exempt bonds would be needed to construct the center.

As Capital Center was built, rivers were about to move, and the state's economy appeared to be percolating, the land necessary for a convention center was assembled. On 20 September 1988 the Authority secured a $42-million loan from Fleet National Bank. This loan was key to buying the Bonanza Bus Station and other state properties, along with two parking lots. On 15 May 1990 the second component of private loans was secured through the Industrial Bank of Japan, which issued a letter of credit to the Authority for a hotel. Like other Japanese commercial banks at the time that were heavily engaged in speculative commercial real estate development in the United States, the Industrial Bank of Japan extended its letter of credit and upped the guaranteed loan amount on 17 November 1990, so that the Authority could leverage a lower interest rate loan (fixed at 5.79 percent) from Fleet Bank. Financing had allowed construction plans to move forward by late 1989. The Authority took steps to build a convention center by issuing a nationally advertised request for proposals. It then selected Metro Partners, a joint venture of Providence-based Gilbane Building Company and Marshall Contractors, to manage the construction and build the Convention Center and an attached south parking garage. Howard, Needles, Tammen and Bergendoff were the architects.

Against All Odds: Moving the Convention Center Forward (1990–1991)

Ironies abound in the building of the Rhode Island Convention Center complex, not the least of which was the re-election in November 1990 of Buddy Cianci to his seat as mayor of Providence after a six-year hiatus.[33] This same mayor who in the 1970s and early 1980s helped put together plans to revitalize the city and, in the words of some renaissance participants, had the good sense not to say "no" and then to get out of the way, single-handedly almost killed the Convention Center. In short measure after his inauguration in January 1991 he reversed the DiPrete/Paolino agreement by withdrawing the city's pledge of financial support out of fear that it would become a long-term drain on the city's finances. Cianci felt that the city did not need another Providence Civic Center, by then considered a financial mess even as discussions about city financial assistance for a mall project were under way.[34] The Convention Center deal unraveled.

Cianci's decision, coupled with the state's fiscal and credit union woes, placed the venture in deep peril by 1991. In November 1991 Cianci and Sundlun were working together to figure out a way for the city property tax to help finance the Mall project.[35] While considerable progress had been made in transforming Providence physically, the city was in disarray, carved up to move the railroads and rivers and build new roads and bridges. Indeed, it was by no means clear that public expenditures had had any impact on the chances for a downtown recovery. One Citizens Plaza on parcel 3 and One Gateway Center on parcel 5 were the only privately financed completed projects in Capital Center, small payoffs by any measure for the hundreds of millions in publicly funded land improvements since 1980.

Governor Bruce Sundlun, who was a very young man during the Great Depression, was an admirer of Franklin D. Roosevelt's New Deal public works policies of the 1930s. Sundlun felt that state government had an obligation to stimulate the economy and put people back to work. He believed that government ought to propel the recovery of the capital city beyond the basic road and rail infrastructure projects that had already been undertaken.[36] "I believe government-aided infrastructure projects have great economic impact on a community. They also put people to work during a recession."[37]

At the same time that Cianci was putting up roadblocks, Sundlun adopted the idea of the Convention Center as the centerpiece of a state-funded initiative that would bring economic multipliers to the depressed metropolitan core and put the construction trades to work.[38] Whereas generous federal funding had picked up 90 percent of the costs associated with constructing the downtown's first ring road and interstate link, railroad relocation, the Civic Center interchange and Memorial Boulevard, Waterplace Park, and the walkways along the Woonasquatucket, Moshassuck, and Providence Rivers, Rhode Islanders under Sundlun's plan would pick up the tab for a new convention center.

Sundlun's task was to persuade a skeptical legislature and an even more skeptical public that state spending on a convention center in the midst of a recession was a realistic course toward recovery. Amid the worst fiscal crisis that had befallen the state in modern history, and with little room to maneuver, he had to move quickly to salvage the project. Because of the so-called Kushner Bill, individual capital expenditures by state agencies were capped at $4 million per project.[39] Anything beyond that limit required legislative approval. Public skepticism over state government's ability to manage the economy and itself was running high. Legislative hearings over the RISDIC debacle revealed that the legislature had been aware of the precarious nature of the credit union system long before its collapse and had failed to act. In addition, the public came to know that the State Department of Business Regulation failed to perform effective oversight of the credit unions. Public support for a new state-funded capital project appeared unlikely.

The legislature recognized, though, that the state had to do something to produce jobs and get the economy rolling once again. State legislative leadership met with the new governor and warned him that authorization of funds for the Convention Center was in jeopardy unless Sundlun took *full responsibility* for the project by personally testifying before the House and Senate to make the case for the Convention Center. The legislature, too, wanted to act, but to marshal the votes to build the project in Providence and increase the state's borrowing required that the governor become the focal point of political criticism.

In April 1991 Sundlun made the public plea for the project, arguing that the economic future of Providence and Rhode Island was in the balance and therefore "the state has to have it."[40] Support for his position came from Convention Center Authority chair Richard Oster, the CEO of Cookson America, who cited a Coopers and Lybrand feasibility study asserting that a convention center would bring in five hundred thousand extra visitors per year, increase tourism in the city significantly, and create up to three thousand construction jobs and five hundred permanent jobs.[41] The Convention Center Authority presented the optimistic feasibility study in 1991 to local government and business leaders, including the executive board of the Providence Foundation. They received a detailed marketing plan briefing indicating that the Convention Center would give the city a "vigorous economic boost" by drawing visitors and stimulating multiple economic sectors, which would benefit the entire state. Following Sundlun's presentation, the state legislature approved the funding package for annual operating appropriations. The Convention Center once again moved forward without city assistance.

The convention center idea was well vetted by this time, and the need for hotel space to accompany it had been widely acknowledged. Providing space for conventions was not good policy if hotel space for convention-goers was not available. Work started on the state-owned Rhode Island Convention Center main building in June 1991 amid much debate over whether a hotel should be included in phase 1 of the complex. The Convention Center Authority hoped to find a private firm willing to pay for and operate a hotel and actively sought bidders. In the absence of tenders, the Authority decided to press ahead with the center without hotel rooms as part of the package.

The attempt to enhance the Convention Center project with hotel construction created a critical crossroads. The bigger the project, the more jobs would be created. Further, the erection of the Convention Center would shift the focus of the Providence renaissance from the financial center that Capital Center envisioned to the creation of a destination city. However, hotels were necessary if the national large-scale convention and exhibition market was to be tapped. A Holiday Inn and the Biltmore were the only two hotels in the immediate vicinity of the planned location of the Convention Center. The ERA/HNTB report that encouraged the much larger-scale convention center project had been clear: additional hotel rooms would be critical to the Convention Center's success.

The economic climate in 1991 was not friendly to hotel financing. Yet time was important because of the need to book convention space in advance. No private company came forward in 1991 to accept the risk of being the first hotel at the new Convention Center complex, which contrasted starkly to 1987, when within weeks of the Authority's creation proposals for hotels blossomed. If a new hotel was to be built in downtown Providence, then the risk would fall to the public.

Relatively quickly the Authority, relying on its own legislatively granted borrowing authority, decided to construct a $57-million, 261-room Westin Hotel and a parking garage. The Authority had entered negotiations with Hyatt Regency, Sheraton, Hilton, and Westin hotels, but Westin offered the best overall deal. Their agreement allowed the authority to appoint senior management, among other administrative prerogatives.[42] Delays caused by ongoing arguments

The Rhode Island Convention Center. Courtesy of Gordon Rowley, Rhode Island College

The Westin Hotel. Courtesy of Gordon Rowley, Rhode Island College

over the hotel's height, consistency with existing buildings, the degree of orna-
mentation on the hotel's facades and roof, and the decision in 1992 to increase the
hotel's size from 261 to 364 rooms slowed hotel construction by almost a year beyond that of the main Convention Center building. The Convention Center
construction itself hit several environmental snags, including the fact that it was
taking place on the former site of the Great Salt Cove. The land was extremely
wet and unstable; the pilings had to be driven several feet deeper than anticipated, which raised costs considerably.[43]

The state continued in its economic doldrums, but the Convention Center
and hotel were pushed rapidly forward by the economic crisis and the willingness of the governor to take the heat if the project went bad somehow. The Convention Center Authority hung a huge banner across the center's north garage in
March 1992 that proclaimed that the construction phase and subsequent operations would create "3,500 New Jobs for Rhode Islanders." The Coopers and Lybrand study projected state revenues of more than $4 million per year from meal,
hotel, and sales taxes.[44]

As the river project was nearing completion and Waterplace Park was within
a year of becoming a reality, the Convention Center Authority's first marketing
document, published in 1993, touted the Rhode Island Convention Center as
"The New England Solution," a less congested and more affordable alternative to
other northeastern venues. "Lower costs, easy accessibility, and Yankee charm"
were the selling points. "Book a City . . . Get a State," the advertising copy concluded.[45] Convention Center Authority chairman Richard Oster promised that
"exciting things" would happen because of the Convention Center.[46] A marketing
analysis for the Authority calculated that the Convention Center and hotel project would produce a $525.3 million net economic benefit to the state by 2027.

Despite construction snags, the structure was built rapidly, perhaps the
most quickly completed large project of the renaissance period. The opening of
the various project components went smoothly and on schedule: the north
garage was finished in January 1993 and the Convention Center's main structure
and the south garage were completed in November 1993. The Convention Center ribbon cutting took place on 24 November 1993. The 364-bed Westin Hotel
was completed on 1 December 1994 and held its first gala in January 1995.

The State Creates a Destination City

The Need to "Do Something" Confronts Skepticism and the Economy

The motivation among the local business and governmental elites to build
the Convention Center was powerful in spite of remaining doubts about the success of similar (and often much smaller) facilities in other medium-sized cities.[47]
They saw the effects of recession and the continuing threats of out-migration

from the old historic core, but there appeared to be substantiation from nationally renowned expert consultants on the feasibility of the project, which gave full support to boosters' claims that a convention center could have nothing but positive effects on the city and state's economy.[48] Whatever the claims of success might be, an energetic governor saw this WPA-type project as essential to putting Rhode Island workers back on the job.

The optimistic reports continued through the mid-1990s, even though the center was heavily booked with local and regional events and was not attracting truly national or international conventions.[49] Nagging concerns appeared in the local press about the increased size of the complex, the rising costs of the proposal, and the viability of the project over the long term in the absence of adequate nearby hotel rooms.[50] Rumors began to circulate even among those close to the project (rumors that persist to this day) that the Convention Center was prewired with the necessary electrical systems to support a gambling casino as a backup plan should the convention business not meet expectations.[51]

The major constraint on the Convention Center project during the 1990s was that it had to be sold to a skeptical public and legislature during a difficult economic time. The idea was not new; the concept had reached contractual status under Mayor Paolino and Governor DiPrete years earlier, only to be undone by Mayor Cianci. Under the Sundlun administration, it was the price tag that had to be confronted amid widespread distrust of government. Yet that same economic climate proved to be a catalyst for Bruce Sundlun to send a positive message to the public: something could be done to respond to the state's economic doldrums.

Hotels remain the key constraint on the Convention Center's success. In 1993, when the Convention Center opened its doors; in 1997, when the first objective reports assessed the economic impacts of the center; and in 2003, when national conventioneers failed to choose Providence for their major events, accessible and affordable hotel rooms were the most significant barrier to success. There are simply too few hotel rooms within walking distance (or even a short taxi ride) of the Convention Center. "The public can only expect us to do so much when we only have 570 committable, walkable rooms," James Bennett, the chair of the Authority, lamented in 1997.[52]

The overall impact to date shows that the Authority's primary goal of increasing convention and allied activities in Rhode Island has been achieved. The Convention Center has increased the state's aggregate business in these sectors by 50 percent over the year prior to its opening, but growth into more lucrative national markets will be limited unless there is a significant increase in hotel rooms with easy access to the Convention Center. Bennet noted:

The voice that Kevin Costner heard in the film *Field of Dreams* told him to "build it and they will come." Unlike Costner's ghostly ballplayers who vanish into an Iowa cornfield, if they come to Providence you have to give them a place to stay. Without adequate hotel space, the [Convention Center] will never realize its potential and the renewal of Providence, that has given us all a sense of pride, will stagnate.[53]

To attract national conventions the center also must expect to spend considerable sums on marketing and outreach. Initially reluctant to do so, Providence spent only $400,000 on its Convention and Visitor's Bureau budget in 1994, while Rochester, New York, spent $1,800,000; Richmond, Virginia, $2,000,000; Baltimore $3,300,000; Charleston, South Carolina, $4,400,000; and Boston $5,300,000.[54] Nevertheless, in September 2000 the Authority declared the period 1 July 1999 through 30 June 2000 a "banner year," while acknowledging that the facility attracted as much business as it possibly could, given the limited supply of hotel rooms in Providence.[55] The hotel room mantra continues and is now a part of conventional wisdom: "We are in desperate need of hotel rooms. I ask myself every day how can we get this done privately?"[56] "There are still so few hotel rooms within walking distance of that place that none of the big conventions want to go there."[57]

Avoiding large operating deficits at the Convention Center and reducing the capital debt on the hotel are now concerns of the state. Selling the Westin has become a possibility. A 1997 report gave no indication that the Rhode Island Convention Center could ever expect to operate in the black and that interest and amortization of the revenue bonds issued by the Authority would result in annual deficits of at least $20 million for close to thirty years.[58] However, the hotel is a prime source of revenue for the Authority. Of the $38 million in total revenue in 2000, $26.6 million came from the Westin Hotel.[59]

A New Purpose for the City as an Outcome

Since the early 1990s the downtown has seen many of the elements that boosters said were vital to the city's success put in place: state-of-the-art office space, high-end retail, easy access and parking, an attractive network of rivers, walkways, and public open spaces, and a convention center. The total cost of the Convention Center project (without the hotel) was $356 million, the second highest in the state's history, after the interstate highway system of the late 1950s.[60] However, despite claims that the center would be essentially a self-supporting enterprise, the Authority routinely requests increases in its state operating subsidy. In recent years the Authority has cited its construction debt as a reason for support.[61] The public nature of the Convention Center is obvious, as it continues to receive an annual state appropriation to underwrite operating expenses of approximately $20 million a year.[62]

As renaissance projects, the Convention Center and Westin Hotel have changed the look of downtown Providence and have had an impact on the economic life of the city. How much is the critical issue. The first officially commissioned report on the actual economic impacts of the Rhode Island Convention Center shows that in 1994, its first full year of operation, the complex brought $2.3 million in tax revenues to the state.[63] In addition, visitors to the complex, including the Westin Hotel, parking garages, and the Convention Center itself, injected $28.2 million into the Providence and Rhode Island economies, and the complex itself spent $22.2 million on wages and purchases. According to the report, "In comparison to other convention centers of similar size, the Center appears to be performing reasonably well."[64]

Yet a review of the Authority's monthly bookings reports to the governor and General Assembly demonstrate that, among the numerous events at the complex, very few major conventions take place in the city each year.[65] A 1995 consultants' report on a revised and "more energized and proactive" marketing plan offered this critique of the nation's cool response to the Providence-based center: "There was . . . a minimal pre-opening sales and marketing program. This has caused great concern about the potential and viability of the facility as an economic generator. Sales efforts did not begin in earnest until . . . 18 months before the grand opening."[66] Bookings consisted of events rather than conventions, such as First Night Providence on New Year's Eve and the Providence Boat Show.[67] The Authority delayed an active marketing campaign because of uncertainty about the number and size of conventions and exhibitions that could be staged, because of the absence of concrete plans for the adjoining hotel and doubts whether other tentative hotel projects would come to fruition.[68]

While tax levies are considered a key measure of success of the Convention Center because they are the only way the complex makes a direct contribution to state coffers, the center has produced a number of direct and indirect benefits: for the fiscal year ending 30 June 1996, non–Rhode Island residents spent $10.6 million at the complex; the center expended $9.7 million on wages and purchases within Rhode Island; and while the center itself lost money, the hotel and parking garages yielded operating profits in the neighborhood of $900,000 collectively.[69] The new chairman of the Convention Center Authority, David Barricelli, argues that patience is warranted and that early findings represent "good news" for the city and state: "I'm happy that it establishes a benchmark. . . . It shows we're doing a decent job. It shows we can improve. We recognize that, and we're trying to do that. Maybe it wasn't a home run. But we didn't strike out, either."[70]

For the mall to be built CCE would have to move, and for CCE to move financing would have to be obtained. In early November 1993 RIPA sold more than $30 million in insured revenue bonds secured by a lease signed by the Rhode Island Department of Administration to renovate Shepard's as a new URI-CCE. The president of URI and the Board of Governors of Higher Education unanimously approved moving CCE, despite some opposition by student groups, faculty, and the administration within CCE. Renovations began in late November 1994. The projected opening date for CCE at its new home was January 1996, and the project came in on time. The mall land was finally assembled.

Sundlun II: Federal–State–Local–Private Interest Arrangements

The mall financing plans had to be flexible. Apparently, Sundlun I, in the public's mind, had provided insufficient insulation from potential financial liability. The Sundlun II financing plan began the shift away from public to more private financing. The new plan called for $225 million to be raised by the developer for the mall. The state would exempt the developers from the 7 percent sales tax on building materials but would remain the "technical" owner; it would retain its air rights while leasing the property back to Providence Place Group for $75 million. The state was willing to enter into a thirty-year Payment in Lieu of Taxes (PILOT) agreement with Providence where PPG would make annual payments of $4.7 million to pay back Providence for the bonds the city would issue for one-half of the garage. The state also would put together in September 1994 a proposal to use federal funds to build its portion of the garage.

The rewriting of the deal did not stop its critics. The owners of the malls

The University of Rhode Island's College of Continuing Education (foreground) and the adjacent Roger Williams state administration building (shown in 1994) would be demolished to make way for Providence Place mall.

Courtesy of Roberta Kaufman

south of Providence filed suit in Rhode Island Superior Court to halt the project on the basis of the governor's acting beyond his authority in signing the agreement between RIPA and the developers and failing to use due diligence in protecting the taxpayer from an unaffordable project. These critics raised questions about Pyramid as the *Providence Journal* published stories regarding Pyramid's legal troubles in other states. The attorney general prevailed upon Governor Sundlun to ask the state's supreme court for an advisory opinion regarding the legality of the contract. The political irony is that the malls whose owners were adamantly opposed to public subsidy for a mall in Providence themselves were the direct beneficiaries of the federal government's construction of the federal highway system. The Rhode Island Mall and Warwick Mall sit at the intersection of Routes I-95 and I-295 just south of Providence, which at the time of their construction furthered the appeal of suburban Rhode Island to Providence residents leaving the capital city.

Throughout the 1980s the federal government was the indispensable financial engine for the railroad, highway, Capital Center, and river projects. Once again state policy makers hoped the FHWA could become a partner in building the mall. The state needed $50 million for the garage and another $25 million for a ramp from I-95 to the mall. "The developers [of the Mall] would've wanted a ramp right into the mall garage!"[13] In June 1994, while Sundlun I was on the table, Gordon Hoxie, still the FHWA regional administrator, notified RIDOT after a partial EIS that he would recommend ISTEA (Intermodal Surface Transportation Efficiency Act) financing for only 500 of the 2,500 spaces the state needed for the garage. The practical result was that the state would have to put up even more of its own resources.

Undaunted, however, after the Sundlun I deal fell apart in August 1994, the state submitted and received preliminary acceptance of a plan that would qualify for FHWA financing for the garage and I-95 ramp improvements. The city for its part continued to approve ordinances that would permit borrowing for the garage. RIDOT began an FHWA-required environmental assessment process. The EPA regional administrator, John DeVillars, urged RIDOT to complete a full EIS, a much longer review that could be ordered only by the FHWA. Public interest groups lobbied for that more stringent requirement but were not successful. RIDOT issued a positive assessment in late 1994, paid for by PPG, that building the garage and access ramps from I-95 to the mall was the best environmental alternative.

Opposition to the garage continued from groups such as the Conservation Law Foundation, a consistent opponent of using any federal money for building the garage, and a Rhode Island transportation watchdog group, RIDOT Watch. Their essential arguments, made in many public forums, was that it was ludicrous to believe that building a garage for five thousand cars would somehow reduce pollution if HOV vehicles were part of the plan. Further, they voiced concern that money for the garage would divert funds from needed road and public transportation work. State officials also expressed some misgivings over how the money would be dispersed: "There's no way that I don't fill potholes because of this project [the garage]."[14] It was this vociferous environmental lobby, and the fact that the regional FHWA office was persuaded by additional local concerns that providing financing for a garage was not a good use of the shrinking road construction dollars, that would curtail FHWA participation in mall financing.[15]

Changing Political Winds

Mall and garage financing injected itself in the 1994 primary season. Public criticism did not abate despite the release by RIPA of a report stating that there was sufficient demand for the project and that two-thirds of mall sales would come from Massachusetts residents.[16] U.S. Representative Ronald Machtley (D-First District Rhode Island), running in the Republican gubernatorial primary against U.S. Attorney Lincoln Almond, who also opposed the mall, petitioned U.S. Secretary of Transportation Federico Peña to deny granting federal funds for the garage because it was a "commercial real estate venture."[17] Sundlun's opponent in the Democratic race, Rhode Island state senator Myrth York of Providence, also ran against the mall. The credit union crisis, the hard decisions engendered by the state's fiscal difficulties, and a fight over the decision to expand Green Airport had taken a political toll on Bruce Sundlun, who was defeated in the Democratic primary in September 1994 in his bid to be nominated for a third term.[18] Lincoln Almond prevailed over York in a tight three-way race in the general election.[19]

Electoral defeat would not deter Sundlun in his pursuit of the mall. In one of his last acts to push the renaissance forward, the "lame duck" Sundlun, as RIPA chair, called a special Port Authority meeting after the election to vote on extending a procedural deadline for FHWA approval of funds and the acceptance date for the environmental assessment report. The contract contained a provision that provided for ending the agreement if those particular deadlines were missed. The Port Authority voted by a 4–3 margin to extend the deadlines, keeping the agreement in place. Whoever succeeded Sundlun would be faced with severe financial penalties if the contract was abrogated.[20]

Opinion polls still indicated a wary public. Sundlun dismissed critics: "We do not have government by polls in Rhode Island. . . . Nothing leads me to believe that it [the mall] is not in the public's interest."[21] Sundlun had support for his position from the Rhode Island legislature. The Senate Commission on Mall Financing released its report in December 1994, which concluded that the deal RIPA had signed with the developers in 1992 was legal and that to abrogate it would cost the taxpayers millions in penalties. Nevertheless, the report severely criticized those who made the deal as "overzealous with regard to achieving completion of the contract and . . . not adequately mindful of protecting the state's interest."[22]

A New Regime Shifts Costs

Candidate Lincoln Almond had been very critical of the closed-door negotiations he claimed characterized the mall development. Within days of his 1995 inauguration, Governor Almond appointed his own task force to review the Port Authority contract, wary of the findings of the Democratic-controlled Senate task force. The Senate commission chair, William Irons (D-East Providence), claimed credit for the Senate task force's having changed the terms of Sundlun I to Sundlun II. Almond was not so convinced that Sundlun II was that beneficial to the state, and so in early February he communicated to J. Daniel Lugosch III, now the principal developer of the mall, that he would not honor the contract. He also continued the Sundlun request to the Rhode Island Supreme Court for a determination of the legality of the contract and asked for an independent, private analysis of the mall's economic prospects.

The governor's study was conducted by HSG/Gould Associates, who issued a preliminary report in March 1995 blunting the criticism of mall opponents on economic grounds by predicting a 12 percent negative impact on surrounding malls. The Gould report forecast a full sales recovery by 2000, on the assumption that the mall would open in 1997. The report also went on to make the strongest public case for the mall on the basis of the following: the mall would recapture the shoppers leaving Rhode Island for Massachusetts stores; there was a projected $2.3 billion in purchasing power that was underserved in the projected mall market; the mall would generate net new sales tax collections of between $4.9 and $6.8 million in 2000 and a consistent twenty-year growth in the revenue stream to the state; an estimated 40–60 percent of new tax revenues would be from Massachusetts residents and convention delegates, tourists, and recaptured Rhode Island spending; the mall would employ 2,840 people on a continuing basis; and the mall's impact on existing retail stores would be relatively light.[23]

The Gould report did not sway public opinion significantly, and ardent critics of the mall were not mollified. However, Governor Almond, concerned over the penalties, reversed his campaign position and endorsed the mall idea. He relented somewhat on the notion that the mall should be entirely financed by private means; he felt that some public investment was needed. He referred to the role of public funds in creating renaissance activities that were nearly complete: "The people rave about Waterplace Park, and its impact on the city, but they forget that public money made it possible."[24]

In April 1995 Almond proposed a new financing plan that sought more tax-payer financial insulation from the project. Federal financing for the garage was abandoned as totally unrealistic. The prevailing notion was that the idea of Rhode Islanders carpooling was an oxymoron.[25] The developer would have to raise the money for the garage. A new financial arrangement was proposed. The PPG would borrow the money to finance the garage, and the state would exempt the mall owners from paying *all local property taxes* for twenty years to pay for that borrowing: a $4.5 million annual subsidy. The mall developers also would keep the first $6 million in net new state sales tax revenues to pay debt service they incurred building the mall, an issue of particular interest to Fleet Bank as the likely lender for the project. Fleet was concerned about the project's cash flow.

The new agreement further distanced the state and city from other liabilities involving the mall and was a test of the developer's commitment to the project. No state or city bonds would be issued, and state liability for PPG expenses would extend only from the new contract date, not back to 1989. Neither the state nor city would be actively engaged in coordinating construction or securing permits. Lugosch signed the new deal. He still had the option of walking away with approximately $16 million in penalties because the previous contract was still legally enforceable. However, for Dan Lugosch Providence Place was a national, attention-grabbing landmark project that would take him to a different level of mall development, and it was still financially feasible.[26] Lugosch's perseverance in the face of this latest fiscal arrangement was the test of his personal commitment to the mall idea.[27]

A Mall "by the State, for the State"

By August 1995 the Almond administration had launched a full-scale public relations effort in support of the mall deal, a full reversal of the stance taken during the 1994 gubernatorial campaign. The mall was too good a thing to pass on, once the reality of governing hit home. "After weeks of negotiations, I'm satisfied the developer has met all of my concerns raised by my special task force which studied the original contract."[28] Also clear was that the level of support statewide was shifting. Fleet Bank, the Greater Providence Chamber of Commerce, the local AFL-CIO leadership, and the *Providence Journal* all endorsed the new approach. The newly implemented gubernatorial four-year term also provided some political breathing room.

The state legislature's level of skepticism remained high, however, during continued public hearings at which supporters and opponents squared off. The Almond administration became an aggressive advocate for the mall with the legislature.[29] Under the new financing arrangement the key obstacle to the mall was a provision in the state's constitution that required a two-thirds majority approval of any deal that specified that a public subsidy would be used for private purposes. During the time it took to hold hearings on mall financing, the legislature initiated a plan to reintroduce state bonding—the very item that most Rhode Islanders said they wanted to avoid—instead of the tax financing subsidy. The governor responded vigorously, publicly calling the plan a "half-baked proposal cooked up at the last minute." Lugosch expressed concern that the "bankers have stopped working on this . . . until we know what's going on with the state. Nobody wants to work on this until it's a real project."[30]

Frustration was growing within the financial community. Rhode Islander Terry Murray, the CEO of Fleet, laid down a gauntlet: "I live here in Rhode Island. This [losing the project] would be such a black eye. We'd be the laughing-stock of the Northeast if we drove this [the mall] out of state." But he added, "It's beginning to get stale. . . . It has to be wrapped up."[31] The Providence Place mall became a likely reality in October 1995, when the legislature voted to permit the developers to have access to the first $6 million of sales tax revenues. Deputy Speaker George Carulo said, "It's a bank-driven deal. . . . it's what they [Almond and Terry Murray] agree to that the developer is able to agree with us [the Assembly]."[32]

Yet another "final" agreement was reached in late October 1995 among the governor, the developer, and the legislative leadership that aimed at capturing the necessary two-thirds vote. A twenty-year sales tax rebate agreement was reached whereby PPG would receive two-thirds of every sales tax revenue dollar generated, up to $3.68 million for each of the first five years and after that $3.57 million, to total $72 million, considerably less than the earlier $120 million proposal. To reduce its cost the garage was reduced from a 5,000- to a 4,000-space mall-owned facility with only 500 HOV spaces. No property tax payments would be made to Providence for twenty years, and the state agreed to pay $85,000 of the $700,000 cost of a walkway link from the mall to Waterplace Park.

The irony is too obvious: to produce a Providence retail renaissance the state decided that the city would sacrifice what the city needed most, property tax revenue. City leaders fumed. The city council threatened not to approve the tax treaty provision because it stood to lose $10 million over twenty years in addition to forgoing the business inventory tax. Representative Paul Moura, the head of the Providence House delegation in the General Assembly, explained the politics this way. To put together a deal acceptable to rural and suburban legislators, "anything we do to help Providence cannot come at the expense of the other communities. . . . There was a strong feeling that Providence was getting too much, that the deal was somehow too sweet."[33]

City-state relations had been tense for some time, but this deal broke open the deep emotions felt by city policy makers. The city council would have to approve any deal that required the city's signing a tax treaty. City council president

Evelyn Fargnoli grumbled that "here we are talking about expanding the city's tax base, and here they are changing the rules." City councillor Patricia Nolan proclaimed, "I see it as an anti-Providence move by the state." City councillor Robert Clarkin viewed the deal as "the state's ripping-off the city."[34] City administrators felt similarly.[35]

The intensity of feelings was exhibited when the question of the mall's impact on other state aid to Providence arose. State policy makers made it clear that if the mall's $48-million property value was added to the Providence tax rolls, the city would forfeit nearly $500,000 of existing school aid because of the formula at the time for calculating that aid. Cianci's response was combative: "They are smart little bastards up there [in the State House]. . . . I don't want the Mall to be the biggest tax-exempt institution we have. If Mr. Carulo [Deputy Speaker] and [John] Harwood [Speaker of the House] want to kill the Mall so be it. . . . We need to be reimbursed for our services. Otherwise, it will not pass the City Council. They will kill it."[36] The Assembly's response to the lost tax revenue was a pledge to increase the PILOT subsidy to the city, based in part on the exemption of the mall's $48 million taxable value. Providence also would be paid construction-related fees by the developers.

Despite public opinion polls showing a nearly 60 percent public opposition to a state subsidy, the House leadership was able to produce passage with the necessary two-thirds majority. PPG received a twenty-year economic development note secured by a capital reserve fund that guaranteed that the state would make the monthly tax rebate payments to the mall developer or put its own credit rating at stake. Lugosch had wanted a full faith and credit bond issued by the state but ran into a resounding "no" from the governor. The prevailing sentiment in the House was articulated by House Finance Committee chair Antonio Pires, who underscored the regional importance of the mall and the mindset of the legislative leadership: "I'm not ready to stand at the Massachusetts border and wave the white flag of surrender."[37] The same rationales surfaced in less contentious Senate hearings. On 9 November 1995 the Senate quickly passed the House bill and Governor Almond signed it into a law that to him represented one "hell of a revenue deal for the state."[38]

Providence found itself in a legislative box. Senator John Roney of Providence captured the irony: "It's bittersweet, the last drops of blood that were wrung out of this deal were wrung out of the City of Providence."[39] Attempts were made to mollify the very angry city policy makers, who were trying desperately to extract the best possible deal for the city from a project that would be impossible to reject after a decade of effort.[40] Despite recent council-Cianci battles over tax increases, collective bargaining contracts, COLAs, and other issues, the mayor's and council's frustration culminated in the city council's resounding rejection of the tax treaty on 13 November 1995. Once again the mall was in trouble.

Ironically, the new financing package for the mall shifted public opinion from opposition to support for the mall. The city leadership now was in a position where they could not kill something perceived as good for the state. The face-saving mechanism for the mayor and city council on the mall financing issue emerged after considerable time was spent on the question of whether two sets of movie theaters would exist in Providence: one in the mall and the other downtown. While opposition to the mall in the 1980s had focused on saving what was left of retailing in downcity, by the mid-1990s the concern was whether the mall would kill fledgling efforts to create a new arts and entertainment focal point for the area.

The mall's relationship to downcity and plans to create an arts and entertainment district suddenly became very important. The mall design included a twenty-screen cinema multiplex (eventually reduced to sixteen screens plus an IMAX theater). Advocates for a downtown cinema project wanted to locate screens on Weybosset Street, far from the mall in the heart of the old downcity. Business leaders did not want Mayor Cianci to hold up the mall over the movie theater issue. Nordstrom, which by now was the lead tenant for the mall, was pushing for the movie theaters in the mall. An agreement was reached whereby the mall developers would help build a smaller movie theater complex in downtown Providence through a $2.5 million investment.[41]

The Ground Is Broken: Coming Full Circle

On 27 October 1996, at the invitation of Mayor Cianci, a Wagnerian-clad soprano, the "fat lady," came out onto city hall steps and sang an ode to salute the signing of the mall tax treaty after the city council approved it.[42] Providence relinquished $136 million in real estate and property tax payments. The political reality at this time was that the city had to allow the mall to be built. No more concessions were made. Ground was broken in March 1997.

Many issues continued to arise during the mall's construction, some of which had the potential to unravel the policy decision to build the mall—but that did not happen. An ownership lawsuit between Lugosch and the original mall developer, Alexius Conroy, was resolved. Fleet Bank withdrew its financing but was quickly replaced by the Japanese financing giant Nomura Capital.[43] Gilbane Construction bowed out as construction manager and was immediately replaced by Morse Diesel. There was even a spirited debate over the wisdom of charging for parking.

Since the beginning the mall's design was an important consideration and remained so in this final phase. Resolving the mall's design once again brought forward a central element in the renaissance story: protecting the heritage of the city while continuing its transformation. The mall's design was the product of six architectural firms whose work was coordinated over the years primarily by the Providence Place project director, Richard Duggan, of Commonwealth Devel-

In 1997 an archeological dig was mandated on the site of the old state prison prior to construction of the Providence Place mall.

Courtesy of Providence Foundation, Inc.

opment Group. His task was to balance costs with the ever-present threat of delay and possible mall-killing demands of those who felt that the location of the mall required special consideration. Perhaps at no other time did Capital Center's Design Review Committee acquire as much muscle as it did in the debate over the mall's design.[44]

The DRC was particularly concerned that the rivers and mall be integrated, that pedestrian activity along Francis Street and its connection to downtown be encouraged, and that the riverwalk from the now completed Waterplace Park reach the mall. The failure by the initial designers to allow street-level pedestrian access to the mall through Nordstrom would become a cause for serious dispute with preservationists in Providence. In the mid-1990s Lugosch invited Friedrich St. Florian to improve the design of the facade of the mall using the existing plans. St. Florian himself did not like the "bulkiness" of the mall design.[45]

Preservationists had never lost their concern over the mall design because of its proximity to the State House. The Providence Preservation Society felt that the design of the CenterPlace Apartments in parcel 5 within Capital Center would have been greatly improved if the PPS had been more involved and not ceded the design review process solely to the DRC.[46] The Rhode Island Historical Preservation and Heritage Commission, while supporting the mall, contin-

Between 1997 and 1999 the Providence Place mall rose from the wetlands on either side of the Woonasquatucket River and the Northeast Rail Corridor, in the shadow of the Rhode Island State House.

Photograph by the authors

ued its architectural and historical watchdog role by insisting that the design of the mall be compatible with the State House and the larger downtown area, be pedestrian-friendly, and take advantage of the new relationship between Providence and its waterways.

The CCC still had jurisdiction over the mall project and had to approve the mall design. The mall's projected opening date was August 1998, so for Commonwealth to have time to obtain building permits and begin construction, the commission would have to approve the design by late May 1997. Pressure was on the CCC, now headed by a Sundlun appointee, Leslie A. Gardner, senior vice president of Hospital Trust and former PPS president, to approve a design. If the federally and state-funded RIHPHC felt that the mall design did not meet federal standards, it could hold up the mall's development.

Continued public hearings yielded a design by 11 July 1997 that resulted in the CCC's unanimous approval, even as pile driving was under way. St. Florian presented the skybridge connecting the mall to the Westin Hotel, which would symbolize the link between downcity and the new retail center of the city. He had already designed the all-glass, domeless "wintergarden" and through this design was able to reunite a retail renaissance with the city's waterways. The wintergarden today is the gathering place for mallgoers to view Providence.[47]

Although the FHWA curtailed its involvement in building the garage, the last act of the mall saga once again illustrates how important federal financing has been to the Providence renaissance story. A ramp from I-95 that would bring traffic toward the mall eventually would appear as part of various upgrades and safety improvements to the new interchange and to Francis Street and Memorial Boulevard that were financed by approximately $30 million in federal interstate highway funds. These improvements included a new ramp leading directly to, but not into, the mall's Cityside garage.

The High Watermark (to Date) of the Providence Renaissance

The Providence Place mall dominates the new Providence urban landscape. It symbolizes the retail rebirth of the city, much as the rivers symbolize the city's link to the past. Along with the Convention Center, the mall is part of an unplanned tourist bubble that makes Providence a destination. The Convention Center and the mall signaled a potential change in thinking about Capital Center. By the time the mall was fully opened in 2000, the Citizens Bank Tower, the last office building constructed in downtown Providence, was a decade old.

Saving Retail and Saving Image

For the city, failure was at its doorstep. Retailing was near death in the city. The risks associated with going forward were overshadowed by the risk of failure. The perception of both private and public actors was that something successful could be and had to be done to save retailing. The mall represented that hope. Failure would mean the continuing flow of retail dollars to neighboring states and the further decline of the capital city as a viable economic entity. Public investment in a commercial project became a critical test of its willingness to assume risk.

Though private developers' motivations obviously were rooted in financial success, Lugosch's perseverance was also attributable to his desire to break new ground in urban mall development. In similar fashion, most of the visible political mall proponents—Sundlun, Paolino, Cianci—in one way or another came to see the mall as too important to be abandoned. Building the mall became a severe test of the willingness of state and local interests and individuals to cooperate even in a highly visible and competitive political environment. Avoiding a major embarrassment became an important objective for public and private policy makers.

Patience and Perseverance Overcome Finances

While there was a high degree of risk with this project, the reality was that if it was not built, the mall would have represented more than a decade of futility. Mall building universally shares the constraints of anchors, garages, and financing, but design was an added constraint in Providence. When the mall was conceived, the economy was good and the increasing suburbanization of Boston was spilling over into Providence. Providence itself was undergoing a physical renaissance.

The Providence political leadership provided an important impetus once it became clear to them that retail was dead in the old downcity, even as the state enjoyed a stronger economy in the 1980s. Once the boom times for the state started to disappear, new financing mechanisms to insulate the taxpayer from future financial liabilities were found to replace more direct sources of public money. Federal assistance was not available to the extent it had been in earlier public infrastructure projects. Once the idea of a mall in downtown Providence began to take a serious place on the policy table, public concern over its economic impact and the cost of financing it dominated the scene. Public officials had to cope with the degree to which the costs imposed were too burdensome.

Keeping the Idea "in Play" through Changing Financial Arrangements

The high degree of personal and institutional motivation was matched by the adept use of varied structural institutional arrangements to move the project forward through difficult moments. The use of the Port Authority and its autonomy to enter into agreements relatively early on provided a certain degree of financial protection for the project, especially with a governor in office who viewed the mall favorably. All of the early financing decisions created a public elite both responsive to public concerns over taxpayer liability and sensitive to the profitability needs of the developers and financers. No matter how badly the money for the project was needed, all parties came to realize the public wanted them to keep their fingers out of local taxpayers' pockets.[48] The object was to find safe money for a risky project from financers and from the public.

The CCC's Design Review Committee provided a public forum for debate over some contentious issues, which allowed concerns over the mall's impact on the fabric of the city to be explored. The DRC debates over the design, particularly in the first stage, actually played a role in cementing the idea that a mall was possible. The focus, rather than being on financing and garages, was on how the mall fit into the future of the city: what purpose it would have and what it would look like as a mechanism to integrate the city. After the contentious financing-related issues were dealt with, the DRC reemerged to "tidy up" the package.

Fulfilling Expectations?

The mall partially opened for business with fifty stores in August 1999 and was fully opened in 2000.[49] To date the $500-million mall has generally met expectations. "New jobs" was the mantra during the thirteen years of mall proposing and building. Estimates ranged from 2,400 to as high as nearly 2,900, a figure cited in the HSG/Gould report in 1995. The number to date seems to range between 2,200 and 2,300.[50] Sales tax revenues also ran behind projections in 1999–2000, when the mall was only partially opened.[51] However, the mall is generating enough sales tax revenue to pay for the state's payment and to generate net new revenue to state coffers.

Another goal of retail advocates for the city was to attract shoppers from outside Rhode Island as well as to keep Rhode Islanders from shopping at out-of-state malls. Anecdotal evidence seems to indicate that progress has been made on that front, with sixteen million visitors to the mall cited.[52] There is no question that the mall is an upscale entertainment and shopping venue. Survey data indicate that mall denizens are younger and represent more minorities than the population as a whole. About 30 to 40 percent of Providence Place shoppers indicate that they have family income greater than $50,000, with about 13 percent reporting incomes of $100,000 or more.[53]

Public opinion concerning the mall is very positive. The mall received overall ratings of excellent or good, especially for the architecture. Parking costs, predictably, were the sorest point among mall shoppers, despite being a mere fraction of the cost of parking in similar upscale Boston malls. Even the tax incentives are generally felt to have been a good investment.[54] Nearly 70 percent credit the mall with creating an upbeat mood for the state. Of even greater significance, given the debate over the mall's impact on downcity, more than half of mall users claim that visiting the mall led them to patronize other stores and restaurants outside of the mall.[55]

Providence Place mall, Stateside aspect (north side), 2003.

Courtesy of Gordon Rowley, Rhode Island College

Conclusion

The Providence Place mall is regarded as the city's "jewel in the crown." In some eyes the "mall was the single biggest factor that pulled everything together and made people feel good about the city."[56] It overcame every obstacle that usually confronts mall projects as well as those unique to the Providence business and political climate. The policy environment was highly politicized: this was no enterprise that slipped by during the dead of night. Advocates and opponents shared the bright light of extensive public awareness.

The project came to fruition for a number of reasons. Perhaps the best way

Providence Place mall, City-side aspect (south side), has a prime location at the intersection of two downtown arterial roads (Francis Street and Memorial Boulevard), the three-lane express connector to Routes 6 and 10, the on-ramps to I-95 North and South, and, one exit south on I-95, to I-195 East. The international lottery giant G-Tech will construct its world headquarters on Capital Center parcel 9, across Francis Street from the mall.

Courtesy of Gordon Rowley, Rhode Island College

to view the mall is as a microcosm of the renaissance itself. The idea of returning retailing to the city had to take root. The persistence of a string of private developers, from Antonio Guerra to Dan Lugosch, in seeking to develop a mall was a necessary condition to plant and nurture the seed. Equally necessary were the public advocates for a mall project who cultivated the seed, especially the relentless Bruce Sundlun. In general there was a feeling that the mall could and should happen. Even those initially opposed, such as Lincoln Almond, came to believe that it was possible to bring retailing back to the city. In sum, the idea of an upscale mall paralleled and became inherently identified with the Providence renaissance.

Patriot Stadium: A Renaissance Fumble?

10

It makes no difference if you're on the *Titanic*
whether you're in the first class section or tourist.

Mayor Vincent A. "Buddy" Cianci Jr.

■ On a freezing January day in 1997, seven thousand New England Patriots football fans stood in Kennedy Plaza facing the city hall portico and steps. The occasion was a gigantic pep rally for the upcoming AFC championship game against the Jacksonville Jaguars, for which Providence was named the host city in the fall of 1996—not Boston. Inside city hall white-gloved waiters passed out hors d'oeuvres as a three-piece band entertained such luminaries as Governor Lincoln Almond, U.S. Representative Patrick Kennedy, and the Patriots owner, Robert Kraft. Outside, the Patriots cheerleaders and a local high school marching band performed.

As they left city hall to attend the host city party a block away at the state-owned Westin Hotel, Mayor Cianci, always ready to seize the moment, announced his dream of bringing the New England Patriots franchise to Providence —permanently! This public pronouncement marked the beginning of a very public campaign to land a huge prize for Providence. An NFL franchise fit well with the arts, entertainment, and destination city theme. The stadium venture was a project of such magnitude that clearly it would affect Providence significantly. The mayor's enthusiasm was bolstered during the week following the rally as Providence received national television exposure through ESPN daily reports from the Jaguar practices held at Brown University. Yet, despite the hoopla, the project never happened.

The inability to close the deal on a new Patriots' stadium makes a valuable counterpoint to the success of the effort to bring about the Providence Place mall. The two projects share some characteristics. They both were pioneering for Rhode Island: luring big, upscale retail back to a city and luring big-time football into the downtown. They both were grand projects in size and cost, requiring complicated financing. Cooperation among state, local, and private officials would be essential. They were destined for the same geographic spot in the city: one slightly east of I-95 and one slightly west—"side by each," in the local vernacular. Both projects were subject to enthusiastic support and genuine skepticism by political and business leaders and by the public.

Coming on the Agenda

The effort to bring professional football to Providence came about because of the difficulty that Robert Kraft, the owner of the New England Patriots, experienced with Massachusetts and Boston in getting a new stadium built. Plans for locating a new facility in South Boston ran up against stiff opposition from neighborhood associations and Boston City Hall. Convincing the Massachusetts legislature that building a stadium was a good public investment was a tough sell, even if the plan was to build a new facility in Foxborough, Massachusetts, the team's home for more than two decades.

While that political and financial give and take was occurring, the AFC playoff games got under way. The Patriots won their championship game against the Jaguars in early January and headed off to the Super Bowl later that month. Mayor Cianci followed the team, met with Kraft, and watched the Patriots lose to the Green Bay Packers. It also appeared the Patriots were losing the stadium battle in Massachusetts. In mid-February 1997 Kraft called Mayor Cianci and Governor Lincoln Almond. Kraft attended a mayors' meeting in Key West, Florida, that month to confer with Cianci. The Rhode Island and Providence courtship of the Patriots began in earnest.

In March 1997 Cianci presented a plan to Kraft based on a survey and site recommendation made by HOK Sport, a Kansas City sports marketing and consulting firm. The 69,000-seat stadium was to be built on a thirty-six-acre site next to I-95, just west of the Providence Place mall, which was under construction at the time. Although the site was often referred to as the "farmer's market," most of it actually would come from tearing down the idle Brown and Sharpe manufacturing buildings owned by the Guerra family, which extended up the south side of Smith Hill. Removing some state offices and a renovated portion of the factory called the Foundry and demolishing about a half dozen century-old houses, including one on the National Register, would have been necessary. In addition to the Brown and Sharpe complex, Amtrak land also would be purchased, along with several of the warehouses on the farmer's market site. This was the same site offered in 1991 by Governor Bruce Sundlun and economic development director Joseph Paolino Jr. when the Patriots made brief rumblings about moving from Foxborough at that time. The 1991 recession and financial collapse of the state's credit union system killed any enthusiasm for the project, which was not pursued or studied further. However, no such recession was evident in 1997 when Providence was undergoing its major facelift.

Stadium Economic Development Rationales and Outcomes[1]

Providence certainly was not the only city in recent decades to venture into the realm of stadium building. In a three-year period in the 1990s, about the time Providence and Rhode Island were flirting with the Patriots, some $7 billion was committed to build or refurbish stadiums and arenas.[2] More than thirty stadiums and arenas were built between 1989 and 1997 at a cost ranging from $200 to $300 million apiece, and much of that money came from public sources.[3] Moving franchises has become very much a part of a new mobile economy. For example, St. Louis built a brand new stadium, the Trans World Dome, for the now St. Louis Rams, after the team's owner, Georgia Frontiere, decided to leave Los Angeles. Monsanto, McDonnell Douglas, and Anheuser-Busch helped finance the new stadium. Baltimore lured the Cleveland Browns' venerable owner, Art Modell, in 1996. The old Browns became the new Baltimore Ravens (the 2001 Super Bowl champions), playing at a new stadium in Camden Yards. Cleveland fans were so irate that the National Football League and the City of Cleveland entered into an agreement to build a new stadium, which opened for the 1999 season with a new "old" Cleveland Browns team.

The typical economic development arguments for building a stadium and for public investment are that these venues generate economic growth through high levels of new spending, thus creating large numbers of new jobs and revitalizing central business districts, and that they bring status.[4] These claims were made to undergird the effort to lure the Patriots to Providence. The challenges to these declarations are that, at best, stadiums break even and that they generate relatively little in local economic activity.[5]

Historically, teams played home games in privately built arenas because team owners did not want public interference. These private franchises, while providing public entertainment and some modicum of civic pride, were clearly run for the economic benefit of their owners and, in recent decades, of their players.[6] However, during the late 1980s and early 1990s it was commonplace for cities to acquire sports franchises by subsidizing stadiums or renovating existing ones.[7] The initial expense of the construction of stadiums is not generally manageable through private financing. Nevertheless, over time teams and their owners do well from ticket sales, broadcasting rights, concessions, advertising, revenue from other events held in the stadium, and tax benefits. Local communities do not do as well, but the lure of being a major league city is difficult to resist.[8]

Improved city status may be the most tangible benefit arising from stadium building, although there is a perceptual clash between the reality of economic development activity actually generated and the expected outcome of civic pride. To quote Gregg Lukenbill, the former owner of the Sacramento Kings (on bringing football or baseball to Sacramento), "The Raiders coming to Sacramento would be an event the magnitude of the Gold Rush."[9] Providence was not immune to such pronouncements. "Rhode Island would be an exception if it rejected the expenditure of public money for a football stadium. . . . It's part of everyone's ego—being a major league city, a pro town. . . . You could have the greatest tool and die plant in the world but it's not going to be written up as news. . . . If you have a pro football team, your city is going to be covered."[10]

There is a correlation between the degree of civic pride and the willingness to use tax dollars to support such projects.[11] This willingness to invest in a stadium fits with the notion that these venues secure intangible benefits to the community such as civic pride, a high-profile image, and national and international publicity. In surveys in which taxpayers indicate a willingness to use "sin taxes" and hotel and car rental charges for building a stadium, those with an added sense of pride were even open to the idea of using sales or property taxes to generate revenue.[12] The sporting events that are most well attended produce the greatest civic pride.

Pursuing the Patriots

The Providence effort to acquire the Patriots fit into no "master plan" of the city. The team's owners threatened to move from Foxborough, Massachusetts, and relocate to Providence, and in an instant the Rhode Island public and political community was engaged. Mayor Cianci was not alone in his enthusiasm for the project. State Senator John Celona stated, "Every time they'll [the Patriots] be on television, there will be shots of Providence or a mention of the state and it will put Rhode Island on the map internationally. Business will look at Rhode Island as an up-and-coming state. It's an advertisement every Sunday."[13] The Senate commission established to determine the feasibility of the stadium concluded that "the economic impact of a stadium and the National Football League Patriots would be significant in and of itself."[14]

The idea was big enough to bring two political rivals close to a level of cooperation. In July 1997 Governor Almond, in a very rare joint telephone interview with Mayor Buddy Cianci, said he supported the construction of the stadium in downtown Providence next to the mall site. "I think that's the site that makes sense. . . . I pitched for it with Kraft. . . . I told Bob [Kraft] that the Providence Place mall will be a success, and that when people come down to the mall, they'll look over and see the stadium and say: 'Why don't we come to a football game next week?'"[15] Even after the negotiations for a stadium in Providence fell apart, the importance of civic pride as an underlying motivation was still apparent in Governor Almond's explanation for the collapse: "To have an NFL franchise in Providence would have given us a lot of significance. . . . If we could have done this, within these principles [no taxes] I think I'd be standing here a hero today."[16]

For Kraft an urban location near corporate headquarters was a publicly stated criterion during the negotiations. An urban area was desirable because of the ability to sell luxury box space. Given Providence's proximity to Boston, it would be possible to sell luxury seats to Boston's business community as well as Rhode Island's and to continue to sell to the national sports press, CBS, ABC, NFL, ESPN, FOX, and others.[17] Kraft also wanted to build a destination complete with hotels, retail, restaurants, and other amenities, not just a stadium. Providence lent itself to that type of development because the proposed site was next to a very busy stretch of I-95 that was within a half mile of the Providence Amtrak station and twenty minutes from T. F. Green Airport.

Telescoped Constraints

A number of constraints had to be overcome relatively quickly for this project to go forward. The financial considerations were daunting. Who would pay for construction of the stadium and how it would be done obviously were key questions. The scale of the project itself was large, raising questions regarding the use of all that land for one purpose, a part-time one at that. Additionally, politics and personalities complicated considerably the efforts to secure the stadium and to overcome financing issues. Finally, in the end, no real consensus was developed that the project should go forward, nor did the project have a single-minded advocate.

Financing the Stadium

Who would pay for the stadium was a difficult question to answer because of the issues of equity and measurability of benefit that accompany a discussion of sport stadiums. Near the end of the negotiations the state of Rhode Island and Robert Kraft publicly had agreed that the state would set up a public stadium authority to build and own the stadium. Public investment would be in the $130–140 million range for construction, land purchases, and road and site improvements. Public fund contributions would come from the state general fund in support of the bonds that would be issued. Expenditures would be offset by income taxes from players and management, the team's corporate income tax, stadium sales taxes, and a 7 percent ticket surcharge, which together were expected to amount to $11–$13 million per year. The team would make $95 million in lease payments over a twenty-five-year period; about 58,000 season ticket holders would pay roughly $43 million, including a one-time purchase of $750 for a seat license, which gave them the right to buy tickets. Naming rights also would be sold.[18] None of the contemplated tools for bringing the project to fruition was unusual. Users of the stadium would thus foot the bill through ticket licenses, surcharges on ticket prices, corporate naming rights, and income and sales taxes attributable to stadium activities.

These mechanisms and others have been part of the stadium building process in the United States for two decades. The public in this instance was being asked to supply the infrastructure (land, roads, and the like), some site development, and debt financing. What was unusual was the principle underlying the attempt to reach an agreement—that the stadium would have to pay for itself—and the Almond administration's willingness to stick to that principle.

This cautious stance was due in part to the recent financial history of Rhode Island. There was considerable debate as to whether the stadium would generate the needed tax revenue for the state to justify its backing.[19] At the time of these negotiations Rhode Island ranked fourth in the nation in debt per capita, approximately $312 million. This circumstance necessitated a raising of the state's sales tax rate and dedicating that additional revenue to paying off the debt. The credit union bailout and the Rhode Island Convention Center accounted for much of that debt.

Further, by 1997 it was clear that the rosy scenario for the Convention Center was not materializing. Given those considerations, Standard and Poor's was wary about the stadium financing. "There was always some risk," said John Swenn, director of economic development for the state. "And maybe if we hadn't done the Convention Center we would have assumed the risk and maybe everything would have turned out fine. The problem is we did do the Convention Center and we got burned."[20] An additional complication was that Fleet Financial Group, a likely source of financing, had recently moved its corporate offices from Providence to Boston, making it sensitive to charges of "stealing the team" from Massachusetts.[21]

Politics

The politics of building a stadium for the Patriots involved two states (eventually three) trying to decide on what terms, if any, the Patriots were worth the effort. By February 1997 Kraft's discussions with Massachusetts and Boston officials seemed dead. The stadium clearly was not going to be built in South Boston. The question was whether it was going to get built in Massachusetts at all. That Massachusetts experience contributed to the Krafts' skittishness about getting involved in another political maelstrom, in which they could become lightning rods for the political agendas of various elected officials.[22] They wanted to keep negotiations between the parties private. Against that political backdrop discussions with Rhode Island began.

Support for the project in the Rhode Island legislature was mixed at best. While there might be credit for success, there also could be a great deal of political pain for either of two outcomes: failure to close the deal, or a failed and costly project. Senate majority leader Democrat Paul Kelly raised some questions concerning state debt but generally supported the idea. The House Speaker, Democrat John Harwood, liked the idea but took no official position. House Finance Committee chair Antonio Pires, also a Democrat, was opposed to adding to the public's debt: "I'd hate to be in a position where we can't do the next deal that comes by that is better because we are already up to our eyeballs in outstanding indebtedness."[23] Nevertheless, the Senate commission to study the issue maintained that the "in-city" location for a stadium along the lines of that built by Baltimore for the Ravens would be welcomed; it recommended that a complete presentation package be made to the Patriots' owners and that "Rhode Island speak with a prudent and clear voice."[24]

City council politics came to the forefront in September 1997, when a number of city councillors voiced concern that the negotiations for the stadium were occurring behind closed doors. The tax "giveaway" orchestrated by the General Assembly and governor that closed the Providence Place mall deal still grated on city councillors. The chair of the city council finance committee, Patricia Nolan, wanted to make sure "we don't take the same ride that we took with the mall. . . . Let's make sure the governor has not sold us down the drain."[25]

Yet another political consideration was that 1998 was a gubernatorial election year. Republican Lincoln Almond, elected by a slim plurality in a three-way race in 1994, faced a difficult re-election bid. The chair of Almond's re-election campaign committee, John Holmes, was ambivalent: "Building a 250 million dollar stadium with bonds and telling Rhode Islanders this was not going to affect their pocketbook would be a tough sell."[26] Almond already was roundly criticized for changing his 1994 campaign opposition to support for the Providence Place mall once he was in office.

Mixed Public Support

General public support for the stadium project was strong at the outset. A telephone poll commissioned by Mayor Cianci showed public support for the stadium in the Providence area running at more than 70 percent.[27] A follow-up poll by the *Providence Journal* showed about the same level of support even if public financing was used.[28] However, during 1997, as the issue simmered on the policy agenda, questions were raised again about the depth of support. Governor

Almond took a politically risky stance opposing the placement of a nonbinding referendum on the stadium project on a special ballot to ascertain the extent of public support for the idea. Although castigated in the local and regional press for this position, the governor was steadfast. Mayor Cianci did not commission another poll, feeling that public opinion had not shifted since the two earlier polls.

While Cianci publicly touted Providence Place mall, there were doubts within his own administration's ranks about the stadium project. For all the publicity benefits that would accrue to the city, the single use of a very large parcel of land next to Capital Center was of concern to many within city hall. And there was the necessity for a garage, which itself posed two problems: financing and design. The design problem was related to the sport itself. Ideas for a multistory garage foundered not only on the money but also on the culture of football spectators. Specifically, where could fans tailgate in the downtown area?[29]

The Providence business community was noticeably absent from public decision making about the stadium. There seemed little public fervor for it from the Providence or statewide business community. In the words of Laurie White, spokesperson for the Chamber of Commerce: "I don't feel there was ever a sense on the part of the business community that it was the Patriots at any cost. The business community felt it would have been nice, but there are other critical issues from an economic development perspective that need to be addressed."[30] Chamber of Commerce president James Hagen thought the stadium would be a boon to the state economy, but the Chamber of Commerce itself took no position: "I think people were waiting to see the specifics. . . . All of the constituencies were waiting until they could see the deal."[31] That private ambivalence did not go unnoticed by the public sector's negotiating officials: "If that kind of grassroots organized enthusiasm to have [the Patriots] come here had generated additional interest from private organizations to put some money in it, it would have made a difference."[32]

Unlike South Boston, where local neighborhood opposition was widespread and organized, the local Providence neighborhood opposition to the stadium was small and slow to get off the ground.[33] A grassroots organization, PASS (People Against Stadium Shenanigans), did form, made up of some homeowners and small businesses on Smith Hill, behind the proposed stadium location. Opinion on Smith Hill was mixed concerning drawbacks and benefits to the area of a stadium. However, before PASS even held their first public meeting, the negotiations concerning the project collapsed.

Competitive Environment and Elite Rivalry

Rhode Island in the 1990s experienced an environment friendly toward sports in general. The Providence College Friars basketball team generated enthusiasm. The University of Rhode Island Rams made an NCAA "March Madness" appearance. The state, with the enthusiastic support of Governor Almond, began studying the feasibility of a convocation/athletic complex for the University of Rhode Island in Kingston, about twenty-five miles south of Providence. Lincoln Almond, the first alumnus of the University of Rhode Island to be elected governor, was a spirited booster of that project. Sports were in the air, but so were questions of paying for all of this activity.

Never far from anyone's mind was the possibility that the Patriots' owner was merely using Rhode Island in his ongoing attempts to jump-start new discussions with Massachusetts officials. Proposals for a new stadium were coming not only from Rhode Island but also from other locales in Massachusetts, including Worcester, New Bedford, Swansea, and, of course, Foxborough. Connecticut weighed in with Hartford. All those suitors were within a one-hundred-mile radius of Providence, so there was potential for intense competition.

Competition among the locales, however, paled when compared to the rivalry between the governor and the mayor. The excitement around the stadium and its eventual demise require an understanding of the relationship between Governor Almond and Mayor Cianci, the two prime public-sector movers of this project. They had a deep and intensely felt rivalry, which was rooted in Almond's prosecution of Cianci municipal aides in the early 1980s when Almond was a U.S. attorney. A number of Cianci aides were indicted, convicted, and jailed during that time.

Kraft had asked the state to take the lead in development and negotiations because he was leery of local leadership after his experience in South Boston. He had spent two years and $4 million fruitlessly and watched as neighborhood opposition killed the plan (which was to be financed with private funds matched by public expenditure for garages, roads, utilities, and a ferry transport service). In effect, however, this request for state leadership pushed Mayor Cianci to the side and focused attention on Governor Almond, his chief of staff, Ed Morabito, and John Swenn, executive director of the Rhode Island Economic Development Corporation.

From April to September behind-the-scenes discussions took place between Almond's negotiators and Kraft's. Cianci, the earliest ardent public booster of the project, was not involved. He was forced to sit and watch as Almond floated ideas for locations other than Providence and other cities in Rhode Island proposed their own communities as sites for an NFL stadium. Cranston, the state's third-largest city (population 35,000), pitched the eighty acres of the former Narragansett Brewery Company.[34] The town of Coventry wanted to replace one of its landmarks, Rhode Island's largest sand pits, with the future home of the New England Patriots. Perhaps most troublesome for Cianci were two suggestions by Governor Almond and his staff: a site off I-295 in Smithfield, northwest of Providence, or Quonset Point in North Kingston, south of Providence. In the first instance Smithfield was considered politically friendly to Governor Almond, who had convinced Fidelity Investments to locate a new facility there. A use for the abandoned defense industry site at Quonset Point in North Kingston was actively being sought during that time.

Nevertheless, in July 1997 the governor and mayor were on the same page, it seemed, despite Cianci's early criticism in February that the governor moved too slowly. In July both politicians in a telephone interview with the *Providence Journal* were singing the same song: the deal is possible. However, by October that unity dissolved into a more familiar tone: recrimination. When the negotiations collapsed that month, a very public exchange between Cianci and Almond provided a glimpse of the feelings each had about the other surrounding this project. Obviously, Mayor Cianci was not happy. He felt that if he had been let in on the negotiations the deal might have had a better chance.[35]

CIANCI: One of the reasons the stadium didn't happen is that he [Almond] wasn't totally immersed in the negotiations. . . . I think it was a matter of getting it done. . . . I like to get things done. I like to set a goal, I like to put my team on the field, a full team and move. . . . The governor, I think, is more reflective and more deliberative than I might be. I like to get things done and show results for the people who pay my salary.[36]

ALMOND: Cianci's plan at the outset didn't even pass the laugh test. . . . Buddy Cianci has yet to call me. He goes to the press a lot. I never received one phone call from the mayor.[37]

CIANCI: Almond is an indecisive leader and prisoner of the suburbs, a man ignorant of urban problems and someone who doesn't dream big or take risks to attract projects to the state.[38]

ALMOND: Remember, the easiest thing in the world is to be a Monday morning quarterback. [On Cianci trustworthiness:] I fight with [state Assembly officials] but once they give you their word, they stick to it and get it done. [Would Cianci abide by a handshake deal?] No, absolutely not.[39]

CIANCI: Here's a guy [Almond] who won't do a stadium deal in Providence because it costs too much but gives them [Pawtucket] $12 million in a deal that has no return to the state.[40] [On being invited into the negotiations at the last minute:] They [Almond's negotiators] wanted to put us in the first-class section, but as I've always known, it makes no difference if you're on the *Titanic* whether you're in the first class section or tourist.[41]

No Stadium for Providence

In September 1997 negotiations for the $250–300 million, 68,000-seat stadium intensified. By 29 September it was reported that verbal agreements had been reached after round-the-clock negotiations but that at the last moment

Robert Kraft refused to commit. Governor Almond called a "time-out" in the negotiations as a result. The sticking point was the ticket surcharge, which the Patriots claimed would hurt ticket sales. On 2 October the negotiations between the state and Kraft ended abruptly. The bedrock principle of the state's negotiating team that the stadium would have to support itself remained in place. Public investment, pegged at no more than $140 million, was to be offset by income taxes from Patriot players, coaches, and the organization, related sales taxes, and ticket surcharges.[42]

The governor would not budge. No tax increases or new taxes would be levied. Only revenues generated from team activity would be used. The Patriots did agree to pay off a twenty-five-year lease if they left town before that time elapsed but refused any part of construction overruns, environmental cleanups, or bond interest expense. The state was unwilling to use up a contingency fund built into the deal. The governor did not want to head into a hostile General Assembly without a rock-solid agreement.

For his part, Kraft did not see the revenues that he would garner from naming rights, concessions, luxury boxes, and such as justifying a move from Foxborough. The stadium and its neighborhood would have to become an attraction. He wanted an additional thirty-five acres for his development, plus an extension of Waterplace Park under I-95 into the stadium area. These costs added $15 million to the $140 million of public investment. The state proposed a 1 percentage point increase in the ticket surcharge, from 7 to 8 percent. The Patriots said no and the game was over. In summing up, Governor Almond answered those critical of the state: "In my heart, I really wanted to see it happen. I thought it was going to be good for the state, and for the city; to have an NFL franchise in Providence would have given us a lot of significance.... We tried as hard as we could with the available revenues to get the job done on the stadium; it was a money issue."[43]

Conclusion

This potential renaissance project failed to happen because it was a big project saddled with an overwhelming number of constraints. It never seemed quite real to many of the participants. First, it was a project that came about almost by accident after the Patriots made the NFL playoffs and encountered difficulties with South Boston. The big Providence renaissance projects have been marked by cooperation among the levels of government and the persistence of interested public and private officials. Cooperation was going to be essential in the stadium project because of its sheer size and the costs involved, and there was no preexisting consensus about the necessity or desirability of a stadium and certainly none about the details of building one.

Second, the project, born of regional economic mobility and competition in a lucrative but narrow niche marketplace, may from the beginning have been doomed by a reluctance by the team's owner to move except under the most advantageous conditions. Simply put, he had alternatives. Third, there was an absence of strong support from the business sector. Fourth, the financial line in the sand drawn by the governor that the private sector had to assume significant financial risk, which worked in the instance of the mall, was not successful in securing the stadium. Fifth, the state was just emerging from the most difficult financial period in its history and was living with a debt burden viewed as extremely serious. This may have killed the project by not allowing any financial wiggle room. Sixth, there was no federal presence to help out. Finally, the city itself had a few reservations about the amount of land that would be consumed. Unlike the mall, where the spin-off benefits potentially were great, it was more difficult to see similar benefits from a stadium, especially in terms of revenue to the state and the city. Absent was the dedicated entrepreneur willing to doggedly pursue this project. Many thought it was worthwhile, but as was not the case with the mall, the rivers, or Capital Center, no one took the lead.

The necessary coalitions that have accompanied other big renaissance projects never had the time or opportunity to develop. Though the project briefly had been talked about in 1991, there had been no sustained discussion of the possibility, no search for funds to accomplish this goal, no planning documents to be circulated, and no infusion of federal money. It was a big stand-alone project, certainly unplanned for, but there was not the time, will, consensus, or luck to make it happen.

Postscript

Throughout 1998 Robert Kraft negotiated a stadium deal with the state of Connecticut and actually entered into a written agreement to build a stadium on the Connecticut River in Hartford, using unprecedented levels of public financial support. However, on 30 April 1999 Kraft terminated that deal, citing pollution on the stadium site and the possibility that it might not be completed by the 2003 season. The Patriots opened their NFL season in 2002 in a newly renovated Gillette Stadium—in Foxborough. The Providence parcel that would have been used for the stadium, in part, is now the site of luxury condominiums.

Measuring
Renaissance Policy

11

If someone wants to build a company here, I'll name
a street after them.

Mayor Joseph Paolino Jr., *Newsweek*, 6 February 1989

Yes, the Renaissance City has become a great place to visit
and a great place to go out and eat. Call me when it becomes
a great place to go to public school.

Bill Reynolds, sports columnist, *Providence Journal*, 23 March 2002

■ Between 1980 and 2000 a series of projects ranging widely in scope were undertaken in Providence. A flurry of construction activity marked by Jersey barriers and the rubbernecking of pedestrians and urban motorists alike produced a
new downtown. The central business district looked better, traffic flowed, parks
were improved, unsightly railroad tracks were moved and buried, the realigned
rivers and riverwalks offered an amenity long unavailable to Rhode Islanders and
Providence residents, new and restored office buildings appeared, hotels and a
convention center sprang up, and the World War I Memorial was carefully restored in a much grander setting than Suicide Circle. The setting for Barnaby
Evans's living sculpture WaterFire and the background shots for NBC's *Providence* were in place. And lo! retail moved to a "new" downtown in the shape of a
massive new $500-million mall. By 1997 registered Rhode Island voters by a 3–1
margin said that Providence looked better than in 1992.[1]

Throughout the two decades of high renaissance activity, policy makers and
entrepreneurs, brimming with optimism, publicly stated time and again that their
high expectations of renaissance efforts involved more than downcity revitalization. For example, in his 1987 State of the City address, Mayor Joseph Paolino's
theme was "An Agenda for *Neighborhood* Progress Through Unity and Pride: A
Providence Renaissance." A scant one page was devoted to downtown development, and only a single paragraph mentioned the river relocation project.[2]

A sampling of more recent comments supports the view that an urban renaissance is supposed to be more than a change in appearance in one city locale—it is a desired change in the appeal of the community and in its underlying fabric. Mayor Cianci touted the accomplishments of renaissance policy this way: "We have moved more than railroad tracks and rivers. We have moved the heart and soul of an entire city."[3]

Specific renaissance success indicators found their way into the mayor's public pronouncements:

The streets of Providence are safer today than they've been in a generation. The crime rate has fallen to levels not seen since the 1960s. Gun-related violence has fallen by a third since the Gun Court [was] created in 1994. . . . Across the city, properties are selling for prices that equal or exceed the lofty levels of the real estate boom of the 1980s. Thanks to the mall, TV series, gourmet restaurants, growing nightlife, we are attracting homeowners; also we have spent $50 million for neighborhoods.[4]

The Providence Place mall is the most visible evidence of the Renaissance. But easing the tax burden on property owners, creating a first-class urban school system, fixing streets, parks, playgrounds and thousands of houses are also extremely important.[5]

Others, such as Robert Mulcahy of Teresphere and Howard Cohen of Beacon Residential Properties, have extolled the virtues of the renaissance:

It's one of the best sites on the East Coast for development [of luxury condominiums]. This is a home-run site. . . . You need three things for development to move forward: a great location, a demonstrable market, and a favorable environment for development—and in Providence you've got all three.[6]

The city's done a very good job providing the infrastructure for downtown revitalization. . . . There's good transportation, both the train station and airport, which is very important to business executives. . . . The mall and other retail plans, and the culture in Providence make it a very attractive place. There are a lot of good things happening. What is really required is a strong housing market.[7]

Declarations of this sort indicate that our definition of renaissance includes elements that renaissance participants themselves would aspire to use to measure successful policy, including a fiscally healthier city; a city that attracts and retains business activity; new jobs and positive changes in income for city residents; stabilized and increased commercial and residential property values; and positive changes in the quality of life for city residents.

The fiscal, economic, and social data are available for an assessment of the a priori assertions made to the Rhode Island citizenry about what to expect from a renaissance. Our goal now is to gauge the amount of fiscal, economic, and social change in Providence between 1987 and 2000, using measures that capture the letter and spirit of policy maker and developer claims and that appear in a much of the commentary concerning city revitalization. The years 1987–2000 are a good analytical time frame for two reasons. Citywide property revaluations were completed during very "hot" real estate markets in 1987 and 2000. Symbolically, 1987 is the year when renaissance activities began to take real shape, as the railroad tracks and river moving efforts were in full swing. By 2000 the most visible economic development symbol of the Providence renaissance, the Providence Place mall, celebrated the end of its first year of full operation after partially opening in 1999.

Change rarely occurs immediately. Time tells whether policy choices produce the desired results. Using trend analysis enables us to plot from known baselines the degree of change in fiscal, economic, and social conditions in the city during the height of renaissance activity. We do not assert that a particular project caused change in any single indicator we use because other variables such as a recession or expansion might intervene. What is inescapable, however, is that much activity began to stir in the late 1970s, was nurtured during the 1980s, and in the 1990s burst out into almost frenzied activity. Whether this activity made a difference to the city is our concern.

A Fiscally Healthy City?

The obvious physical change in the city between 1987 and 2000 occurred as Providence experienced serious fiscal troubles. The success of renaissance policy must be measured to some extent by the overall fiscal health of the city. We used generally accepted measures of municipal fiscal health to gauge the city's fiscal condition after years of intense renaissance activity: the value of property; a decline or growth in property tax revenues; degree of dependence on intergovernmental assistance; increasing or decreasing operating expenditures; fund balance condition; and the level of municipal debt.[8]

The Providence Property Value Paradox

Whether property value has grown throughout the city during the renaissance period is a question of paramount importance to the city. For any municipality heavily dependent on the property tax, *growth in taxable property or an increase in value of existing taxable property* is crucial. Because of its relative inelasticity, though, any revenue growth from property tax systems comes from some combination of an increased amount of taxable property, a rise in the assessed value of property, and higher tax rates. Consequently, the renaissance hope of Providence policy makers is for a positive trend in the value of property and the property tax revenue derived therefrom. Property tax revenue is the only own-source of direct tax revenue Providence can receive in hefty quantities from a successful renaissance.

A close examination of the condition of Providence real estate unveils the paradoxes that face the city. There are hopeful signs of a property value renaissance because between the 1987 and 2000 revaluations, the average value of real estate parcels in Providence grew in all classes of property, with the exception of two-family houses (see table 11.1). However, it was during the time of the infrastructure projects, the moving of the rails, the creation of Capital Center, and the early river-moving planning when phenomenal growth in parcel values was realized. This period was marked by rampant speculation on what were considered very low-value properties throughout the city, which contributed to the rapid spike in values by 1987.

In large measure the nearly sizzling Providence residential real estate market fuels this current growth. The housing market in Providence is much different now from that in the 1980s, when prices were driven upward by speculators and absentee landlords. Today much of the residential market is owner occupied. Demand is strong and staying that way. Housing in Providence is strongly influenced by the high-priced Massachusetts market and by the willingness of people to commute by car, bus, rail, and air.[9]

The city would like to see this hot market continue for a long, sustained period. The rising median sales price of single-family houses in Providence (see

TABLE 11.1
PROVIDENCE, RHODE ISLAND, AVERAGE PARCEL VALUE
Percent Growth in Current Dollars

Property class	1980–1987	1987–2000
Single family	482	28
Two family	578	–2
Apartments	979	19
Commercial I	325	10
Commercial II	400	35
Industrial	195	17

Source: Rhode Island Office of Municipal Affairs. Authors' calculations.

table 11.2) is evidence that a rebound from the real estate doldrums the city and state experienced in the early to mid-1990s is under way. By 2000 the median sales price of houses in Providence had reached the peak of the 1987 boom market. Houses on the East Side of Providence by 2000–2001 were selling at prices far outstripping those in the rest of the city and state and significantly higher than the 1987 prices. Renaissance advocates point to the higher sales prices as a sign that renaissance policy will have a positive effect on revenues when revaluation begins to capture these improvements in the housing economy. The trend continued into 2001, when the median sales price of a house on the East Side was $359,500, a 22 percent growth over the previous year and the third-largest growth rate in the state.

There is a good news/bad news paradox in this rise in residential values. The good news is the potential for revenue growth based on increased property values. The bad news is the potential for a continuation of a dramatic, worrisome shift of the tax burden from commercial and industrial taxpayers to residential ones. In 1988, the last year of the pre-1987 tax classification system, residential property accounted for 35 percent of tax revenues and commercial property about 37 percent. By 2000 those numbers were 57 percent and 28 percent, respectively (see table 11.3). Whether the renaissance will change the relative importance of residential property compared to other classes is not exactly clear at the moment. The hope certainly is that by attracting more businesses to occupy more valuable land, the city will lift some of the revenue burden from residential taxpayers.

Assuming that renaissance policy does produce more valuable property, another important paradoxical fact of property tax life in Providence may offset future gains. Almost half the property in the city is exempt from taxation, for two

TABLE 11.2

MEDIAN SALES PRICE OF SINGLE-FAMILY HOMES, RHODE ISLAND, PROVIDENCE, AND EAST SIDE, 1987–2000 (SELECTED YEARS)

Year	Rhode Island	Providence	East Side
1987	$120,000	$83,000	$164,750
1990	125,000	85,000	185,000
1993	115,000	76,100	169,000
1996	116,600	68,500	185,000
1998	122,600	72,000	190,000
1999	126,000	75,000	248,500
2000	135,976	83,000	294,000

Source: Rhode Island Realtors Association.

reasons. The first is that the city's homestead ordinance, designed to provide some property tax relief for resident homeowners in Providence, allows a 33 percent tax exemption of the assessed value of a dwelling of six or fewer units.[10] In 1997 more than $1 billion in residential property value, approximately 20 percent of all taxable property, was exempt from taxation.[11]

The second is that Providence is the capital and principal city in Rhode Island. As such, within its boundaries is property owned by a broad array of federal, state, and municipal agencies and private not-for-profit higher educational institutions, medical facilities, and religious and charitable bodies. In 1997 approximately 40 percent of the property making up the city's tax base was owned by tax-exempt organizations, up from 35 percent in 1989.[12] Taxable property is routinely turned over to tax-exempt organizations. Recent examples include the Old Stone Bank building sold to Brown University; the Outlet Communications property bought by Johnson and Wales University; Miriam Hospital's purchase of the Providence Sears building; Citizens Bank's donation of property in a prime downtown location to the private nonprofit Trinity Repertory Theater; and Sovereign Bank's property donation to the Rhode Island School of Design for that school's library expansion. There are many others. The obvious problem is that the burgeoning nonprofit and governmental sector in Providence puts an onus on the residential property owner to pick up the resulting additional revenue burden, which forces the city to provide some tax relief through the homestead exemption and thus further reduces the city's revenues.

Because of the amount of nonprofit, tax-exempt property in Providence, the city receives more than 60 percent of the state aid that is available through Rhode Island's PILOT program. State policy is to rely on PILOT to reimburse communities for the tax-exempt property within their boundaries that is owned

TABLE 11.3
SHIFTING TAX BURDEN, PROVIDENCE, R.I.
Percentage of Tax Revenue

	1988	2000
Residential	35	57
Commercial	37	28
Industrial	8	5
Utilities and RR	6	4
Motor Vehicles	13	6
Other	1	21

Source: Official Statements of the Providence Building Authority, Appendix: Information Statements of the City of Providence, Analysis of Tax Revenue, 1989, 2001. Authors' calculation.

by nonprofit educational institutions, nonprofit or state-owned hospitals or veterans' residential facilities, and correctional facilities, which are exempt by state law. This PILOT program is supposed to act as a cushion for local communities from loss of taxable property to tax-exempt property owners. In truth, it pays for only a fraction of what the city would derive if these properties were taxed. Recently, the new mayor of the city, David Cicilline, has made the need to derive revenue directly from the nonprofit higher education institutions a more central part of his long-term budgetary strategy.

Property Taxes in the Renaissance City

A reliance on property tax increases to generate more revenues was not the promise of renaissance policy advocates, but, more or less, that is what has happened in Providence. Property tax revenue grew between 1987 and 1999, but it was higher property tax rates, not increased property values or a growth in taxable real property, that were responsible for property tax revenue increases during this period.

There are three distinct periods in the Providence property tax revenue history in recent years. From 1989 through 1992 the real estate tax rate, following the tax reclassification implementation in 1988, rose 17 percent, from $23.88 per thousand to $28.17. The revenues generated rose from $133.6 million to $165.8 million, a 24 percent increase. No revaluation took place within this time frame, so the increase in revenues primarily resulted from these tax increases, which outstripped inflation.

The story was quite different in the subsequent four years. Between 1992 and 1996 there was no property tax revenue growth at all, and revenue actually dropped between 1993 and 1994 (see table 11.4). The explanation is quite simple: between 1992 and 1996 city policy makers did not approve any hikes in the $28.17 rate set in 1992. Revenues were flat because the tax rate was flat. The city was fortunate indeed that during this period inflation was approaching historically low levels, moderating the loss of purchasing power from the property tax revenue the city did garner.

The period 1996–2000 offers further evidence that property tax rate increases are the cause of improved revenue yields. Between those years there was a 21 percent aggregate increase in property tax revenues, which grew at rates greater than inflation once again. Tax rates were raised 18 percent, from $28.17 to $33.44 per thousand. When policy makers raised the tax rate, revenues from the property tax went up, generally beating inflation. When they opted to hold the line on the rates, revenues were flat or declined, but fortunately during this period inflation remained in check.[13] Overall, city policy makers over the decade exercised restraint in the authorized levy, the amount the city had to generate from its property tax after accounting for external and other non–property tax revenues. The levy mirrored the property tax revenue stream's hills and valleys.

Revaluation politics will play a role in the success of tax policy that evolves as the renaissance unfolds. Between 1988 and 2000 no revaluation of property occurred. It took thirteen years to complete a revaluation after 1987, despite a state requirement that one be accomplished every ten years. Providence, not unlike other Rhode Island communities, is a "reval" procrastinator. If the politics is not favorable, revaluation just goes undone. So, for example, preliminary mid-1990s indications were that commercial and industrial property values, like residential values, had plummeted throughout the city, which further accelerated the shift of the cost of city government onto residential property owners. The 1998 municipal election year and looming statewide elections in 2000 caused a delay in revaluation because of the potential for voter backlash directed at Providence municipal and state delegation officials. Waiting proved a successful strategy, as property values generally have recovered quite substantially in the city since 1997.

In theory Providence will be able to measure changes in the value of the city's property much more frequently and uniformly than it has in the past, because the state enacted legislation in 1997 that requires municipalities to complete a triennial statistical revaluation and full revaluation every nine years.[14] An improved revaluation process holds out the promise of less homeowner "sticker shock" and the potential for an improved revenue stream that is based on im-

TABLE 11.4
PROVIDENCE PROPERTY TAX REVENUE, 1989–2000

	Revenues	Rate
1989	$133,586,000	$23.88
1990	138,843,000	23.88
1991	148,708,000	25.50
1992	165,821,000	28.17
1993	165,987,000	28.17
1994	165,388,000	28.17
1995	163,804,000	28.17
1996	165,665,000	28.17
1997	177,920,000	30.42
1998	189,130,000	31.99
1999	192,300,000	31.99
2000	203,241,000	33.44

Source: Official Statements of the Providence Building Authority, Appendix: Information Statements of the City of Providence, City Finances—Schedule of Revenues, Other Financing Sources, 1990–2001.

proved property values, without tax rate hikes. Therein lies the promise of renaissance policy makers.

The "City-State": State Intergovernmental Assistance

While improved property values and increasing property tax revenues are the hope of renaissance policy makers, Providence could not survive without significant amounts of state aid. Measuring renaissance policy through the lens of intergovernmental assistance is a special challenge because few communities, whether economically successful or impoverished, are likely to turn their backs on state financial assistance. However, because policy changes at other levels of government can have severe revenue consequences, the financial and policy stability of a funding source is a major worry for any community whose operating revenue increasingly is made up of intergovernmental revenues. Providence must continue to garner a rather large infusion of cash from the state to help keep the city afloat as it awaits its own revenue renaissance.

An indicator of successful renaissance policy over time is a moderated demand *for increasing levels of support from the state to finance local operations.* If renaissance fiscal success is realized, then the city would become less dependent on state assistance to support operations because of an improved stream of own-source property tax revenues derived from improved property values and a growing tax base.

The financial relationship of the state and Providence has been contentious. Whether the issue is building renaissance projects or securing state aid for education, the State House and its capital city sometimes are at loggerheads. City policy makers again and again make the claim for more state aid because the state can expect revenue windfalls from a successful Providence renaissance. In Rhode Island only the state can tax the income of workers and businesses; levy the retail sales tax; and collect tax revenue derived from a range of goods and services that tourists and others coming to the Renaissance City consume—meals, beverages, cigarettes, and fuel.[15] In 1997 efforts by the city to be granted permission by the state legislature to levy a local option commuter tax for Providence never made it out of committee.

State lawmakers have not turned away from Providence. The city is the single largest recipient of the state's two basic forms of assistance to local communities: direct aid and education aid. Other Rhode Island communities have proportionately lost shares of education and direct state aid as Providence has gained them, a situation that further fuels a statewide skepticism concerning the city's financial condition and the reliability of the state as a financial partner. For example, in 1987 about 15 percent of total education aid went to Providence, whereas in 2000 it was 25 percent. By 2000 the Providence share of all other forms of direct state aid had risen to nearly 40 percent, up from 18 percent in

1987; this leaves about 60 percent to be divided up among the thirty-eight other cities and towns in Rhode Island.[16]

Currently, for Providence increasing state aid, particularly for schools, is the difference between financial failure and draconian tax increases and service reductions. Between 1987 and 1994 about 60 percent of the city's total revenues were derived from property taxes. Since then property taxes have dropped to about 50 percent of total revenues, while state education assistance has grown from roughly 20 percent of city revenues to well over 30 percent. Other state aid totals 5 percent of Providence revenues, and other own-source revenues such as fines, fees, and federal grants make up the revenue balance (see figure 11.1).

Rhode Island's Direct Aid Programs

The capital city is a primary recipient of Rhode Island's four principal forms of direct state assistance to local governments (see figure 11.2). Providence garners roughly one-quarter of the available state general revenue sharing (GRS) dollars, a formula program based on per capita income and the local tax effort. Providence also receives a substantial share of the revenues generated from the Public Service Corporation Tax imposed on telegraph, cable, and telecommunications corporations exempt from local taxation. The state's formula-based Distressed Communities Relief Program sends more than half of its available funds

FIGURE 11.1
Providence Revenues, 1987–2000

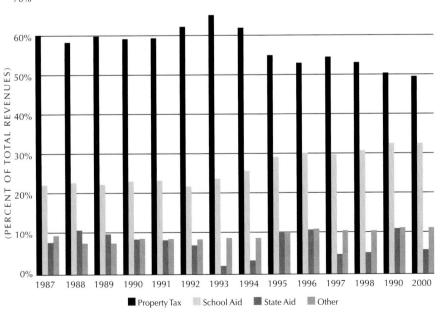

FIGURE 11.2

Rhode Island Direct Aid to Local Governments: 1987, 1992, 1997, 2000

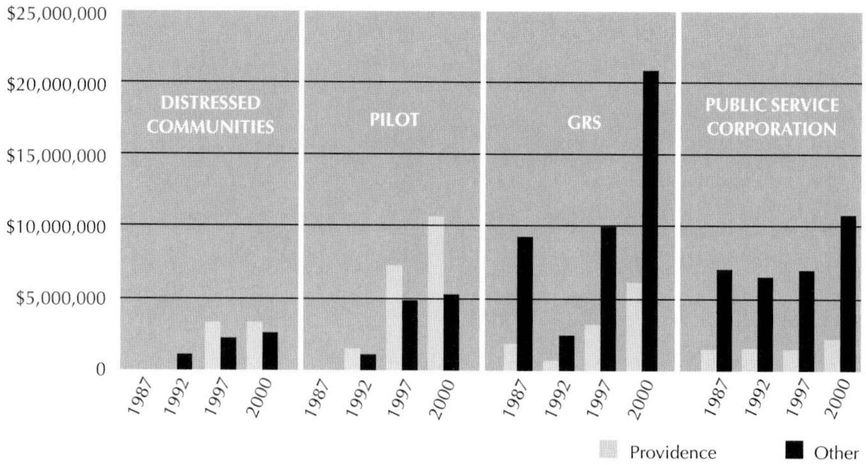

Source: House Fiscal Advisory Staff, *Rhode Island Educational Aid,* November 2000; Rhode Island Department of Administration, Budget of the State of Rhode Island, Executive Summary, 1991–2000.

to Providence. Providence receives more than double the amount of PILOT aid than all other Rhode Island communities combined.

The importance of the financial condition of the funding source is clearly documented by Rhode Island state government's simultaneous struggle through the recession and state credit union crisis of the early to mid-1990s. Local governments took it on the chin when the state reduced GRS state aid. In 1992 alone Providence lost nearly 50 percent of its GRS dollars. Providence paid for this fluctuation in aid and for its policy decision not to raise taxes between 1992 and 1996 by negotiating with municipal workforces to receive no pay increases during that period. Newly vacant positions went unfilled. Budget gimmicks included the sale and leasing of assets, principally the Port of Providence and the city-owned Triggs Municipal Golf Course, and slowed payments to the city's pension funds.

Education Assistance

State aid to fund the Providence public school system is the dominant form of state intergovernmental assistance to Providence, as it is for all Rhode Island municipalities. It is also the single most contentious state aid policy issue in Rhode Island. Providence has incrementally increased its share of state education dollars from 15 percent in 1987 to about 25 percent of all state education assistance in 2000. By 2000 more than 60 percent of educational expenditures in Providence were paid for by state dollars, making the city's dependence on state largesse for education acute. Simply put, Providence would be incapable of financing its current school effort without large property tax increases if state education aid was significantly reduced.

While awaiting a revenue renaissance, the Providence school system remains chronically in financial difficulty and continues in its sometimes contentious city-state relationship. It is a common lament by many Rhode Island local government officials that the state education aid decision process is so slow and uncertain that it sometimes forces local communities to assess levies and to set the property tax rates before it is known how much state aid will be forthcoming for the fiscal year at hand. The state's funding formula is the product of a political struggle that pits urban and suburban communities against each other. As has happened in many other states, legal challenges to Rhode Island's education funding formula have played a role in redefining state educational financial assistance.[17] The state has changed the educational formula no fewer than five times to accommodate the growing clamor for more assistance, a response made possible until very recently by an unprecedented growth in the state's economy and a resulting inflow of tax revenues.

There is a cost to Providence, however, for this growing dependence on state funding, which other communities will not be subject to: much closer scrutiny of the Providence School Department spending. Stories concerning school crossing guards earning upward of $30,000 per year, misuse of federal grant money, and the Plunder Dome federal corruption investigation of city hall emboldened the legislature in the late 1990s to demand more oversight in return for the increasing amounts of aid. An end to the city's residency requirement for teachers also became necessary, as was strict attention to the state's overall educational accountability system enacted by the legislature in 1997.

Spending and Saving in Renaissance Providence: Expenditures and Fund Balances

In Rhode Island, as elsewhere, local governments are required to have a balanced budget. A successful renaissance, at least in theory, would produce enough revenues to ensure that spending obligations are met each year and that the municipality would produce enough of a surplus to make certain an appropriately modest growth in the fund balance. Most cities do find a way to achieve the required balance but often not without fiscally hair-raising moments. Those periods of fiscal stress are what renaissance policy is supposed to help prevent.

How a successful renaissance affects expenditures is not so clear. For example, if the renaissance is a success and more businesses view the municipality as a place to operate and people want to live there, then upward pressure on expenditures will be felt. More schools, increased public safety and public works, and amenities such as parks, bike paths, and such indicate a more livable city. Therefore, higher expenditures would be a positive sign. The expectation is that the growth in the taxable base would pay for the increased expenditures and perhaps a bit more. However, if expenditures rise and there is no corresponding growth in property value or the taxable base is yielding less revenue (or both), then a fiscal renaissance is difficult to achieve. A worst-case scenario is that expenditures rise because the city is viewed as a nice place to visit but not as a place to live or locate a business.

Checking the propensity to spend may also prove difficult even if a fiscal renaissance does occur. Providence's real, noninflationary spending increases during the renaissance period grew at a rate greater than inflation (see figure 11.3). These noninflationary increases occur in the big three spending areas—the local share of education costs, public safety, and finance and administration—while spending in other categories has remained flat or actually declined.

On average, each year general fund revenues outgrew expenditures but just barely. This surplus is contributed to the city's fund balance. A positive unreserved fund balance can be thought of as savings for a rainy day. For a city like Providence, always seemingly on the verge of a fiscal crisis, *a positive unreserved fund balance as a percent of total general fund revenues* would be a positive indicator of successful economic development. In other words, a fiscal renaissance should provide a financial cushion.

FIGURE 11.3
Providence Total Expenditures, 1987–2000

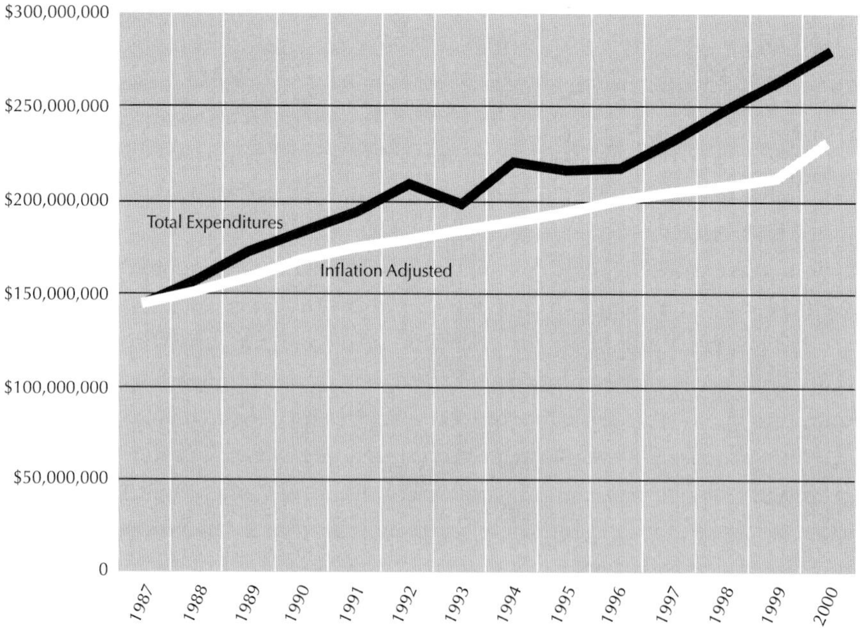

Source: Official Statements of the Providence Building Authority, Appendix: Five-Year Comparisons, Schedules of Revenue, Other Financing Sources, 1987–2000.

Providence sits on a thin, if slightly improved, financial reed. When the books were closed in 1987 a negative unreserved general fund balance of slightly more than $1 million confronted city officials. Since then Providence has managed to eke out minimal surpluses almost every year during the 1990s to produce a positive unreserved fund balance of $6.8 million at the end of fiscal year 2000.[18] This cushion leaves little room for errors in policy judgments, economic development policy making, managing state aid changes, or weathering an economic downturn.

The COLA Struggle[19]

Expenditures do not just "happen." Choices are made and dollars are spent. The following case has a single lesson for urban policy makers: all the hard work that goes into conceiving, planning, and implementing an economic development strategy can be undone by ill-considered policy decisions that create large expenditure dilemmas that even a successful renaissance could not cure. Providence barely survived such a fiscal disaster that would have effectively bankrupted the city and downgraded its bond offerings to below junk status. Its cushion would have been of little help.

The Providence contributory pension plan retirement system is the source of much union-management policy friction, debate, and litigation. It covers more than three thousand active employees and nearly the same number of retirees. Pension politics came to a head just as the renaissance was heating up. On 6 December 1989 the union-dominated retirement board of the Employees Retirement System of Providence voted to provide pension cost-of-living adjustments (COLAs) and other benefits to current and retired city employees. The city administration, then under Mayor Paolino, asserted that the retirement board did not have the power to make the changes and refused to implement the retirement board's action.

Predictably, several legal actions were filed. To settle the litigation, on 18 December 1991 Mayor Cianci and the retirement board entered into a consent decree to settle the suit.[20] It turned out not to be such a good deal for the city. The backbreaking financial realities of the consent decree emerged relatively quickly. The city reversed its position and challenged the decree in superior court and finally in the Rhode Island Supreme Court, asking the high court to nullify the agreement.

As the "COLA wars" were waged, in 1995 the city council won a hard-fought legal battle against the mayor to secure for the council an interpretation of the city charter that made all labor agreements negotiated between the mayor and collective bargaining units subject to council approval. Ironically, it was the Rhode Island Supreme Court decision, one that the Cianci administration bitterly fought, that provided the legal legs for the mayor to challenge the validity of the consent decree, which had never been submitted to the council for approval.

Late in 1995 the Rhode Island Supreme Court dealt the city a blow by holding that the consent decree was final and binding. It remanded the case to superior court because the decree was entered into *prior to* the city council's prevailing in its suit. For the next five years this pension fight went back and forth within the Rhode Island legal system. In April 2000 the Rhode Island Supreme Court decision lessened the city's future burden somewhat by distinguishing one group of retirees from another: those who retired before 1991 and those who retired in subsequent years.[21]

While the city still faced a larger than desirable pension liability, its financial pain was lessened somewhat because the court limited the scope of those entitled to the decree's windfall. In 2000, according to the city's actuarial consultant, the market value of the total assets of the pension fund totaled more than $351 million, with an unfunded accrued liability of more than $450 million.[22] While not quite the immediate financial cataclysm it once was, the unfunded pension liability is still a looming menace. The lesson is clear: an enormously successful economic development policy will be needed to yield revenues to pay for this pension issue or any other expansive spending program that the city brought on itself. Renaissance policy cannot overcome even well-intended folly.

Dealing with Municipal Debt

Providence has not borrowed money to any noticeable extent to pay for its grand renaissance projects. The city did not have to mortgage itself as the renaissance activities unfolded. For example, early efforts to involve the city directly in borrowing for the Convention Center and Providence Place mall were abandoned. Nevertheless, city borrowing has occurred for other purposes, including its capital improvement program. Borrowing totaling more than $100 million was undertaken for neighborhood development projects during the 1990s.

Borrowing creates debt service, the amount of principal and interest that a local government must pay each year on its debt. Debt service is a fixed cost, and if it increases as a percent of revenues, it reduces the amount of financial flexibility of a local government. Successful renaissance policy would permit a municipality the financial flexibility to ensure its timely payment of debt service, a condition that ensures favorable treatment by credit rating agencies and lenders. Four debt-related indicators of a successful renaissance policy are *strong bond ratings; decreasing debt per capita; decreasing direct debt service as a percent of tax revenues; and a drop in long-term debt as a percent of assessed valuation.*

General obligation bond borrowing by Providence is subject to terms and conditions established by state law. For example, without a local referendum and a majority vote of the city council (which is subject to the mayor's veto), general obligation borrowing cannot exceed the 3 percent of the taxable property debt limit established by the state legislature. The city has created structures such as the Providence Public Building Authority to provide some borrowing flexibility.[23]

In general, over the twenty years of renaissance-related activity, the general obligation bonds issued by Providence are treated as medium, investment-grade bonds by bond rating companies. Moody's, for example, rates Providence-issued general obligations as Baa1 bonds.[24] The security of these bonds is generally adequate, but over time there may be some unreliability.[25] In other words, to bond rating companies the creditworthiness of Providence has remained the same as renaissance activity unfolded.

During the period between 1990 and 2000, even as the city struggled with large spending commitments and a shrinking tax base, Providence's policy makers remained committed to managing the city's debt. No tax anticipation notes have been issued since 1987, and long-term debt as a percent of net assessed value has remained consistently low, but the percent debt service to tax revenue increased considerably in the mid-1990s (see figure 11.4), though by 2000 it drifted back to where it had been in 1988. The net debt per capita generally drifted upward throughout the 1990s but in 2000 stood at $594 per resident, about the same as in 1988. In general, Providence's debt service has remained within the industry standard for maintaining the city's bond rating for more than a decade. For Providence, with its small reserves, these trends in debt service need to be watched closely.

Tax Treaties

Tax stabilization agreements, "tax treaties," are a well-known tool of economic development and a source of much controversy. They can take many forms but generally involve a city's forgiving all or some portion of the tax liabil-

FIGURE 11.4
Providence Debt Trends, 1988–2000

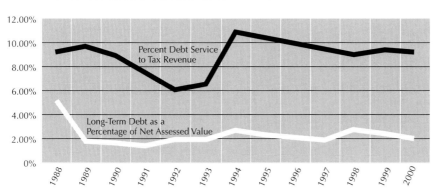

Source: Official Statements of the Providence Building Authority, Appendix: Information Statement of the City of Providence, Debt.

ity of a business in the city or one moving to or expanding in the locale. In return, cities require benefits, usually in the form of hiring local contractors and an increase in jobs in the city, especially for city residents. More hiring of women and minorities often is included in the terms of the agreements. Enforcement has been a problem in Providence, as granting abatements requires significant monitoring, a task that generally has not been fulfilled there.[26]

Providence has used tax stabilization agreements to engage in renaissance economic development. For example, the American Express Building (parcel 5) and the Courtyard by Marriott (parcel 1) in Capital Center were granted stabilization agreements by the city. The state required the city to enter a tax treaty with the Providence Place developers, and, most recently, the state negotiated a tax treaty with G-Tech Corporation to encourage that corporation's move into Capital Center. The city has granted tax treaties for industrial park development (Silver Spring), housing (Village at Elmhurst), individual companies (Vargas Manufacturing Company), and others. The general belief within Providence throughout much of the 1990s was that the benefits of the stabilization treaties outweighed the costs, which were generally minimal and had little impact on the tax rate.[27]

A Stabilized and Improved Urban Economy?[28]

Economic conditions are usually outside the immediate control of a municipality's political and business leadership. The goal of urban renaissance policy making presumably is to produce a new economic base for the city that will help the city and its residents better weather inevitable adverse economic conditions. There is some preliminary indication that renaissance activity is associated with positive changes in the city's economy when business activity, local employment, resident income, property activity, and tourism data are analyzed. There also are some warning signs that the city's economic health is still in question.

Attracting and Retaining Business

Increased business activity is a paramount goal of renaissance policy. The hope is to create an upward spiral of increased business activity leading to demand for space within the city and eventual improved property values. Business activity–related indicators of a successful renaissance policy in Providence are *business start-ups; gross retail sales; office vacancy rate; rental costs per square foot; and available class A and B square footage.*

Providence is bustling indeed. If we look at business start-ups, the 1990s represented a period of optimism in the city's future. The preparations of the 1980s for the activity of the 1990s appeared to be paying off. In the five years between 1990 and 1994, business start-ups increased by two-thirds over the previous half decade. The average number of business start-ups continued to increase through-

out the 1990s, averaging 322 annually from 1995 to 1998. The 421 business openings in 1995 marked the single highest number of new business openings in two
decades, which was followed by 392 in 1997.[29] Certainly businesses left and failed
to thrive in the same decade; virtually every car dealership and lumberyard has
vacated the city because of the extraordinarily high business inventory tax.[30]
Other companies closed their doors, as well: Old Stone Bank is a prime example.
However, the overall amount of activity is encouraging.

Optimism based on business start-ups is tempered somewhat by the poor
showing to date of an equally important success indicator: gross retail sales (see
figure 11.5). Gross retail sales have continued to slide downward in spite of the
renaissance activity, while statewide they increased until 1998–99. All eyes will
be watching the retail numbers in Providence closely because the Providence
Place mall, which celebrated its one-year anniversary in September 2000, represents a $500 million wager that retail can return and act as a catalyst for further
retail activity.

A more hopeful sign for renaissance boosters is the improving conditions related to office space and rental in the central business district (see table 11.5).
Total available class A square footage is rebounding in the city. A demand for
that office space in Providence is beginning to be felt, a positive renaissance indicator. Between 1995 and 1999 the vacancy rate for class A and B office space
dropped. Class A space has become more expensive, although the more available
class B space has remained at roughly the same rental price per square foot.

Local Employment

The increased business activity in the city bodes well for future employment. The employment base of the city is defined as the rate of unemployment
of its citizens and the number of jobs within the community. A successful re-

FIGURE 11.5
Rhode Island and Providence Gross Retail Sales, 1987–1999

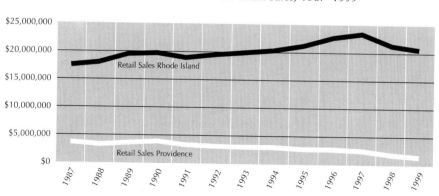

Source: Rhode Island Economic Development Corporation.

TABLE 11.5
PROVIDENCE OFFICE SPACE, CENTRAL BUSINESS DISTRICT, 1994–1999

	1994	1995	1996	1997	1998	1999
CLASS A OFFICE INVENTORY						
Total square footage	2,809,042	1,741,104	1,741,104	1,741,104	1,948,302	1,968,790
Vacant	598,326	280,318	214,156	200,227	200,675	192,941
Vacancy rate	21.3%	16.1%	12.3%	11.5%	10.3%	9.8%
Rental rate (average)	$17.00	$17.00	$23.00	$23.00	$23.00	$24.00
Class highest	$26.00	$28.00	$28.00	$28.00	$30.00	$32.00
Class lowest	$16.00	N/A	$21.00	$20.00	$20.00	$21.00
CLASS B OFFICE INVENTORY						
Total square footage	N/A	2,049,527	2,093,056	2,103,418	2,260,620	2,284,029
Vacant	N/A	461,166	493,961	422,787	262,232	194,143
Vacancy rate	N/A	22.5%	23.6%	20.1%	11.6%	8.5%
Rental rate (average)	$15.00	$17.00	$16.00	$16.50	$16.50	$17.50
Class highest	$16.00	$28.00	$16.50	$19.00	$19.00	$20.00
Class lowest	$12.00	N/A	$14.00	$14.00	$15.00	$16.50

Sources: Society of Industrial Research, Reports, 1995–2000.

naissance policy would produce *a lower unemployment rate and yield more private industry jobs.* Certainly, factors other than local economic development play a role in determining the unemployment rate within a community. An economy in recession produces higher unemployment more than a failed renaissance policy does. However, so many renaissance projects are touted as "job creators" that employment-related outcomes must not be ignored as a measure of success.

During the last half of the 1980s the Rhode Island unemployment rate (3.8 percent) was considerably less than the 6.2 percent national average but slightly higher than that of the New England region (3.4 percent) (see table 11.6). The Providence unemployment rate was 4.4 percent, still better than the nation but higher than the state's rate. The years 1990–95 were difficult ones for Rhode Island workers. The national recession and state credit union crisis prompted the unemployment rates of Providence and Rhode Island to zoom past the national and New England averages.

There is some evidence that renaissance policy is contributing to an improved employment climate in Providence. In 1999 the Rhode Island unemployment rate (4.1 percent) edged below the national rate for the first time since 1989. Providence's unemployment rate in 1999 was the lowest since 1989, at 5.4 percent. This welcome unemployment news also is reflected and most clearly felt in the retail industry; by 1999 Providence retail jobs increased to levels not seen in more than a decade. Service jobs appeared in restaurants, drinking establishments, and

TABLE. 11.6
ANNUAL AVERAGE UNEMPLOYMENT RATES, 1987–2000

	1987	1988	1989	1990	1991	1992	1993	1994	1995	1996	1997	1998	1999	2000
U.S.	6.2%	5.5%	5.3%	5.5%	6.7%	7.4%	6.8%	6.1%	5.6%	5.4%	4.9%	4.5%	4.2%	4.0%
New England	3.4%	3.1%	3.8%	5.7%	8.0%	8.1%	6.8%	5.9%	5.4%	4.8%	4.4%	3.5%	3.3%	2.8%
Rhode Island	3.8%	3.1%	4.1%	6.8%	8.6%	9.0%	7.8%	7.1%	7.0%	5.1%	5.3%	4.9%	4.1%	4.1%
Providence	4.4%	3.3%	4.4%	7.6%	9.5%	9.9%	8.9%	8.3%	8.4%	6.5%	6.7%	6.2%	5.4%	4.1%

Source: U.S. Department of Labor.

hotels as well as in the full range of shopping venues typically associated with malls.

Service employment continues to dominate manufacturing in Providence (see table 11.7). Manufacturing jobs were cut in half over the decade, replaced by employment in private health, business, educational, engineering, social, and other services. An alarming trend is that the share of employment attributable to finance, insurance, and real estate decreased. Should that direction continue, the employment-related promises of the early renaissance would be difficult to attain. The irony is that Capital Center was designed in part to attract the financial industry. On the other hand, the upward trend of retail employment reflects the presence of Providence Place.

These decade-long trends are evident in an employment snapshot of Providence businesses and organizations. Since 1990 the employment base of the city has become dominated by nonprofit agencies that typically provide health-related or higher education services. Six of the ten largest employers in the city—Rhode Island Hospital, Brown University, Women and Infants Hospital, Roger Williams Medical Center, Blue Cross/Blue Shield of Rhode Island, and Johnson and Wales University—are nonprofit organizations.

The hospitals, colleges, arts organizations, and countless smaller private,

TABLE 11.7
PROVIDENCE PRIVATE INDUSTRY EMPLOYMENT, 1989–2000
(Selected Industries)

	1989	2000
Service Industry	46,852	56,874
Manufacturing	23,719	10,709
Finance, Insurance, R.E.	11,961	9,845
Retail Trade	11,566	14,165

Source: Rhode Island Economic Development Corporation, Research Division.

nonprofit organizations, as well as the government agencies and state higher education institutions that make up the public nonprofit community, contribute jobs and a certain amount of prestige to the capital city. What they do not do, of course, is provide property tax revenue, and as discussed earlier, as more of Providence's property is removed from the tax roles, pressure is put increasingly on residential property owners. Some of the largest corporate taxpayers no longer are the largest employers. Narragansett Electric remained the city's largest taxpayer between 1990 and 2000, yet its workforce fell from the fifteenth largest to eighteenth in 2000. Fleet Financial Group, the second-largest taxpayer, fell from the sixth- to tenth-largest employer. Other private commercial businesses have similar profiles—they pay taxes but are employing fewer people.[31]

Personal Income in the Renaissance City

Increased business activity and more employment, regardless of economic sector, potentially establish a climate where more personal wealth is created and the city becomes more attractive to individuals of some means to come and live, even if they work elsewhere. If a renaissance is under way, then the personal economic circumstances of families and individuals living in Providence should improve. Positive changes in *adjusted gross income* for Providence taxpayers, as well as an improved income *per capita, per household, and per family*, should result. *Wage rates* should improve, as well.

The residents of Providence experienced a positive change in personal wealth during the last half of the 1990s. The Providence adjusted gross income (AGI) for resident filers for the period 1995 to 2000 grew by 7 percent. Their tax liability to the state grew by about 15 percent, even as Rhode Island continued to lower very incrementally its personal income tax rates. Rhode Island grants a tax credit to residents for taxes paid to other states, and this credit grew by 12 percent.[32] Yet as Providence residents become somewhat wealthier in this period, other Rhode Island residents are generally doing even better: statewide AGI rose by 24 percent, state liability by 33 percent, and the state credit for payments to other states by 44 percent.

During the 1990s increasingly wealthier individuals and families did come to live or remained in Providence, as the overall income improvement suggests. This growing wealth in the city is evident when per capita income, median family income, and median household income are compared. Even as the population in the city grew, per capita income rose from $11,838 in 1990 to $14,260 (inflation-adjusted) in the year 2000.[33] This increase in real income is a sign of a potential renaissance for individual city residents, as was the more than 20 percent rise in median household income, from $22,147 in 1990 to $26,867 for 2000.[34] Family income grew by about 6 percent, a slower rate that actually lost ground to inflation. (Household income refers to money received by all members occupying a housing unit, family income to money received by all members of a family unit; more than one family may occupy a housing unit.) Nevertheless, there are more households and families with incomes over $49,000 in 2000 than there were in 1990 (see table 11.8).

Wages dropped in Providence during the early to mid-1990s after having risen for most of the second half of the 1980s, although individuals who earned those wages did not always live in Providence. However, in the second half of the 1990s wages recovered in Providence and, at least for a time, were growing at a pace faster than the rest of Rhode Island and the United States as a nation.[35] An analysis of wage patterns over the period 1998–2000 indicates that in those renaissance-thematic areas such as restaurants and hotels, retail, health, and financial and human services, wages paid to entry-level workers have generally increased.[36]

Property in Providence

There is some willingness of businesses and homeowners to invest in Providence. The potential economic strength of an urban center and the confidence of investors is reflected in an increase in *industrial and commercial construction and actual square feet of construction*. The condition of the *housing market* in the city indicates whether there has been an impact of the downtown renaissance on neighborhoods in the city. These indicators suggest that a property renaissance in Providence is under way.

Investors, commercial and residential, are showing a willingness to take a chance on the Renaissance City. The total number of building-related permits issued in 1999–2000 increased incrementally over the 1987–88 boom. However, the amount of commercial construction that occurred in Providence between 1997 and 1999 dwarfs that of the years 1989–96 and constituted the lion's share of commercial construction statewide (see table 11.9). The list of construction proj-

TABLE 11.8
CHANGES IN PROVIDENCE FAMILY AND HOUSEHOLD INCOME, 1990–2000

Providence Family Income Percent Change (N=35,657 [1990]; 36,187 [2000])			Providence Household Income Percent Change (N=58,530 [1990]; 62,327 [2000])		
	1990	2000		1990	2000
< $49,000	78.2	67.9	< $49,000	83.6	73.6
> $49,000	21.8	32.1	> $49,000	16.4	25.9

Source: U.S. Census Bureau, Profile of Selected Characteristics, Rhode Island Statewide Planning. Authors' calculation.

ects includes the projects discussed earlier as well the Providence Courtyard by Marriott, the Radisson at India Point, and a flurry of construction by nonprofits such as Johnson and Wales University, Brown University, and the Rhode Island School of Design. Providence's commercial and industrial construction value of nearly $22 million in 2001 was the equivalent of slightly more than 1 percent of the previous year's full property value and was considerably less than the previous six-year average of more than $100 million.[37]

Housing is an important barometer of the city's economic future, because it is the housing market that contains evidence of individual commitment to live in the city. Obviously, Providence does not have the open space available for development of new housing that is found in the suburbs and rapidly developing rural areas of Rhode Island. That fact is reflected in the paltry number of new single- and multifamily housing units authorized in Providence between 1991 and 2000, compared to statewide figures for the same period as well as to the last few years of the 1980s real estate boom (see table 11.10). Expanding the housing market in Providence is a difficult uphill struggle.

The cost of housing is also a measure of the economic health of the city, because it indicates the willingness of people to live in a locale where a larger portion of disposable income is spent on a basic necessity. As discussed earlier, the rising median sales price of single-family houses in Providence is evidence that a rebound from the real estate doldrums the city and state experienced in the early to mid-1990s is under way (as was illustrated earlier in table 11.2). The sudden in-

TABLE 11.9
RHODE ISLAND AND PROVIDENCE COMMERCIAL CONSTRUCTION, 1989–2000

	Providence (sq. ft.)	Rhode Island (sq. ft.)	Providence percent of construction
1989	34,000	2,292,119	2
1990	—	1,056,637	0
1991	1,330,000	1,953,429	68
1992	392,128	2,080,836	19
1993	—	1,051,049	0
1994	219,015	1,447,903	15
1995	65,000	1,305,359	5
1996	75,000	1,190,392	6
1997	1,310,000	2,301,758	57
1998	2,573,400	3,808,459	68
1999	1,498,543	3,584,553	42
2000	269,039	1,993,946	13

Source: Rhode Island Economic Development Corporation: Research Division, Local Government, City of Providence, "The Economy/Trends."

terest in the development of high-end condominium projects on the eastern (Pilgrim Mills) and western (the Jefferson) edges of Capital Center is another indicator that Providence is thought by investors to be able to sustain its renaissance momentum. A proposed upscale luxury residence project to be built in Capital Center was announced in October 2002.[38]

The Providence rental market continues to tighten despite the overall number of occupied units growing by about 8 percent. The number of vacant housing units dropped during the decade of the 1990s by more than 30 percent, from nearly 8,000 units to about 5,500. About 8 percent of Providence's housing units were vacant in 2000, in contrast to nearly 12 percent in 1990. Over the decade of the 1990s the rents obtained by property owners increased such that more than half of renters now pay more than $500 per month (the median is $526), whereas in 1990 more than half the renters paid less than $500 per month (the median was $469).[39]

Destination City[40]

Because city leaders tout Providence as a destination city, measuring the success of the renaissance rests on people visiting the city. This tourism renaissance occurs against the backdrop of a general boom in Rhode Island tourism.[41] The three largest industries in Rhode Island are health services, miscellaneous manufacturing, and tourism. By 1999 employment, wages, and firms grew faster in

TABLE 11.10
RHODE ISLAND AND PROVIDENCE RESIDENTIAL CONSTRUCTION, 1989–2000

	Providence New Housing Units			State	Providence
	Single	Multi	Total	Total	percent of total
1989	87	318	405	3865	10
1990	108	205	313	3042	10
1991	29	44	73	2377	3
1992	30	16	46	2592	2
1993	22	12	34	2575	1
1994	53	18	71	2539	3
1995	33	26	59	2127	3
1996	32	48	80	2462	3
1997	37	38	75	2672	3
1998	21	18	39	2642	1
1999	25	56	81	3304	2
2000	31	78	109	2596	4

Source: Rhode Island Economic Develvment Corporation, Research Division, Local Government, City of Providence, "The Economy/Trends."

tourism than in the other two leading industries.[42] Providence boosters hope for the destination theme to work to the advantage of Providence and yield a significant amount of tourist activity. Indicators of the success of the destination city theme include *hotel occupancy and daily rates* and *increased levels of employment in tourism-related industries.*

The indications are that more people are visiting Providence. WaterFire, the Convention Center, Providence Place mall, Trinity Repertory and other local theater companies, the many restaurants that have attracted national attention, and the plethora of architectural styles in the city have increased tourism. In turn, the mean and median occupancy and daily rate of hotels in the city have increased substantially. These are heartening figures for downtown destination city proponents and for developers of other hotel projects. The number of hotels built in the city will determine to a large extent the long-term success of the Convention Center as a tourism engine for the city and state. Not surprisingly, since 1998 employment for desk clerks and maids in the city's hotels has increased substantially.[43]

Since the 9/11 attacks, concern over the future of tourism in urban areas has been very high. In another hopeful sign for the city, since 2000 the Providence gross metropolitan product and tourism-related employment have remained stable in spite of 9/11 and the mild regional economic setback.[44] The city itself felt that the renaissance might be jeopardized by 9/11, and so the Mayor's Special Commission on Business, Tourism and Culture was created. That commission reported in April 2002 that despite the terrorist attacks, "the average occupancy at the city's five hotels exceeded the average for the same months [October, November, December] in 2000."[45]

A Better Quality of Life for All City Residents?

Controlling the economic conditions that affect cities poses a significant challenge. The quality of life within its boundaries is also often beyond the immediate control of a city. A principal claim by urban policy makers for participating in renaissance activities is that the overall quality of life will be improved for *all* the city's residents.[46] Such claims hark back to Paul Peterson's assertion in *City Limits* (1981) that there is a unitary interest among urban residents in the pursuit of aggressive urban economic development policy. The supply-side argument that a rising tide lifts all boats underpins much of what has driven downtown economic development since the early 1980s.[47] The Providence political leadership is no less adept than any other civic boosters across the nation at linking the pursuit of infrastructure projects, top-ranked hotels, convention facilities, high-end office space, and tourist attractions to broader quality-of-life outcomes for residents.

Renaissance boosters argue that the only way to increase the supply of jobs, reduce the residential property tax burden, and improve the quality of public education and municipal services is for the public sector to become aggressively engaged in economic development activities. However, given the highly competitive nature of capital, labor, and land markets, the likelihood of equal distribution of the payoffs from renaissance activities cannot be presumed. Uneven spatial development is a well-documented phenomenon in American cities.[48]

If an enhanced quality of life for all city residents is a principal justification for pursuing economic development policies, then some measure of improved city living standards should be evident following a period of sustained activity. This analysis compares data from the mid-1980s to the present in three important urban policy areas: public safety, education, and health and welfare. Two dynamics affect the analysis. First, we are ever cognizant that many quality-of-life indicators can lag significantly behind economic changes and that events in the city's larger economic environment can work to accelerate or decelerate change.

Second, the level of government responsibility for each of those areas differs in Rhode Island. The city is primarily responsible for funding and providing public safety. The state fiscal and oversight responsibility for elementary and secondary education in Providence has grown considerably. Rhode Island's state government is almost exclusively responsible for health and welfare services. As a result of this mix of responsibility, and of other decisions beyond the control of either state or local policy makers, such as increased immigration and altered federal policy, changes in the quality of life for city residents can be difficult to link directly to renaissance activity.

Public Safety

Mirroring national trends, both violent crime (murder, rape, assault) and nonviolent crime (motor vehicle theft, larceny) declined in Providence throughout the renaissance period. Violent crime peaked in 1991 and has since declined. The pattern is similar for nonviolent crime, which has declined by nearly 40 percent since its peak in 1990. Some negative indicators persist, however; juvenile arrests for violent crimes have remained high, even as adult arrest rates fall.[49]

Concerns over safety remain paramount despite falling crime rates. Policing the new venues at Waterplace Park and concerns over safety in the Providence Place mall virtually guarantee that the costs associated with public safety in the Renaissance City have increased. Providence, however, has moved to address those concerns. The city has bolstered its police department by slightly more than 22 percent since 1992, while increasing the number of sworn officers by more than 13 percent during that period.[50] By 1999 Providence and Newport had the highest number of sworn officers per thousand residents in the state.[51] A new state-of-the-art public safety facility to house police and fire commands opened in 2002, built not downcity but across I-95. This building anchors the end of what are hoped to be revitalized Victorian-era streetscapes.

Public Education

A detailed discussion of public education in Providence would fill volumes, judging by the innumerable studies and reports already published.[52] The Providence School System was described in chapter 3, and the discussion on state aid makes clear that the resources that Providence must have to serve its school-age population are well beyond the city's means, hence the state's role in financing and its increasing control of the district. It is the largest system in the state by far, with the highest percentage of students from low-income families: 80 percent versus 30 percent statewide. Only about one-third of eligible three- and four-year-old children in Providence enroll in Head Start programs, compared with almost one-half of such eligible children statewide. Thus for many children school readiness is a major issue.

Compounding school readiness concerns is the fact that 20 percent of public school students in Providence have limited proficiency in English, compared with only 6 percent statewide. Providence residents come from many, often poor, regions of the world. This enriching mix of students from Africa, Central and South America, the Caribbean, and Southeast Asia represents what a renaissance can create—a destination city. It also poses a challenge to the city and state to provide an effective learning environment for these children. Grades 4 and 8 results on Rhode Island's Metropolitan Achievement Test are well below statewide averages in many instances and demonstrate that Providence and state policy makers still have a long way to go before Providence begins to match statewide student performance.[53]

As a result of the twenty-year or longer pattern of Latino and Southeast Asian immigration, Providence has experienced the most significant growth in its school enrollments among Rhode Island's core urban districts. Providence's enrollment growth rate between 1991 and 2000 was more than twice that of the state; it is thus imperative for the state to buttress the financially strapped city as it tries to build the needed classrooms. The culturally diverse school-age population has increased the need for costly enrichment and support programs. The per-pupil cost for instruction generally and for special education services specifically exceeded the statewide average but for general instruction lagged behind the state average by a considerable margin.[54]

Those financial measures of social change are mirrored in data reflecting the likely educational success of students. An education renaissance will improve such yardsticks as the likelihood of attending school on a regular basis, remaining consistently enrolled in the same school and district, and graduating from high school. In the ten urbanized areas of Rhode Island,[55] in 1999 Providence ranked third highest in student mobility with the poorest average student attendance record and the third-highest dropout rate.[56] In 2001 the Providence high school graduation rate was 64 percent, 30 percent less than the statewide rate.[57] Presumably, mobility would change if residents of Providence found consistent employment that allowed for renting or purchasing affordable housing, which would moderate the dropout rate.

Health and Welfare

The improved quality of life for many of the lower-income residents of Providence is dependent on state and federal human services policy rather than on the economic development efforts of the city. Success of the renaissance economic development policies can help by providing opportunities to work, thereby assisting the state and federal government in their efforts to combat persistent poverty and its attendant problems. Naturally, there are lags between policy formation and policy implementation—between the immediate benefits of downtown economic development policies, such as increased employment and wages, and the effects of those changes on the overall quality of life in the city, such as improved health among infants and young children.

One health-related area of significant concern to state policy makers has been lead paint poisoning. Urban regeneration and architectural renewal that might accompany an urban renaissance have a long way to go to improve housing in the city's poorest neighborhoods. With its aging housing stock and high percentage of multifamily rental units, Providence has a problem with lead paint in homes.[58] One of every four kindergarten-aged Providence children screens positive for lead levels considered unacceptable by the EPA, greater than 10 mg per deciliter of blood. Statewide the number is 13 percent. Fortunately, both percentages represent a slight decrease over the past decade.[59]

Other indicators reveal that children and families in Providence continue to experience the health problems associated with persistent poverty. Women living in the state's capital on average delay prenatal care at rates far higher than women statewide, although there is an encouraging trend toward earlier exposure to prenatal services. While statewide there is a slight improvement in the areas of prenatal care and infant mortality, women in Providence are more likely to give birth to low-weight babies and have a higher incidence of infant mortality than women from other communities in Rhode Island. These gaps between Providence and the state have persisted for decades, even though there has been improvement. That improvement is not so clear in the case of teen birth rates, which have increased over the last decade in Providence. In this area, as well, a big gap exists between Providence and the state as a whole.[60] According to 2000 U.S. census figures, Providence was home to 8,642 families living in poverty, which represented 24 percent of all families in the city and was an increase over the 18 percent reported in the 1990 census.[61]

None of the issues just detailed, or the many others, will be ameliorated quickly or at all by a Providence economic development renaissance. Nonetheless, they deserve mention here because in the zeal to pursue renaissance policy and make large financial investments in the city, the claims that benefits will trickle down to city residents may only be possible with proportionately large investments in public safety, education, and health and welfare.

Summary

Has the fiscal health of the city improved? This discussion shows that it remains as it has been: in a state of uncertainty. On the basis of analysis of the data available, we can see that there is hope that a fiscal renaissance could happen, but warning signs remain. Among the positive fiscal signs are:

+ The value of the city's residential property improved between 1989 and 1999.
+ Debt remained manageable throughout the 1990s.
+ The state showed some willingness to help the city overcome fiscal difficulties at times.

The negatives, though, are still present:

+ Providence's property tax capacity remained low and its effort remained high throughout the 1990s; there was a shift of the tax burden to residential tax payers.
+ The shift of property from tax-paying to tax-exempt institutions continued.
+ Higher tax rates, more often than not, accounted for increases in the city's inadequate own-source revenues; the city was thus forced to become generally more dependent on state aid and in particular on state aid for education throughout the 1990s.
+ The city has little financial cushion to absorb prolonged periods of fiscal stress.
+ Pension policy remains troublesome.

Has the city's economy improved? There are some strong indicators that this is so. Sustaining that improvement and building upon it is the next challenge.

+ The city's unemployment rate is the lowest it has been since 1989.
+ Retail employment has grown steadily, as have service-related jobs, while manufacturing continues its decline and some weakening in financial sector employment has appeared.

- The Providence economy continues a shift from private commercial to private and public nonprofit.
- Entrepreneurs have indicated a willingness to invest their business capital in Providence, but the jury is still out as to the success of the retail investment in the Providence Place mall.
- There is reason to hope that residential properties are recovering their value lost throughout the early 1990s.
- Tourism has increased markedly.

Has life changed for residents of Providence? There is still a great need for effort to improve conditions.

- The city is safer than it was.
- Its educational system has considerable ground to make up before it is on firm footing financially and programmatically.
- There is still a considerable distance to go before the health and welfare of all its citizens realize a renaissance.

Future renaissance activities will take on added importance as the focus shifts from the feel and look of a Renaissance City to a measurement of what actually has changed for those who find themselves living in Providence.

Opportunities, People, Policy

12

Already it has achieved what many larger cities, with far greater resources, have failed to do—renew itself without obliterating its past.

Dallas Morning News, 26 November 1989

Providence is a treasure trove of early American architecture . . . and a spiffed up downtown. . . . It easily merits a day or two of relaxed rambling.

New York Times, 30 October 1994

WaterFire is an exceptional example of how Providence is turning into a destination city. It's a great revival of a former desolate town.

Anonymous WaterFire visitor book entry

Perfect timing. Every city should have such events. It is an excellent show of peacefulness and collectiveness in a community.

WaterFire visitor book entry, 15 September 2001

■ In 2002, searching for a revived policy agenda for downtown Providence, the Providence Foundation commissioned a series of presentations and workshops by Richard Florida, professor of economic development at Carnegie Mellon University. Florida's book, *The Rise of the Creative Class and How It's Transforming Work, Leisure, Community and Everyday Life* (2002), has as a central theme that a highly talented and diverse labor pool is the key variable in urban economic growth, because the creativity inherent in that pool will translate into the development of new and economically relevant forms of knowledge. He argues that knowledge and information are the essential ingredients of creativity and that positive innovation, whether in the form of technological breakthroughs or new business models, will result.[1]

In his analysis of Providence Florida identified five main "market clusters" that drive the local economy: medical research, knowledge creation, design and business innovation, creative technology, and arts and culture. "Providence," the report claims, "is bringing art and science to the market."[2] Underpinning these clusters are a series of strengths and solid opportunities that Providence needs to maximize to ensure a stable future: entrepreneurship derived from research; architectural legacies that are authentic and desirable; a rich cultural base and artistic vibrancy; a creative infrastructure of colleges and universities; a critical population mass that can support diversity, networking, and partnerships; and the as yet unrealized raw materials to position and market the city.

Florida's work is designed to stimulate ideas about what's next for Providence. By engaging Florida the Providence Foundation, the organization created in 1974 to help bring an NEA grant to Providence to fund *Interface Providence*, returns to its roots as an idea catalyst after a number of years helping to move along many brick-and-mortar projects. The foundation and Florida appear ready to advocate that the renaissance in Providence be attentive to what Florida refers to as the four T's: talent (brains, skills, and creativity); technology (research and innovation); tolerance (respect for diversity); and trees (a sense of place).

Our purpose in this chapter is to determine the degree to which the two questions that guided our inquiry into the Providence renaissance have been answered: (1) What is an urban renaissance and how does it start and sustain itself? (2) Has all the effort made a difference for the well-being of the city, or is it all just a massive case of civic cheerleading, good salesmanship, marketing, or, worse, the self-aggrandizing or enriching behavior of a privileged few? Our answers to those questions can be used as a jumping-off point to assess the degree to which the renaissance in Providence can sustain its momentum and what it might do to create a fertile environment for the types of suggestions contained in Florida's work.

What Is the Urban Renaissance in Providence?

We defined urban renaissance as a sustained effort by private and public individuals, groups, and institutions that for a variety of reasons act to reverse urban physical, fiscal, economic, and social decline often brought on by forces outside their control. These collective efforts result in undertakings that when viewed in the aggregate produce measurable changes in a city:

- The city's physical appearance improves—the canvas looks different;
- Enough revenue is generated to provide a satisfactory level of city service and the city remains solvent;
- Commercial and residential property values are stabilized and increase as the local economy improves;
- An improved economic environment promotes business retention and attracts new business; and
- City residents realize real jobs, changes in income, and an improved quality of life.

In partial answer to our second question, it is clear that the renaissance efforts have made a difference to the city. Without question, downtown Providence's appearance has changed dramatically for the better. Infrastructure projects have resulted in improved roads, traffic circulation, and pedestrian walkways; the reappearance of the city's rivers; and new construction and restoration of older buildings that together have created a physical atmosphere conducive to a feeling of rebirth. Commercial retailing has returned to Providence, and the idea of Providence as a destination city has taken hold among local policy makers and is symbolized by the Rhode Island Convention Center and by WaterFire. This feeling of rebirth has extended to the older downcity, where investments by the higher education community, the state, and private developers offer the hope of a renaissance led by students and those wishing to return to a city offering many cultural attractions—in what was once thought to be a dead zone. In effect, Florida's fourth "T"—a sense of place—has been the focus of renaissance attention, one of the strengths of Providence pointed out in the Foundation's report.[3]

There is some preliminary indication from business activity, local employment, resident income, property activity, and tourism data that renaissance activity is associated with a positive change in the city's economy. Local employment has improved in the city, as rising income levels and a lower unemployment rate strongly suggest. The city's fledgling success at becoming a destination city is reflected in the extraordinarily high hotel room occupancy and rental rates. This tourism service industry also has created a better employment base, albeit a lower-paying one. The city still retains a significant portion of jobs statewide, and the growing presence of large nonprofit educational and medical industries in the city holds the promise of more professional employment.

There is a willingness of businesses and homeowners to invest in Providence, as an increase in business start-ups and in commercial and residential construction indicate. The improved condition of the housing market in the city hints that there has been some impact during the renaissance period on neighborhoods in the city. A property renaissance in Providence is under way. When coupled with the growing dominance of higher education and medical services in the Providence economy, the basis for two other "T"s, tolerance and talent, is potentially within the Providence policy orb.[4]

Despite an improved city economy, the city's fiscal health remains in a state of uncertainty. The city has staved off cataclysmic fiscal events but always teeters on the brink. Its tax base continues to shrink as nonprofit institutions increasingly dominate the local economy. The decision to enact the homestead ordinance contributes to the declining tax base even as the value of property in the city increases. More frequent revaluations may help to increase revenues but only, of course, if property values continue to climb. Tax abatements also contribute, to a degree, to loss of revenue from new businesses moving into the city. The consequence is that the city has become a virtual ward of the state: it depends on statehouse politics to resolve city fiscal problems with ever-increasing school aid and other forms of state direct aid, which, as history has demonstrated, can be fickle. What the state gives, the state can take away. While the city has managed to hold its debt burden in check, expenditures threaten to spiral out of control. The city has little saved for a rainy day, should either the state pull back its aid or the city be unable to check its expenditures.

The feel of the city is different and is improved for many of its residents, but there is still a considerable distance to go before their welfare realizes the promise of renaissance policy. The education and welfare policy arena are not something that the city can do very much about: the state controls the latter directly and the former increasingly. Public safety remains the principal area of local responsibility, and Providence has become a safer city over the last decade.

In summary, the Providence renaissance is an improved physical appearance not yet accompanied by enough own-source revenue to provide a satisfactory level of city services and remain solvent unless considerable state assistance is available. The local economy improves as jobs become more plentiful, income rises, and commercial and residential property values stabilize and increase; and the improved economic environment promotes business retention and attracts new business. City residents are on average somewhat wealthier today, partly because the city has attracted new, more affluent residents, and partly because there have been changes in income. Still, a significant portion of the city's population needs better schools, better incomes, and a better overall quality of life.

How Did the Renaissance Start? In Theory and Practice

Our central theme is that the twenty-five years of activities associated with what is called the Providence renaissance evolved somewhat serendipitously and often hinged on critical events over which participants may have had little control but were well positioned to take advantage of decisively. The rather inelegant garbage can policy framework offers a way to understand renaissance decision making in Providence: how it appeared on the agenda; the way alternatives were specified; and why certain choices were made. The garbage can framework accommodates well what we have come to view as the hallmark of the Providence renaissance: that opportunities arose when the right people in the right place at the right time had what appeared to be the right idea and were willing to exert the leadership to try to bring that idea to fruition. This circumstance was particularly true for the early stages of Providence renaissance activity. Bringing ideas to reality, however, required considerable give and take by participants. Once the idea of a renaissance took root, nurturing that overarching policy goal led to a series of decisions that initiated one project idea after another—but ideas not necessarily brought to fruition successively. Projects overlapped (rails and rivers), sometimes stalled (the mall), and sometimes went up rapidly (Convention Center); others continue to struggle (building hotels) while still others move ahead (I-195 relocation).

There was no dearth of ideas about what to do about the threat of urban decay facing Providence. From the *College Hill Study* through the *Downtown Providence 1970* urban renewal planning process and *Interface Providence* there was a great deal of focus on ideas that involved the importance of a new physical configuration for downtown and a new transportation system, including doing something with the railroads. That particular idea was discussed in many forums, and a consensus was reached early on in all sectors about the importance of relocating the rails *if ever* the opportunity arose. The importance of Providence's architectural and historical legacy crept into discussions and in small ways began to appear on the agenda in projects such as the preservation of College Hill and the restoration of the Providence Performing Arts Center.

These ideas constituted the earliest moments of a "primeval soup" in which ideas originate, compete, evolve, prosper, and perish in a somewhat jumbled fashion. Motivations varied considerably. Yet time and again the many individuals in and out of government who had to make decisions, particularly in the period from the mid-1970s to the early 1990s, held in common a powerful, if unspoken, unifying theme of "doing the right thing" for Providence and making a difference. "The players all loved Rhode Island and shared an old-fashioned virtue of civic humanism: 'I do it because it is good.' There was a strongly held sense of civic identity, a reservoir of deep affection among both the old elites and elected officials for the city—that it was worth saving. That's what drove it."[5]

Somewhat serendipitously, issues, politics, and policy came together at an opportune time and opened a policy window; interested participants could offer alternatives to a specific policy issue. Discrete national events, specifically the national rail crisis, energy crunch, and environmental concerns, opened windows of opportunity for Rhode Island policy entrepreneurs, civic elites, elected and appointed officials, and others to reach back for ideas that had been discussed in public and private forums but for which there had been no opportunity for implementation. Moving railroad tracks, demolishing the Chinese Wall, and creating Capital Center were the result of changed *national* policy regarding rail passenger service. In turn, a broken policy logjam led to building an eight-movement highway interchange with federal money not used because *state* voters turned down proposed highway projects. The opportunity to put a new idea on the policy table, the uncovering and moving of rivers, became part of the Providence renaissance only because those other prior events occurred.

In Providence policy decisions were made at opportune times. The right idea, the river relocation and Memorial Boulevard extension projects, addressed the traffic congestion problem but also created a historic Providence and destination city theme that in turn led to WaterFire, the signature piece of the Providence renaissance. The right decision makers, a cadre of federal, state, and local administrators with the backing of elected and appointed officials, were receptive to an available solution: uncover and move the rivers. Policy makers and implementers developed the capacity to perform effective assessments of the political feasibility of their actions and the array of political forces shaping or curtailing various opportunities. At first glance, incrementalism appeared to rule the day, but in fact policy choices made in Providence were not done at the margins but involved a significant rethinking of what the city could become.

The post-1990 period is not quite as linear as this earlier renaissance phase. Ideas and opportunity still were important ingredients, but so were persistence and ideology, along with events over which the city and state had little control. The regional recession and state banking crisis led directly to the building of the Convention Center, because the government felt the need to prime the pump and stimulate the state's construction trades. Completing that project effectively solidified the idea that Providence could become a destination city, but at the same time, because of its scale, it also created the need for more hotel space. In other words, the unanticipated consequence of becoming a destination city was to redirect Providence away from financial services and toward tourism. As a consequence the city has endured any number of hotel and residential proposals but with few results as of 2004.

Since then proposals for the destination city have had mixed results. The Providence Place mall opened after more than a decade of efforts and was the result of a developed consensus that a mall could be built in downtown. The Patriots' stadium never developed a similar consensus because of the meteorlike rise and fall of the proposal. The long periods of discussion, studies and reports, shelving of ideas, and consideration of alternatives, all to garner enough political support in favor of a particular policy, never took place for the stadium. Extensive bargaining and conflict resolution among competing interest groups were compressed into a very narrow time frame.

An important hallmark of the Providence renaissance was that policy entrepreneurs were found in many positions and places. They brought together these streams of policies and processes. Entrepreneurs are persistent, tenacious, and willing to spend enormous amounts of their own resources on the issues of importance to them. The Providence renaissance would not have happened without Senator Pell's enthusiasm for rail travel. But his enthusiasm could not have borne fruit without policy entrepreneurs such as Ron Marsella and William Warner, who were advocates willing to invest their time, resources, and talents to promote a position in the hope of some future return.

Also important were leaders who emerged from the public and private sectors and played critical roles at crucial times. Government administrators were essential to the Providence renaissance. A surprising aspect of the Providence story is the nonconservative choices that a number of nonelected government bureaucrats made to effect change in the city. Whether these bureaucrats were politically appointed, such as Ed Wood, Bob Bendick, or Bill Collins, or career civil servants such as Gordon Hoxie, Joseph Arruda, or Samuel Shamoon, their use of discretion to make things happen was key to the renaissance as it unfolded. The civil servants, particularly those with access to public funds, were often as important to the Providence renaissance as were the more public movers and shakers. These implementers were close to the decision-making processes, so there was never a great distance between ideas and those responsible for putting them into action. Private-sector participants such as Bruce Sundlun, Ken Orenstein, J. Daniel Lugosch III, and Barnaby Evans brought their particular interests and passions to the policy table. In fact, the case could be made that Florida's third "T," talent, has been firmly in place throughout the story of the Providence renaissance.

The motivations of these assorted actors varied considerably. Certainly personal ambition and profit were involved, but so was a desire to promote the value of community responsibility—of doing something good for the city. Certainly the love of the "game" motivated others, including Providence's own irrepressible Mayor Buddy Cianci, perhaps the best renaissance booster in its entire twenty-five years. Bill Collins reflected, "Sure, making money and political success were important, but because of those types of motivations they could have cut each other to shreds, but instead, somehow, they came together."[6] The Capital Center and river relocation projects were relatively easy to get implemented because, as Gordon Hoxie recalled, "private commercial people stood to make a lot of money and it solved so many problems for so many interests who were able to get together in short order and figure out who would get what. It also helped that we had good professional people."[7]

In sum, Providence during this period had a number of individuals from a cross section of civic and private life who could command the city's ear because they were politically connected experts and good negotiators who sat in positions of authority. Most important, they were all "on the same page," more or less. What had happened in garbage can terms is that the window of opportunity had opened; for a time ideas prospered because differing motivations came together unified by the core idea that the city could be saved.

A striking characteristic of the Providence renaissance as it unfolded is that the effort was not coordinated by a central agency. Instead, renaissance projects and the partnerships that created them were the product of opportunity, adaptability, and ever-changing relationships among institutions and individuals.

Many public and private entities have been part of the general story of the renaissance. However, the plans, ideas, approvals, sources of funds, designs, discussions, and decisions took place in a variety of forums too numerous to recount. They ranged from conversations in a local eatery to formal urban renewal plans drawn after years of discussion. The nonprofit Providence Foundation, the quasi-governmental Capital Center Commission and its Design Review Committee, the formal federal, state, and local planning and regulatory bureaucracies, and the continued use of waterfront study teams ensured the opportunity for influence in decision making by public and private interests. These organizations were important as rallying points for individuals and groups as incubators of ideas, vehicles of financing, and mechanisms for airing differences concerning projects and the politics surrounding them. They sometimes were highly visible and at other times barely detectable. Some organizations remained active throughout the renaissance period, while others came and went with projects. As an example, by the time the Memorial Boulevard/River Relocation project was done, federal, state, local, private nonprofit and for-profit officials, and agency "stakeholders" had participated on a regular basis in its conceptualization and implementation.

Relying on the garbage can framework does not preclude recognizing the fact that elements of an active growth machine and an active governing elite were taking advantage of opportunities to promote policy agendas friendly to various coalitions or individuals. Central to the Providence story is that over nearly three decades a remarkably steady set of public, quasi-public, and private institutions and actors have played key roles in these activities. Certainly elites were involved in decisions. A few prominent individuals appeared again and again at crucial decision-making points. There was money to be made and electoral success to be gained. However, money and electoral success could have been achieved without the effort to recreate the city, although perhaps not in the same ways or to the same extent. The renaissance endeavors involved considerable risk, as well.

During the prime redevelopment phase (1980–2000), well-forged *contingent coalitions* among private-sector individuals and organizations and local, state, and federal appointed and elected officials materialized. The idea of a renaissance was firmly implanted among these various actors. While they might not all have agreed on a single "vision" and perhaps had different motivations, these alliances had enough combined strength to bring a number of projects to fruition. Opponents emerged not because they opposed revitalization or desired to thwart a renaissance but because their idea of renewal was different.

Our analysis led us to conclude that the Providence renaissance occurred not because of a growth machine, a controlling elite, group competition, an agenda driven by planners and bureaucrats, or incremental policy choices. The renaissance started because ideas that had been percolating among many individuals and organizations over the years suddenly had the opportunity to be tried by people who were in positions to make decisions and influence the flow of resources, sometimes as the result of unpredictable events. The ability to come together quickly as a result of a preexisting consensus was critically important. Whatever the mix of motivations, the common theme was that a successful effort to save Providence would yield potential benefits to many.

Sustaining the Renaissance: Lessons Learned

First Lesson: Government does make a positive difference. Without the capital provided by the federal government (and the state to a more limited degree), what is called the Providence renaissance would not have happened. The central role of the federal-state-local financial arrangements in sustaining urban economic development is critical. A corollary is that it pays to have a congressional delegation influential enough to direct federal resources to renaissance projects.

A second corollary is that compared to the public's willingness to spend, the private sector is nearly risk averse. Government is the entrepreneur forced to develop creative financing tools to sustain development efforts. With the exception of the Providence Place mall, private investment in the core of the Capital Center district has occurred at a snail's pace, although there is continued interest in development within that district. Capital Center is being handed to the private sector with billions of public investment dollars, yet it has been very difficult to entice private investors. It is nearly impossible to obtain private financing for a hotel, and changes in the financial industry make the idea of investing in an office building in an urban office park most unattractive.

Second Lesson: A renaissance is the product of people who vary in their motivation. In Providence there were policy entrepreneurs, people whose ideas were powerful enough to gather support and who had or made access to other groups. The presence of dedicated individual visionary entrepreneurs who could sustain momentum and act as advocates for a project or for the city was essential.

There was always a group who sustained momentum because they cared about the city. Either by birth, by profession, or by a sense of obligation, a leadership elite who for the most part lived in the city and was committed to the future of Providence surfaced to play important roles at varying times. Other groups who wished to profit financially, gain electoral success, or have access to patronage (jobs and contracts) were present within specific projects. Any success they experienced occurred as the result of the policy entrepreneurs and elites being willing to sustain momentum. The role of the bureaucrats was critical in finding and fine-tuning solutions brought to the policy table. While the big picture was set by business and government elites, most of what happened did so because of staff members.[8] They, too, had to be as dedicated as the leadership elite to the overall success of renaissance policy.

Third Lesson: A renaissance is not a linear, planned event or the product of a policy regime. Accidents of location, economics, and policy that produce markets and money are needed to sustain renaissance policy. More than a little luck is involved: the right people with the right idea must be in the right place at the right time. Being able to form coalitions quickly when an opportunity for change presents itself is important. Those coalitions must at their core be devoted to the betterment of the city and not be overly concerned about how to protect or seek benefit for some narrow, parochial interest.

Fourth Lesson: The ability of those public- and private-sector elites and organizations to mobilize rapidly to undertake a project when an opportunity appears adds to likely renaissance success. These contingent alliances are temporary, shifting coalitions in support of a project, though such alliances can be sustained over the life of other projects. Individuals are as important as organizations, but they are often dependent on events beyond their control. Consequently, individuals must be willing to shift their preferences, make accommodations, and rise above self-interest to look out for the public interest. Elites and organizations must be enlightened and use their accumulated influence and power to do good. In sum, leadership makes a difference.

Fifth Lesson: While the elements of a long-term public development strategy may be difficult to plan, receptivity to good ideas around which a consensus emerges produces the environment in which it might be possible to build one project on another. That consensus must come from public-private cooperation and partnerships in which the public sector is willing to assume some risk and keep the private interests engaged. Risk taking and leadership are necessary, as are committed CEOs, skilled professionals, and organizations committed to the implementation of plans sometimes forged years earlier.

Sixth Lesson: Activity leading to physical and aesthetic rebirth does not determine the full meaning of success. While a city may change physically, ultimately a successful renaissance must be measured by positive fiscal, economic, and social changes that occur. Those kinds of change do not occur instantly. Patience and continued dedication of institutions and individuals to the city's future are essential for long-term achievement. State and federal policies that produce positive outcomes in social welfare, education, and public safety also must accompany the renaissance. Stable tax policies are needed in the city. Similarly, the marketplace must produce the environment for the creation of lasting businesses and employment. Public works projects boost local economies, certainly; but for a renaissance to sustain itself, more permanent employment is necessary.

On the other hand, a renaissance does not necessarily produce social indicators that change rapidly or without persistent effort. The inner city revival is generated less by young struggling families than by singles, couples without children or with very young children, and empty nesters whose time in suburbia is done.

Improved inner city schools are likely to be one of the last aspects of urban revival to arrive. A realistic sequence might be safe streets, commerce, efficient public transportation to get people to work and home, and enough families to create a critical mass sufficient to improve schools.[9]

Sustaining the Renaissance: What's Next?

The city's efforts at sustaining its renaissance have not halted. The lessons learned in the period 1975–2000 can assist policy makers as they continue the efforts to sustain the city's renaissance. There are projects currently under way or contemplated that are signs of the city's ability to sustain its physical renaissance.

I-195 Relocation: First Rails, Then Rivers, Now Roads

The grandchild of the railroad relocation project of the late 1970s is the $320-million I-195 relocation that is currently under way; its expected completion date is 2007. The federal government will pay 90 percent of the cost, which suggests its genetic heritage as a renaissance project. The current I-195/I-95

The current route of I-195 cuts a swath through downtown Providence, carving residential streets off from the waterfront and separating the downtown from neighborhoods to the south. Its twists, turns, bends, and difficult-to-negotiate on/off ramps cause daily congestion and frequent accidents.

Courtesy of Providence Foundation, Inc.

merge is the second-busiest intersection in New England. The I-195 roadway forms a physical and visual barrier between two historic Providence neighborhoods by segregating Fox Point from the waterfront and cutting the jewelry district off from downcity.

The idea to move the highway had been contemplated for some time and was actually put on the back burner in order to pursue the river relocation project. When the state signaled its intent to resume work on addressing the problems posed by I-195, Bill Warner went to see Rob Freeman, then director of the Providence Foundation, with the idea of continuing the efforts to reconnect Providence with its waterways. In 1990 the Providence Foundation responded to a RIDOT "scoping" process initiated to seek ideas to relieve I-195–related congestion problems. On the assumption that I-195 would be moved, Rob Freeman did a quick feasibility study on relocation in advance of a foundation-authored NEA grant.[10]

These events led to the 1992 Old Harbor plan and to another federally required EIS. Three road alignment ideas were proposed. The first was to repair the existing road and bridges but not address the congestion issue. The second was to align a new road just south of the Providence hurricane barrier, the core of the Old Harbor plan. The third was to build a new bridge virtually alongside the existing one, a less expensive but also less appealing alternative. The EIS was completed in 1996, and the state selected the second alternative because of safety and community development needs. The EIS concluded that the hurricane barrier alignment alternative would improve traffic flow and safety as well as repair the fabric of surrounding neighborhoods; it could be built while the existing highway remained in place.[11] In 1998 the Federal Highway Funds Bill was passed, and Senator John Chafee helped to secure the funds for this road project through a T-21 formula increase of $50 million that was in the bill. In March 1999 the state began buying land.[12]

The project is under way, but the state will need another $200 to $250 million to complete it. There are clearly defined outcomes expected from this project, including opening almost forty acres of land with riverfront access; reunification of the jewelry district with the center city; a safer highway that eliminates seven traffic weaves; better access to Rhode Island Hospital; an enhanced marine/bicycle/pedestrian system; and reduced noise and visual impact of the highway on the historic parts of the city.

Several lessons of the renaissance can be found in this project. Massive amounts of federal money garnered through John Chafee's efforts will be used. This project is where the strength of the current Rhode Island congressional delegation will be tested. Policy entrepreneur Bill Warner and the idea incubator and catalyst, the Providence Foundation, continue their efforts to resurrect Providence's relationship with its waterfront. Because of the preponderance of federal

The proposed route of I-195, slated for completion in 2007, will place the highway on a new bridge south of the Fox Point hurricane barrier and open up new downtown land under the former road for public and commercial development.

Courtesy of Providence Department of Planning and Development

money in the project, the critical question will be how the resulting land will be used. How will it contribute to the themes that have emerged—destination city, historic and residential Providence, higher education, and the service economy? Or will some new direction emerge? What alliances will form, and will the unifying theme of "the good of the city" remain paramount? The resulting land obviously will be available for development and potentially yield a better tax base for the city. Whether it will actually do so may be the product of as yet unforeseen struggles between state and city policy makers and the economic interests that come to find Providence an interesting place to be.

Destination City: The Masonic Temple

Hotel financing has been scarce for several years because of the conviction of financiers that there is a national surplus of hotel rooms. However, Providence has a shortage of hotel rooms and must rectify this in order to be a destination city. There have been proposals to convert the Masonic Temple into a hotel; whether this happens may be an important predictor of whether the Providence renaissance can sustain itself. Successful adaptation would signal renewed interest in helping Providence achieve its goal of becoming a destination city. The Masonic Temple project is not the only hotel possibility; there have been many other proposals, but all are still just that—proposals.

The history of the Masonic Temple is tortuous. In 1928 the Rhode Island Scottish Rite Freemasons began construction of a planned $2.5-million temple in Providence, across the street from the Rhode Island State House. The project was to be financed privately, but the organization ran out of money and could not get further bank financing. Construction of the temple came to a halt in 1929, the year of the stock market crash, and never was restarted. The shareholders seemed unwilling to authorize more stock. The specter of embezzlement by the treasurer of the local Freemasons began to hover over the project.[13] In June 1933 the Freemasons' treasurer was sentenced to eighteen months in prison by the Rhode Island Superior Court after pleading no contest to two counts of embezzling funds from the Masons. Because of its colossal Ionic colonnade and prominent location across the street from the Rhode Island State House, the abandoned building is a very visible eyesore.

The Masonic Temple, located on Francis Street across from the Rhode Island State House, was abandoned in 1929 and never completed. Several developers have submitted proposals for a luxury hotel conversion in recent years, but none has yet been adopted.

Courtesy of Providence Department of Planning and Development

State decisions and the economy control the fate of the temple. In 1945 Rhode Island purchased the property with voter-approved bond money, and in 1949 the state reconstructed the adjacent auditorium; today it is called Veterans Memorial Auditorium. The auditorium is home to a number of local arts organizations, such as the Rhode Island Philharmonic, and over the years has undergone various refurbishments, but the temple has sat deteriorating. In 1966 Governor John Chafee recommended razing the building, but the cost was prohibitive.[14]

The auditorium continued to attract advocates even as the temple continued to deteriorate. The former underwent a $6.35 million refurbishment, completed in 1990 as the result of efforts by local preservationists and a newly formed Veterans Memorial Auditorium Preservation Association (VMAPA). The Masonic Temple, which is attached to the auditorium, continued to fall into disrepair, regularly losing parts of its copper roof to daring thieves. In 1993 the Providence Preservation Society managed to get the temple placed on the National Register of Historic Places. In 1996 the PPS sponsored a public charrette to save the temple, which resulted in a recommendation for mixed use of the site, not a hotel.

In 1997 it was clear that the Providence Place mall was going to be built virtually next to the temple. Governor Almond appointed a fourteen-member Masonic Charrette Implementation Task Force to search nationwide for a developer for the temple. The PPS actively participated in the process of soliciting interest by providing a list of developers with a specific interest in rehabilitating old buildings. Tours of the property were arranged in May 1997. The state made a $500,000 commitment to protect the temple from further deterioration. Eight proposals were received by June 1997.[15]

Converting the temple into a hotel was seriously discussed for the first time as a result of these proposals and became the task force's preferred alternative. Converting the building into state offices was rejected because of the considerable public expenditure involved.[16] The VMAPA's suggestion to create a "temple of the arts" with retail and office space foundered on the estimated $15 million price tag and opposition by the Veterans Memorial Auditorium executives, who thought the idea was redundant because the auditorium had received a Rhode Island Foundation grant to establish a similar project next door.[17]

Algen Corporation proposed an upscale hotel. Governor Almond and the Charrette Implementation Task Force liked the plan because it did not require a massive infusion of public money, the same policy stance that the state took in its negotiations with the New England Patriots during the same year.[18] The public reaction was mixed, but nevertheless by January 1998 some preliminary agreements were reached with Algen to build a $20–25 million, 170-bed hotel named the Providence Grand Hotel.

The Algen proposal and many subsequent iterations of it perished. Despite the 1998 optimism, the many obstacles to the project thwarted it, including the lack of private capital for hotel financing. Other constraints arose, and no organization or individual advocate has yet been able to muster the strength to overcome those constraints. The inability of the developers to qualify for federal tax credits for preserving the historic structure, which required myriad building and site design approvals from federal and state agencies, including the Capital Center Commission, held up the project for a considerable amount of time. The policy position by the Almond administration that no state funds would be invested created another financial obstacle for the project. Design issues also have been a major impediment, as developers sought to integrate the architecturally significant elements of the remaining three original walls into a new design to accommodate or overcome height restrictions that exist because of the site's proximity to the State House. Parking remains a problem, as well. In March 2002 Governor Almond announced he was giving up on trying to save the Masonic Temple. His chief of staff, Joseph Larissa, stated, "It's been over seventy years and that temple has never been habilitated. . . . There may be a point soon where the temple cannot be habilitated without an astronomical cost that nobody would pay."[19]

The probable benefits of a completed Masonic Temple project are plain. Signing over the temple from the state to private hands raises potential for city tax revenue. The much-needed hotel spaces for the Convention Center make the success of that project and the marketing of Providence as a destination city more likely. Concern for the most visible and threatened city landmark would be eliminated, which would add significantly to the State House and mall locations and in the process perhaps help to bring a few jobs to the Smith Hill neighborhood and stabilize property values.

The constraints the project faced certainly are no greater than the obstacles associated with moving railroads and rivers and building malls and convention centers; the benefits of those projects might actually have been less certain at the time of the initial proposals. What is absent is a catalyst for the project. No policy entrepreneur is willing to expend time and capital to make the project happen. The one seriously entertained hotel proposal by Algen did not mobilize public- and private-sector elites and organizations to undertake the project. No contingent alliance ever formed. The one tool available to help move the project forward—federal tax credits—was inadequate to overcome the legion of issues associated with the project. No underlying consensus about what the project should be was achieved, and certainly the temple as hotel idea was never well vetted over the decades. It just sat there. As a consequence, the Masonic Temple tests the degree to which the elements that created the initial excitement of the renaissance remain within the community. In early 2003 another proposal for the temple restoration from Sage, a Colorado company that specializes in historic rehabilitation, surfaced in the seventy-fifth anniversary year of the start of construction of the Masonic Temple.

Without significant public investment, private capital will not come to the rescue. While there may be a market for hotel space in Providence, the economy has not produced the money to sustain a project. The Rhode Island Convention Center Authority, already the owner of the Westin Hotel, has proposed becoming a partner in a new hotel to be built across the street from the Convention Center. The authority wants permission from the legislature to borrow $27 million in revenue bonds to support the project. The partner would be a former state representative turned developer. If that proposal comes to fruition, once again direct public investment would win the day over private investment with indirect public assistance.

Downcity: The Renaissance within a Renaissance

Planning for downcity continued in the early 1990s as the Capital Center district efforts began to take on a retail and destination city theme instead of the originally envisioned focus on financial services. The effort to rebuild downcity is perhaps the most significant experiment in the Providence renaissance because, if successful, Providence will have essentially two downtowns: the Capital Center district and downcity. The renaissance in downcity is now dependent on a successful link among arts and entertainment, higher education, and residential development to produce foot traffic and the climate to attract urban residents. The city, for its part, has contributed to downcity development through changes in zoning, a property tax rebate program for residential conversions, and obtaining from the state an artist property and sales tax rebate program for those artists who live and work in downcity.[20]

Charrettes conducted by Andres Duany during 1993 emphasized an "arts and entertainment" district for downcity that would take advantage of the rejuvenated Trinity Repertory Theater, the upgraded Providence Performing Arts Center, and the nearly completed Rhode Island Convention Center. Special tax incentives and zoning modifications that would encourage the development of artists' lofts, practice studios for musicians, and gallery spaces were contemplated in the plan that emerged from this process. According to participants in these charrettes, Duany contributed to opening up the development process to new ideas, particularly the notion that the city could pin part of its development future on higher education, tourism, and the arts while protecting its urban character.[21]

Residential development still is in its infancy. The current phase is very slow, building by building. St. Florian recently remarked, "I feel very confident. . . . Luckily, the right people are coming back here: singles, couples with no children, students, wealthier retirees who winter in Florida but who want top quality and high security and will buy real luxury in the downtown."[22] Buff Chace, a member of one of the old families of Providence, has undertaken the renovation of two nineteenth-century downcity buildings (the Smith Building and the Alice) into residential units, one of the hopeful signs that people will move downcity, but "what to do with the first floors" (that is, the obsolete retail spaces on the ground floors of these buildings) remains a problem.[23] There will be two hundred Chace-rehabbed apartments in the blocks bounded by Weybossett, Mathewson, and Eddy by the end of 2003.

Long-sought downcity movie theaters have not materialized. An attempt to lure Hoyts Cinemas to build a six-screen "art" theater on the edge of the new district, as part of the mall negotiations, was rejected by city officials at the urging of some downcity groups. Instead, a bid was made to attract Robert Redford's Sundance to downcity. The hope was that Sundance would come to town with all of the national recognition it would bring. That effort failed when General Cinema, Sundance's source of capital, declared bankruptcy. [24]

The emergence of a significant higher education presence in downcity has taken place quietly. Johnson and Wales University, located in the heart of the old downcity, followed through on an ambitious Duany-inspired expansion master plan. Roger Williams University planned its move onto Washington Street in Providence. The presence of the Rhode Island School of Design and Brown University a short walk from this proposed district made a further argument for a focus on both the arts and entertainment and higher education themes. The state's decision to locate the University of Rhode Island's College of Continuing Education in a $35-million refurbished Shepard's department store produced a downtown urban campus on Washington Street.[25]

Moving to the Neighborhoods

There are plenty of other projects located in and outside of Capital Center and downcity that deserve to be watched. While Capital Center remains in flux, proposals for residential and office buildings continue to come and go. Most recently, G-Tech Corporation has expressed its intent to move its corporate headquarters to parcel 9. The fact is that Capital Center as an office park has not materialized yet, while its potential as a hotel and residential zone has not been fulfilled, either, with the exception of the completed Courtyard by Marriott on parcel 1. A proposal by developer Eastman Pierce for a residential compound, including a hotel within Capital Center, continues to be reviewed by the Design Review Committee in 2003.

There has also been development on the periphery of Capital Center. Just to the west of the mall, a 330-unit luxury residential complex called Jefferson at Providence Place, developed by Starwood Wasserman, a Providence real estate development company, has risen. Just a bit farther west up the Woonasquatucket, the Eagle Square project is bringing a suburban-style shopping plaza to the heart of the Valley neighborhood and preserving (after considerable debate) a number of former mill buildings. In the same neighborhood the Rising Sun Mills, a 151-loft apartment complex with one hundred thousand square feet of commercial space, is planned. At the bottom of College Hill, just outside Capital Center, luxury condos have been carved out of existing nineteenth-century buildings, and what was once called the "Mickey Mouse" building, a law firm whose senior partner had his tongue firmly implanted in his cheek, has been taken down. The former Blue Point Oyster Bar building is part of the new development along this South Main Street project corridor. In the city's jewelry district three-thousand-square-foot luxury loft condominiums are being developed.

The Future of the Renaissance in Providence: Messages from the Participants

In 2003 the developers of the newly constructed Jefferson at Providence Place, located on the banks of the Woonasquatucket immediately behind the mall, began to seek buyers for their upscale condominiums.

Courtesy of Gordon Rowley, Rhode Island College

Many of the basic positive elements that existed twenty-five years ago still hold true for Providence. The agglomeration of highways, a burgeoning Greater Boston market, its waterfront location, and large numbers of wealthy and middle-class residents are all very much part of the Providence landscape. The city has a number of assets, including its universities and colleges, its built environ-

ment and aesthetic, its numerous arts and entertainment venues, its restaurants, its roads and transport system, and its proximity to Boston. And, of course, the image of the city has changed dramatically.

There are some negatives, however, chief among them the loss of the local banks and businesses tied to the city's fortunes. Former locally owned banks whose CEOs took active roles in the renaissance have been consolidated out of existence or bought by corporations outside Rhode Island. These shifts are perhaps most powerfully symbolized by the move of Fleet Bank's headquarters from Providence to Boston and the sale of Fleet's downtown office buildings. At the same time a generation of political and business leadership has retired, leaving behind a legacy but not necessarily successors. Providence needs a renewed civic leadership and a creative wave involving business leaders whose egos do not get too much in the way of the broader city interest. The business community must follow through on goals and commitments to make sure that the deals that do get made match the goals. Incentives must match priorities. Perhaps what is most important is a need to "rediscover the camaraderie," the human capital, that grew out of the small projects of the 1970s. The motivation is still alive, although not as fervent as before.

The renaissance has entered a new phase. The original excitement and focus

The benefits of renaissance policies in the central city area have, to a limited extent, spilled over into surrounding neighborhoods. Upriver from Providence Place mall and the new Jefferson apartments, Eagle Square has been redeveloped into a retail district on the site of underutilized mill buildings along the banks of the Woonasquatucket River.
Courtesy of Gordon Rowley, Rhode Island College

on what could be has been replaced over time with shopping for the "deal" and much more microregulation born of the important role that the Capital Center Commission and its Design Review Committee played in the late 1980s and 1990s, in particular with the mall. The danger is that ideas that could move the city forward become less the focus than micromanaging the details of proposals not yet fully developed and preserving regulatory schemes. Further, the city today seems just to wait for proposals and then react by cobbling together tax breaks rather than developing a set of criteria and expectations for projects. Of course, tax breaks for the readaptive use of older buildings remain an important ingredient for the renaissance to continue.

The future requires a critical mass of people to get things moving again. In doing so the city can develop more economic depth and diversity. In turn, property values will continue to rise as demand outstrips the supply in a highly desirable waterfront city. The ongoing shift in focus to residential development has turned Providence into something of a suburb of Boston, that is, Providence is to Boston as Stamford, Connecticut, is to New York. If these trends continue and become a development focus, the city will capture a workforce in industries such as computer research and development, higher education, and health and medicine. The city (and state) will then be able to retain a higher percentage of degreed and highly skilled people.

Conclusion

Our examination of the processes by which railroad and river relocation projects came about leads us to agree in substantial measure with analysts who have argued that local political and policy choices matter a great deal.[27] One cannot simply ascribe the fortunes of cities to structural forces operating at the regional, national, or global scales in the face of which local policies make little or no difference.[28] The fact that these forces have been harnessed by local regimes to promote increases in economic activity is indicative of the potentially powerful role of municipal government in economic development: in short, state and local politics matters.

Where we differ from the mainstream regime theorists is in their focus on traditional governing coalitions (or growth machines) between city hall and local business elites.[29] Our analysis suggests a more complex alignment of interests whose institutional configuration involving federal, state, and city agencies, a new state-city alliance in the form of the Capital Center Commission, and a blending of public and private interests was not as clear-cut in Providence as elsewhere. The creation of the Capital Center district, the relocation of rails and rivers, and the creation of an extensive urban park went much further than traditional local economic development policy in the United States. The Providence renaissance is the product of opportunities to use ideas that were waiting in the wings. Project followed project once it became clear that a fertile environment existed in which the ideas could flourish. Local institutions composed of local talent produced the vision of a Providence renaissance by following this nexus of ideas and opportunity.

How to encourage the likelihood of a renaissance? Encourage ideas, because the well-vetted, well-understood idea allows for a quick, clear consensus on which projects to pursue. Foster the sense of community so that a critical mass of individuals choose to live in a city because they like it, not because they are forced by circumstances to remain. Much of the early renaissance is the product of home-grown intellectual capital and, to a certain degree, local business capital. The boards of the Providence Foundation, Chamber of Commerce, study groups, and the like were in part composed of leaders from local institutions. Perhaps that is the biggest problem posed by a global economy: local talent will be replaced by anonymity—people and institutions not tied to the future of a city.

Transforming Providence from a smudge to the Renaissance City has taken almost thirty years, and there is still a considerable distance to go. In our opinion the real renaissance has been the ability to convert narrow private and public interests to a much larger public good. Providence represents a successful effort to create a policy environment where the total is greater than the sum of its parts.

Appendix

Providence Renaissance: Chronology of Selected Milestones

1636	Roger Williams founds Providence.
1764	The first drawbridge in Providence is built by lottery subscription.
1815	The Great Gale destroys the last drawbridge across the river connecting Weybosset with Providence.
1828	The Providence Arcade, the first indoor shopping mall in the United States, is completed.
1832	Providence is incorporated as a city.
1844	The Great Salt Cove is reduced to a water basin and park with a promenade to accommodate the newly formed Providence and Worcester Railroad.
1860s	The Woonasquatucket and Moshassuck Rivers are canalized.
1898	Union Station is completed; the cove basin is filled and the railroad tracks moved and elevated onto a viaduct—the "Chinese Wall."
1904	The Crawford Street Bridge is completed. The Rhode Island State House on Smith Hill is completed.
1928	The Masonic Temple is under construction.
1929	Construction of the Masonic Temple is halted.
1931	Theodore Francis Green Airport opens.
1959	Antoinette Downing, William Warner, and Laichlin Blair write *College Hill: A Demonstration Study* to preserve College Hill.
1961	*Downtown Providence 1970* is published; it suggests using federal urban renewal planning funds to move railroad tracks, among other projects.
1965	I-95 and I-195 are completed; the federal High Speed Ground Transportation Act is passed with Claiborne Pell as primary sponsor.
1972	The Providence Civic Center opens after a fifteen-year effort.
1973	The federal Regional Rail Reorganization Act creates the Northeast Corridor; Roger Williams National Memorial Park is com-

pleted with Senator Pell as sponsor; the Providence and Worcester Railroad becomes an independent regional freight railway.

1974   *Interface Providence*, written by Gerald Howes and others, is published; it suggests using federal NEA grant money secured by Senator Pell to change transportation patterns in Providence. Vincent "Buddy" Cianci Jr. is elected mayor. The Providence Foundation is formed.

1976   The federal Railroad Revitalization and Regulatory Reform Act is passed, including Title VII, Northeast Corridor Improvement Project, which contains funds for upgrading tracks and rehabilitating stations.

1978   The Loews Theater on Weybosset Street is restored as the Providence Performing Arts Center through the use of both private and public funds; it is among a number of other Urban Development Action Grant and federally funded projects brought together by the Providence Foundation and the mayor's office.

1978–1979   A local feasibility "track moving" study by C. E. Maguire is undertaken at the behest of the Providence Foundation; the federal Department of Transportation gives provisional approval to move the tracks.

1979–1982   The Capital Center District and Capital Center Commission are formed.

1979–1987   T. F. Green Airport is expanded.

1982   William Warner applies to the NEA for a waterfront study grant; the Providence Foundation pledges its support.

1983   The Providence Home Rule Charter takes full effect; the Westminster Street Pedestrian Plan is written; William Warner sketches plans for the Memorial Boulevard extension project to create bridges over the rivers. The NEA awards the waterfront study grant. Governor Garrahy cancels plans for an I-84 link to Hartford, leaving federal highway money available for other uses.

1984   Open meetings on the waterfront plans are held; William Warner begins his Waterplace Park feasibility study.

1984–1986   The railroad tracks are relocated and the "Chinese Wall" demolished.

1986   The Carr, Lynch/Levine Providence Development Strategy is written; Antonio Guerra makes his proposal for a mall.

1987   Providence Station is completed; the Capital Center parcels are laid out and the river relocation project begins; Waterplace Park is incorporated into the plans; the Westminster Street Pedestrian Mall fails; Alexius Conroy proposes a mall adjoining Capital Center. The Convention Center Task Force is established and reports on the feasibility of a large convention center; the state legislature establishes the Convention Center Authority.

1988   The legislature transfers the URI-CCE site to the Rhode Island Port Authority; the Providence Place Group takes options on the Amtrak property and RIPA state land.

1989   Union Station (parcel 1) restoration is completed as Cookson America headquarters.

1989   The American Express building is completed as Gateway Center.

1989–1994   Rhode Island suffers a fiscal crisis and credit union collapse; there is a national recession.

1990   CenterPlace and Citizens Bank Tower are completed; the developers of Providence Place mall withdraw, but Pyramid steps in.

1991   Work on Waterplace Park begins; Providence withdraws from the convention center deal with the state; Governor Sundlun convinces the legislature to prime the pump with a stand-alone convention center and hotel project.

1992   The Old Harbor plan for the I-195 relocation is completed.

1993   Andres Duany charrettes for downcity.

1994   The Convention Center/Westin Hotel are completed; WaterPlace Park opens; the plan for an arts and entertainment district is completed; the first WaterFire presentation takes place on New Year's Eve.

1994–1996   Three financing arrangements for the mall are negotiated.

1996   The second WaterFire presentation takes place; URI-CCE is moved to the downcity Shephard's building; land is cleared for Providence Place mall.

1997   Work begins on the mall; the Patriots' stadium deal arises and collapses.

1998   The Fleet Skating Rink opens in Kennedy Plaza.

1999   Providence Place mall opens; Senator John Chafee secures highway funding for the I-195 relocation; the *Providence 2000* comprehensive community plan is published.

1999–2004   Several downcity residential projects are under way or completed.

2000   The Courtyard by Marriott opens.

2002   I-195 relocation is under way.

2003   A new proposal to complete the Masonic Temple arises; a proposal to build G-Tech's world headquarters on parcel 9 in Capital Center is made.

2004   Upscale residential apartments are proposed for the Foundry.

Notes

PREFACE

1. Vincent A. Cianci, quoted in "Operation Plunder-Dome: Providence Development Will Weather This Storm," *Providence Journal* (6 April 2001): A-1.

CHAPTER 1

1. Stephen P. Morin, *Wall Street Journal*, 28 June 1983.

2. Jane Jacobs in the 1960s blamed policy makers and city planners for destroying cities as human communities and substituting for neighborhood vibrancy and eclecticism urban wastelands of office parks, towers, and highways. See Jane Jacobs, *The Death and Life of Great American Cities* (New York: Vintage, 1961). James Howard Kunstler in 1993 wrote about urban "dead zones" in which "every place is like no place in particular," *The Geography of Nowhere* (New York: Touchstone, 1994), 67.

3. David Rusk, *Cities without Suburbs* (Washington, D.C.: Woodrow Wilson Center Press, 1993); John O. Norquist, *The Wealth of Cities: Revitalizing the Centers of American Life* (New York: Perseus Books, 1999). See also Myron Oldfield, *Metropolitics* (Washington, D.C.: Brookings Institution Press, 1997); William Julius Wilson, *The Truly Disadvantaged: The Inner City, the Underclass, and Public Policy* (Chicago: University of Chicago Press, 1990); Anthony Downs, "The Challenge of Our Declining Big Cities," *Housing Policy Debate* 8, no. 2 (1997): 362–64.

4. *Money* is not alone in its praise of Providence. Consider this list of publications in the last few years touting the Providence renaissance: *New York Times* (six articles); *USA Today* ("one of the country's five Renaissance cities"); *Travel and Leisure* (praising the city's zoo); *Girlfriends* (one of the ten best lesbian cities); restaurant praise found in *Food and Wine, Bon Appetit*, and the *National Culinary Review*; and other favorable comments in *National Geographic, Arts and Antiques, Film and Video, Shopping Center Executive, Working Woman*, and *Governing*.

5. Mayor Vincent A. "Buddy" Cianci as quoted in Charles Mahtesian, "Buddy's Town," *Governing* (October 1998): 29.

6. *Comeback Cities* is the title of a recent book by Paul S. Grogan and Tony Proscio (Boulder, Colo.: Westview Press, 2000).

7. See Dennis R. Judd, "Constructing the Tourist Bubble," in *The Tourist City*, ed. Dennis R. Judd and Susan S. Fainstein (New Haven: Yale University Press, 1999), 35–53; Briavel Holcomb, "Marketing Cities for Tourism," in Judd and Fainstein, *Tourist City*, 54–70.

8. Bruce Ehrlich and Peter Dreier make the claim that Boston's success as a tourist destination "occurred almost by accident" in "The New Boston Discovers the Old Tourism and the Struggle for a Livable City," in Judd and Fainstein, *Tourist City*, 155.

9. Rachelle L. Levitt, *Cities Reborn* (Washington, D.C.: Urban Land Institute, 1987), and Grogan and Proscio, *Comeback Cities*, detail the efforts of a number of cities to reinvent themselves.

10. D. Massey and R. Meegan, eds., *Politics and Method* (London: Routledge and Kegan Paul, 1986), 13.

11. Duane Lockard, *New England Politics* (Princeton: Princeton University Press, 1959).

12. John Mollenkopf, *A Phoenix in the Ashes* (Princeton: Princeton University Press, 1992).

13. For a description of the tourist bubble see Judd, "Constructing the Tourist Bubble," 35–53.

14. Mark T. Motte and Laurence A. Weil, "Of Railroads and Regime Shifts: Downtown Renewal in Providence, Rhode Island," *Cities* 17, no. 1 (2000): 7–18.

CHAPTER 2

1. Floyd Hunter, *Community Power Structure* (Chapel Hill: University of North Carolina Press, 1953), is the seminal expression of elite theory. Also see Thomas R. Dye and L. Harmon Ziegler, *The Irony of Democracy*, 8th ed. (Monterey, Calif.: Brooks/Cole, 1990).

2. Robert Dahl, *Who Governs? Democracy and Power in an American City* (New Haven: Yale University Press, 1966), is the classic statement of pluralist theory. Also see David Truman, *The Governmental Process* (New York: Knopf, 1951), and Earl Latham, *The Group Basis for Politics* (New York: Octagon Books, 1965). Critics include E. E. Schattschneider, *The Semisovereign People* (New York: Holt, Rinehart and Winston, 1960).

3. Harvey L. Molotch, "Strategies and Constraints of Growth Elites," in *Business Elites and Public Policy*, ed. S. Cummings (Albany: State University of New York Press, 1988); P. Schumaker, J. Bolland, and R. Feiock, "Urban Economic Development and Community Conflict," in *Research in Urban Policy*, ed. T. Clarke (Beverly Hills: Sage, 1986); Bruce Ehrlich and Peter Dreier, "The New Boston Discovers the Old Tourism and the Struggle for a Livable City," in *The Tourist City*, ed. Dennis R. Judd and Susan S. Fainstein (New Haven: Yale University Press, 1999), 157; J. M. Levy, *Economic Development Programs for Cities, Counties and Towns* (New York: Praeger, 1990).

4. Paul P. Kantor, "The Dependent City: The Changing Political Economy of Urban Economic Development in the United States," *Urban Affairs Quarterly* 22 (1987): 493–520.

5. Hunter, *Community Power Structure*; C. W. Mills, *The Power Elite* (Oxford: Oxford University Press, 1956); Charles Lindblom, *Politics and Markets* (New York: Basic Books, 1977); T. Barnekov and D. Rich, "Privatism and the Limits of Local Economic Development Policy," *Urban Affairs Quarterly* 25 (1989): 212–38.

6. For neo-Marxist literature on urban development see Susan Fainstein et al., eds., *Restructuring the City: The Political Economy of Urban Redevelopment* (New York: Longman, 1983); William K. Tabb and Larry Sawyer, eds., *Marxism and the Metropolis* (New York: Oxford University Press, 1978).

7. Paul E. Peterson, *City Limits* (Chicago: University of Chicago Press, 1981).

8. Clarence N. Stone, "Summing Up: Urban Regimes, Development Policy, and Political Arrangements," in *The Politics of Urban Development*, ed. Clarence N. Stone and Heywood T. Sanders (Lawrence: University Press of Kansas, 1987), 269–88.

9. See Harold Seidman and Robert Gilmour, *Politics, Position and Power*, 4th ed. (New York: Oxford University Press, 1986).

10. See Anthony Downs, *An Economic Theory of Democracy* (New York: Harper and Row, 1957); and Charles M. Tiebout, "The Pure Theory of Local Expenditure," *Journal of Political Economy* 64 (October 1956): 416–24.

11. See Charles Lindblom, "The Science of Muddling Through," *Public Administration Review* 19 (1959): 79–88.

12. A more complete explanation of the "garbage can" in the policy process is found in John Kingdon, *Agendas, Alternatives and Public Policy*, 2d ed. (New York: Little, Brown, 1995). Also see Michael D. Cohen, James G. March, and John P. Olsen, "A Garbage Can Model of Organizational Choice," *Administrative Science Quarterly* 17 (1972): 1–25.

13. Michael J. Wolkoff, "Is Economic Decision-making Rational?" *Urban Affairs Quarterly* 27 (1992): 340–55; Harold Wolman, "Local Economic Development Policy: What Explains the Divergence between Policy Analysis and Political Behavior?" *Journal of Urban Affairs* 10 (1988): 19–28.

14. Stephen L. Elkin, *City and Regime in American Politics* (Chicago: University of Chicago Press, 1987).

15. For factors impelling activity and its growth see such sources as Peterson, *City Limits*; Todd Swanstrom, *The Crisis of Growth Politics: Cleveland, Kucinich and the Challenge of Urban Populism* (Philadelphia: Temple University Press, 1985); John R. Logan and Harvey L. Molotch, *Urban Fortunes: The Political Economy of Place* (Berkeley: University of California Press, 1987); Clarence N. Stone, *Regime Politics: Governing Atlanta* (Lawrence: University Press of Kansas, 1989); Michael A. Pagano and Ann O'M. Bowman, *Cityscapes and Capital* (Baltimore: Johns Hopkins University Press, 1995); Bryan D. Jones and Lynn W. Bachelor, *The Sustaining Hand*, 2d ed. (Lawrence: University Press of Kansas, 1993); Dennis R. Judd and Michael Parkinson, eds., *Leadership and Urban Regeneration* (Newbury Park, Calif.: Sage, 1990).

16. Mark Schneider, in *The Competitive City* (Pittsburgh: University of Pittsburgh Press, 1989), makes the case for the revenue outcome; John P. Blair, Rudy H. Fichtenbaum, and James A. Swaney, in "The Market for Jobs: Locational Decisions and the Competition for Economic Development," *Urban Affairs Quarterly* 20 (1984): 64–67, are more insistent on employment outcomes.

17. See P. Furdell, *Poverty and Economic Development: Views of City Hall* (Washington, D.C.: National League of Cities, 1994).

18. Ann O'M. Bowman, *The Visible Hand: Major Issues in City Economic Policy* (Washington, D.C.: National League of Cities, 1987); H. J. Rubin, "Shooting Anything That Falls: Conversations with Economic Development Practitioners," *Economic Development Quarterly* 3 (1988): 236–51.

19. C. Spindler and J. Forrester, "Economic Development Policy: Explaining Policy Preferences among Competing Models," *Urban Affairs Quarterly* 29 (1993): 28–53; Lynn W. Bachelor, "Regime Maintenance, Solution Sets, and Urban Economic Development," *Urban Affairs Quarterly* 29 (1994): 596–616.

20. The range of economic development techniques and tools can be found in the following: R. C. Feiock, "Urban Economic Development: Local Government Strategies and Their Effects," *Research in Public Policy Analysis* 4 (1987): 215–40; I. Rubin and H. J. Rubin, "Economic Development Incentives: The Poor (Cities) Pay More," *Urban Affairs Quarterly* 23 (1987): 37–62; Laura A. Reese, "Local Economic Development in Michigan: A Reliance on the Supply Side," *Economic Development Quarterly* 6 (1992): 383–93; Laura A. Reese, "Categories of Local Economic Development Techniques: An Empirical Analysis," *Policy Studies Journal* 21 (1993): 492–506; Harold Wolman with D. Spitzley, "The Politics of Local Economic Development," *Economic Development Quarterly* 10 (1996): 115–50.

21. Laura A. Reese, "Municipal Fiscal Health and Tax Abatement Policy," *Economic Development Quarterly* 5 (1991): 23–32.

22. Paul P. Kantor and S. David, *The Dependent City* (Boston: Foresman/Little, Brown, 1988).

23. Stone, "Summing Up."

24. Paul P. Kantor and H. V. Savitch, "Can Politicians Bargain with Business?" *Public Affairs Quarterly* 29 (1993): 230–55.

25. E. Goetz, "Type II Policy and Mandated Benefits in Economic Development," *Urban Affairs Quarterly* 26 (1990): 170–90.

26. Laura A. Reese, "Decision Rules in Local Economic Development," *Urban Affairs Quarterly* 28 (1993): 501–13.

27. E. B. Sharp and M. Bath, "Citizenship and Economic Development," in *Theories of Local Economic Development*, ed. R. D. Bingharn and R. Mier (Newbury Park, Calif.: Sage, 1993); K. Wong, "Economic Constraints and Political Choice in Urban Policymaking," *American Journal of Political Science* 32 (1988): 1–18.

CHAPTER 3

1. Quoted in Margaret D. Uroff, *Becoming a City: From Fishing Village to Manufacturing Center* (New York: Harcourt, Brace and World, 1968), 5.

2. William G. McLoughlin, *Rhode Island: A History* (New York: W. W. Norton, 1968).

3. M. Woodward and E. Sanderson, eds., *Providence: A Citywide Survey of Historic Resources* (Providence: Rhode Island Historical Preservation Commission, 1986), 4.

4. A comprehensive history of the economic and social changes occurring in Rhode Island and Providence in this period is found in Peter J. Coleman, *The Transformation of Rhode Island, 1790–1860* (Providence: Brown University Press, 1963); and Joseph S. Gilkeson Jr., *Middle-Class Providence, 1820–1940* (Princeton: Princeton University Press, 1986).

5. Uroff, *Becoming a City*.

6. Farhad Atash, "City Profile: Providence," *Cities* (February 1988): 24–32.

7. Woodward and Sanderson, *Providence: A Citywide Survey*, 2.

8. Mayor's Office of Community Development and the Department of Planning and Development, City of Providence, *Neighborhood Profiles* (1976, 1984).

9. Woodward and Sanderson, *Providence: A Citywide Survey*, 4.

10. Uroff, *Becoming a City*.

11. Rhode Island Department of Elementary and Secondary Education, *Information Works* (2000).

12. William E. Collins, interview by authors, Providence, R.I., 7 August 2002. This phenomenon stands in direct contrast to the experience of Hartford, Conn., where wealthy Asylum Hill residents abandoned the city in droves.

13. Collins interview, 2002; Kenneth Orenstein, interview by authors, Providence, R.I., 20 August 2001; Bruce Sundlun, interview by authors, South Kingstown, R.I., 25 September 2002.

14. Orenstein interview, 2001.

15. What was locally referred to as the "mixed-up mile" used to require those coming from central Massachusetts into Providence to meander through the city looking for a street to lead them to I-95.

16. Sundlun interview, 2002; Collins interview, 2002; Thomas Deller, interview by authors, Providence, R.I., 25 October 2002.

17. Uroff, *Becoming a City*.

18. W. K. Tabb and L. Sawers, *Snow Belt/Sun Belt* (New York: Longman, 1987).

19. Susan Fainstein, Norman Fainstein, R. C. Hill, Dennis R. Judd, and M. Smith, *Restructuring the City: The Political Economy of Urban Redevelopment* (New York: Longman, 1986), 4.

20. Rhode Island Public Expenditure Council, *The City of Providence: Tax Policies, Economic Outlook, and Competitive Performance: Final Report*, Nexus Associates (13 March 1997): 4–7.

21. Department of Planning and Development, City of Providence, *Providence 2000: The Comprehensive Plan* (1992).

22. A principal change was to shrink the city council from twenty-six members to fifteen ward-based councillors.

23. Other "quasi-public" city agencies include the Providence Water Supply Board, which owns and manages the Scituate Reservoir, about fifteen miles west of the city, the principal water supply for many communities in Rhode Island; and the Providence Housing Authority, which owns and manages public housing in the city. The Dunkin' Donuts Center, formerly the Providence Civic Center, operates under the aegis of the Providence Civic Center Authority and is managed by a private corporation (see chapter 4). Roger Williams Park is operated directly by the city, and its nationally recognized zoo is directed by the nonprofit Friends of Roger Williams Park Zoo.

24. Though the state successfully consolidated the formerly municipal health departments into one state department and brought wastewater facilities under the aegis of the state, core functions such as fire, police, and, in particular, schools have resisted any efforts at consolidation.

25. This definition is adapted from Steven Gold, *The Fiscal Crisis of the States* (Washington, D.C.: Georgetown University Press, 1995), 43.

26. John H. Bowman, Susan MacManus, and John L. Mikesell, "Mobilizing Resources for Public Services: Financing Urban Government," *Journal of Urban Affairs* 14 (1992): 317.

27. Rhode Island Public Expenditure Council, *A System Out of Balance: Rhode Island's State and Local Tax System* (May 2000), 16.

28. Rhode Island Office of Municipal Affairs, Department of Administration, *Tax Capacity and Tax Effort: Fiscal Year 2000* (2000).

29. The state also adopted certain property classification requirements designed to bring more uniformity among the thirty-nine cities and towns of the state, an eight-year phaseout of the local motor vehicle property tax, and a ten-year phaseout of taxes on retail, wholesale, and automobile inventories.

30. David R. Berman, *State and Local Politics*, 8th ed. (New York: M. E. Sharpe, 1997), 53. Following the 2000 decennial census, redistricting occurred and Providence gained population. However, under a 1996 constitutional reform, the state General Assembly reduced its membership by one-third to one hundred, reducing the Providence delegation from seventeen to thirteen.

31. *The City of Providence: Final Report*, 13, 30.

32. Michael Stanton, "The Only Game in Town," *Providence Journal* (10 December 2002): A-14.

33. Cianci successfully charged that two city council members, Robert Haxton and Anthony Merola, had to be removed from office because of their convictions in criminal cases. One other opponent was serving time, shrinking the anti-Cianci majority to 12–11. Through a series of parliamentary maneuvers Cianci was able to get several blocked appointees approved. Though the courts eventually overturned the action, the public gave Cianci a 56 percent win at the polls.

34. Mayor's Special Commission on Alternatives to the Property Tax, *Report on Financing Providence: Alternatives to the Property Tax* (February 1989): 1.

35. Subsequently state law required that no more than 33 percent of the property tax be forgiven under the homestead provision program.

36. Gary Sasse, quoted in Charles Mahtesian, "Buddy's Town," *Governing* (October 1998): 30.

CHAPTER 4

1. David Easton, "An Approach to the Analysis of Political Systems," *World Politics* 9 (April 1957): 383–400.

2. Friedrich St. Florian, interview by authors, Providence, R.I., 7 April 2003.

3. For a full account of the effort to save College Hill and the development of the College Hill plan, see Gene Bunnell, *Making Places Special* (Chicago: Planners Press, 2002), 158–73.

4. Bunnell, *Making Places Special*, 168.

5. William E. Collins, interview by authors, Providence, R.I., 7 August 2002; Kenneth Orenstein, interview by authors, Providence, R.I., 20 August 2002.

6. City of Providence, City Plan Commission, *Downtown Providence 1970* (1960), xii.

7. Ibid., xxx.

8. Ibid.

9. Kenneth Orenstein, interview by authors, Providence, R.I., 14 June 2001.

10. Samuel J. Shamoon, interviews by Mark T. Motte and Lawrence Weil, Providence, R.I., July–September 1997, reported in Mark T. Motte and Laurence A. Weil, "Of Railroads and Regime Shifts: Downtown Renewal in Providence, Rhode Island," *Cities* 17, no. 1 (2000): 7–18. See also John Perrotta, "Machine Influence on a Community Action Program: The Case of Providence, Rhode Island," *Polity* 9, no. 4 (1977): 481–502; Martha Bailey, "After Ten

Years, Mayor Doorley Finds Himself in a Dogfight," *Providence Journal* (14 September 1974): G-1.

11. Mayor Joseph Doorley, quoted in *Providence Journal* (10 September 1970): A-14.

12. Orenstein interview, 14 June 2001.

13. Mike Stanton, "A Providence Civics Lesson," *Providence Journal* (9 December 2002): A-8.

14. Ibid. At the time Richard Daley, the son of Mayor Richard Daley of Chicago, had been sent to Providence College.

15. Thomas Deller, interview by authors, Providence, R.I., 5 October 2002.

16. William Warner, interview by authors, Exeter, R.I., 22 August 2002; Orenstein interview, 14 June 2001.

17. Samuel Shamoon, interview by authors, Providence, R.I., 26 March 2003.

18. For a detailed discussion of the Providence Civic Center see Thomas Anton, "Understanding Urban Revitalization: The Case of Providence," paper presented at the annual meeting of the New England Political Science Association, Hartford, Conn., 5–6 May 2000.

19. Governor Dennis Roberts, Transmittal Letter to the Rhode Island General Assembly, Proposed Civic Center, Providence, Rhode Island, 19 March 1958. In addition to the Civic Center, this plan envisioned tearing down the nineteenth century seat of local government and constructing in its place a new city hall and state and federal office building.

20. John Chafee lost his bid for a fourth two-year term after a contentious election battle focused to a large extent on his state's sales and income tax plans.

21. Stanley Bernstein, Kenneth Orenstein, and Samuel J. Shamoon, interviews in Motte and Weil, "Of Railroads and Regime Shifts," 7–18.

22. Orenstein interview, 14 June 2001.

23. Bailey, "Mayor Doorley Finds Himself in a Dogfight," G-1.

24. Virtually all of those interviewed concerning this period were adamant that urgency was the correct way to characterize the feeling in Providence among business and government officials.

25. Orenstein interview, 14 June 2001.

26. Ibid.; William E. Collins, interview by authors, Providence, R.I., 22 August 2002.

27. Rhode Island School of Design, *The First Circular* (1878). RISD was founded through the efforts of the Metcalf family, prominent Providence manufacturers and eventual owners of the *Providence Journal*.

28. See M. Charles Bakst, "Claiborne Pell: A Unique Legacy," *Providence Journal* (8 December 1996): D-1.

29. Kenneth Payne, interview by authors, Providence, R.I., 20 September 2002.

30. Ibid.

31. Ibid.

32. Romolo Marsella, interview by authors, Providence, R.I., 30 October 2002.

33. Daniel Baudouin, interview by authors, Providence, R.I., 11 March 2003.

34. Orenstein interview, 20 August 2002; "Providence Waterfront Study/Memorial Boulevard River Relocation Project: Ingredients for Success/Overcoming Obstacles & Lessons for Other Communities," unpublished document, 2003.

35. Kenneth Payne, interview by authors, Providence, R.I., 17 September 2002.

36. Assistant state prosecutor Cianci was the lead investigator on the prosecution that indicted and brought to trial the then prominent New England crime figure Raymond Patriarca in 1972. Patriarca was acquitted. Stanton, "A Providence Civics Lesson," A-9.

37. Patricia McLaughlin, interview by authors, Providence, R.I., 23 December 2002.

38. Edward Sanderson, interview by authors, Providence, R.I., 28 April 2003.

39. Ibid.

40. Marsella, transcript of interview with Linda Wood, Providence, R.I., 20 November 2002, p. 8.

41. Collins interview, 7 August 2002. The foundation's first director was Joseph Madonna of Detroit, who had worked on the renaissance project in that city.

42. Romolo Marsella, quoted in Doug Riggs, "Into the Future," *Providence Sunday Journal Magazine* (25 October 1992): 10.

43. Sanderson interview, 28 April 2003.

44. Marsella interview, 30 October 2002.

45. Marsella, transcript of interview with Wood, p. 6.

46. Marsella interview, 30 October 2002.

47. Clarence Stone, "Regime Analysis and the Study of Urban Politics, a Rejoinder," *Journal of Urban Affairs* 20, no. 3 (Summer 1998): 249–61.

48. Payne interview, 17 September 2002.

CHAPTER 5

1. Samuel J. Shamoon, interview by authors, Providence, R.I., 15 June 2001.

2. Louis Thompson, Federal Railway Administration Regional Administrator, quoted in Russell Garland, "Federal Official, in from the Start, Checks Rail Shifting and Likes What He Sees," *Providence Journal* (12 July 1985): A-1.

3. U.S. Department of Transportation, Federal Railroad Administration, *Northeast Corridor High Speed Rail Passenger Service Improvement Project: Task 1 Demand Analysis*, a final report prepared by Bechtel Corporation (Washington, D.C.: April 1975), 3-1.

4. M. Charles Bakst, "Claiborne Pell: A Unique Legacy," *Providence Journal* (8 December 1996): D-1.

5. President Kennedy had secured a small study grant for the high-speed rail idea prior to his assassination in November 1963.

6. Bakst, "Claiborne Pell," D-1.

7. See *Destination Freedom: The Newsletter of the National Corridor Initiative: Special Edition* 1, no. 12 (30 June 2000).

8. In addition, a TurboTrain established a New York–Boston run.

9. U.S. Congress, Senate, Committee on Commerce, Subcommittee on Surface Transportation, *Passenger Train Service: Hearings on S. 674*, 91st Cong., 1st sess., 1969, 30, 70, in Lloyd Musolf, *Uncle Sam's Private, Profitseeking Corporations* (Lexington, Mass.: D. C. Heath, 1983), 50.

10. The story of Amtrak's successes and failures is documented in David Nice, *Amtrak: The History and Politics of a National Railroad* (Boulder, Colo.: Lynne Rienner, 1998).

11. Also known as the 3-R Act, it created the United States Railway Association. Penn Central was reorganized out of bankruptcy and what became a quasi-government corporation known as Conrail was created. For a full account of the railroad crisis in the United States during the 1960s–70s, see National Academy of Public Administration, *The Great*

Railway Crisis: An Administrative History of the United States Railway Association (Washington, D.C.: National Academy of Public Administration, 1978).

12. *Northeast Corridor High Speed Rail Passenger Service Improvement Project*, 1-1.

13. Skidmore, Owings and Merrill, *Capital Center Project: Development Plan*, prepared for the Providence Foundation in association with the City of Providence and State of Rhode Island (1 May 1979), 7.

14. Bruce Sundlun, interview by authors, South Kingstown, R.I., 25 September 2002.

15. Kenneth Orenstein, interview by authors, Providence, R.I., 20 August 2001.

16. Joseph Arruda, interview by authors, Coventry, R.I., 14 April 2003.

17. Romolo Marsella, interview by authors, Providence, R.I., 30 October 2002.

18. Marsella interview, 30 October 2002.

19. Milly McLean, "Moving Heaven and Earth," *Rhode Island Monthly* (February 1989): 33; Marsella interview, 30 October 2002; Bruce Sundlun, interview by authors, South Kingstown, R.I., 21 June 2001.

20. Marsella interview, 30 October 2002.

21. Bruce Sundlun, interviews by authors, Providence, R.I., 24 August 1999 and 25 September 2002; Marsella interview, 30 October 2002.

22. Arruda interview, 14 April 2003; Shamoon interview, 15 June 2001.

23. Gordon Hoxie, interview by authors, Providence, R.I., 13 September 2002.

24. Kenneth Payne, interview by authors, Providence, R.I., 17 September 2002.

25. J. Joseph Garrahy, interview by authors, Providence, R.I., 10 June 2003.

26. Governor J. Joseph Garrahy as quoted in McLean, "Moving Heaven and Earth," 33.

27. Garrahy interview, 10 June 2003.

28. Vincent A. "Buddy" Cianci as quoted in McLean, "Moving Heaven and Earth," 33.

29. McLean, "Moving Heaven and Earth," 34.

30. Ibid., 32; Marsella interview, 30 October 2002.

31. McLean, "Moving Heaven and Earth," 32; Arruda interview, 14 April 2003.

32. Marsella interview, 30 October 2002.

33. Skidmore, Owings and Merrill, *Capital Center Project: Development Plan*, 50.

34. The station at Stamford, Conn., was the other.

35. Payne interview, 17 September 2002.

36. Gregory Smith, "A Conversation with Capital Center Chief Engineer Wendell Flanders," *Providence Journal* (1 July 1996): C-1.

37. A dispute between the state and Amtrak over ownership and easement rights eventually would be resolved.

38. For the creation of the nineteenth-century railroad network in Rhode Island and southern New England, see Stewart P. Schneider, "Railroad Development in Rhode Island during the Nineteenth Century," *Rhode Island History* 61, no. 2: 37–47.

39. Eder and DiStefano met because the latter worked for the Del Sesto and Del Sesto law firm that was representing Eder in his attempts to establish a gasoline distributorship and retail outlet. Eder had gone to Harvard Law School with former governor Del Sesto's son. William E. Collins, "Joe DiStefano Is the Man to See in Capital Center," *Ocean State Business* 5, no. 3 (12–25 September 1988): 1–16; Joseph R. DiStefano, interview by authors, Providence, R.I., 12 June 2003.

40. The New Haven Railroad and the Penn Central Railroad would both go bankrupt.

41. DiStefano interview, 12 June 2003.

42. Capital Properties assembled the land through claims based on the 1892 lease agreement and a 1935 lease agreement, the Providence Terminal Agreement. Collins, "Joe DiStefano Is the Man to See," 1–16.

43. Arruda interview, 14 April 2003.

44. Romolo Marsella, interview by Mark T. Motte and Lawrence Weil, Providence, R.I., 12 August 1997.

45. Gene Bunnel, *Making Places Special* (Chicago: Planners Press, 2000), 177–78.

46. Marsella interview, 30 October 2002.

47. William E. Collins, "Joseph R. DiStefano: City Builder," *Ocean State Business* 6, no. 6 (16–29 January 1989): 7.

48. DiStefano interview, 12 June 2003.

49. William E. Collins, interview by authors, Providence, R.I., 7 August 2002.

50. W. Edward Wood, interview by authors, Hopkinton, R.I., 4 October 2002.

51. Arruda interview, 14 April 2003.

52. Collins, "Joseph R. DiStefano: City Builder," 7.

53. Marsella interview, 30 October 2002.

54. Orenstein interview, 20 August 2002; Sundlun interview, 25 September 2002.

55. Hoxie interview, 13 September 2002.

56. Shamoon interview, 15 June 2001.

57. Chester Smolski, "Downtown Revitalization," *Town and Country Planning* (May 1980): 153–56.

58. Jacques V. Hopkins, Esq., letter to Robert E. Freeman, Executive Director, Providence Foundation, 21 January 1992.

59. Skidmore, Owings and Merrill, *Capital Center Project: Development Plan*, 9.

60. In the 1990s, after its formative work was completed, Governor Sundlun shifted the team into the Department of Transportation.

61. James R. Capaldi, interview by authors, Providence, R.I., 30 September 2003.

62. In 1983 the authorizing legislation would be amended to add three more members: from the Rhode Island House, appointed by the Speaker; from the Senate, appointed by the majority leader; and an additional governor's appointment.

63. Orenstein interview, 20 August 2002; Sundlun interview, 21 June 2002.

64. Skidmore, Owings and Merrill, *Capital Center Project: Development Plan*, 9.

65. Ibid., 13.

66. Orenstein interview, 20 August 2002.

67. Bunnell, *Making Places Special*, 202.

68. Edward Sanderson, interview by authors, Providence, R.I., 28 April 2003.

69. Edward Sanderson, quoted in Bill Van Siclen, "There Is Room for Improvement," *Providence Journal* (30 May 1997): A-1.

70. Capital Center Commission, *Design and Development Criteria* (Providence, October 1980), 1.

71. Ibid., 33; Skidmore, Owings and Merrill, *Capital Center Project: Development Plan*, Section 4.

72. The design and development regulations were amended twice prior to 1985 and sub-

stantially revised in 1985 in response to the river relocation project; again between 1989 and 1995 in response to Providence Place mall plans; and later in 2003 in response to a number of residential proposals.

73. Wendell Flanders, quoted in Smith, "A Conversation with Wendell Flanders," C-1.

74. Arruda interview, 14 April 2003.

75. Louis Thompson, quoted in Russell Garland, "Federal Official," A-5.

76. Bunnell, *Making Places Special*, 185.

77. Collins interview, 7 August 2002.

78. Joseph Paolino, interview by authors, Providence, R.I., 11 June 2001.

79. Office of the Governor, State of Rhode Island, *Retail Market Analysis: Providence Place*, Final Report prepared by HSG/Gould Associates (May 1995), 6–7.

CHAPTER 6

1. William D. Warner, "An Abbreviated History of the Waterplace Park and River Relocation Projects" (unpublished manuscript); William D. Warner, interview by authors, Exeter, R.I., 22 August 2002; Friedrich St. Florian, interview by authors, Providence, R.I., 7 April 2003.

2. Warner, "Abbreviated History," 3.

3. William D. Warner, interview by authors, Exeter, R.I., 13 December 2001.

4. Kenneth Orenstein, interview by authors, Providence, R.I., 20 August 2002.

5. W. Edward Wood, interview by authors, Hopkinton, R.I., 4 October 2002. Wood articulated this idea most forcefully, but every other person interviewed also made the same point about Warner and his work.

6. Gregory Smith, "Capital Gains," *Providence Journal* (1 November 1999): C-1.

7. Peter Phipps, "Along Providence's Rivers, City's History Ebbs and Flows," *Providence Sunday Journal* (19 April 1998): D-1–2.

8. Ibid.

9. Michael Holleran, "Filling the Providence Cove: Image in the Evolution of Urban Form," *Rhode Island History* 48, no. 3 (August 1990): 65–85; Providence Preservation Society, Historical Guides to Providence, *Downtown Providence: Celebrating the Past, Meeting the Future* (1997).

10. Providence City Plan Commission, *Master Plan for Thorofares* (22 July 1946).

11. William D. Warner, "The Providence Waterfront, 1636–2000" (unpublished manuscript, 1985).

12. Skidmore, Owings and Merrill, *Capital Center Project: Development Plan* (1 May 1979), 22.

13. Capital Center Commission, *Design and Development Criteria* (October 1980), 31.

14. Paul Philippe Cret, a French veteran of World War I and graduate of the Ecole des Beaux Arts in Paris, was commissioned in 1924 by the American Battle Monuments Commission to design three World War I monuments in Europe and to supervise the Monument Commission's architects. He also designed the Federal Reserve Building in Washington, D.C. The Providence monument was dedicated 11 November 1929 at a ceremony featuring Sgt. Alvin C. York, the celebrated World War I infantryman, as the main speaker.

15. Warner interview, 13 December 2001.

16. Gordon Hoxie, interview by authors, Providence, R.I., 13 September 2002.

17. James R. Capaldi, interview by authors, Providence, R.I., 30 September 2003.

18. Joseph Arruda, interview by authors, Coventry, R.I., 14 April 2003.

19. Keith Lange, interview by authors, Providence, R.I., 20 September 2002.

20. That the senators were the driving force in securing funds for the project and that the various first and second congressional representatives assisted both senators was a point made by most of those interviewed.

21. Capaldi interview, 30 September 2003.

22. Ibid.

23. J. Joseph Garrahy, interview by authors, Providence, R.I., 10 June 2003, ; Wood interview, 4 October 2002.

24. Wood interview, 4 October 2002.

25. Hoxie interview, 13 September 2002.

26. Ibid.

27. Ibid.

28. Ibid.

29. Wood interview, 4 October 2002.

30. Warner, "Abbreviated History," 3.

31. Wood interview, 4 October 2002. Garrahy wanted Wood to replace William Harsch as director of the newly formed DEM when Harsch left to work for the Carter administration.

32. Garrahy interview, 10 June 2003. A number of Garrahy appointees made this same point: that the governor granted considerable latitude in decision making concerning road and associated transportation projects.

33. Wood interview, 4 October 2002.

34. Warner, "Abbreviated History," 3.

35. The application asked for funding to study the Seekonk River eastern shore; Fox and India Points on the southern shore of the East Side of Providence; and the Providence River up to Memorial Square.

36. Gene Bunnell, *Making Places Special* (Chicago: Planners Press, 2000), 180; Kenneth Orenstein, interview by authors, Providence, R.I., 14 June 2002; Warner interview, 13 December 2001.

37. Warner interview, 22 August 2002.

38. Capaldi interview, 30 September 2003.

39. Wood interview, 4 October 2002; Arruda interview, 14 April 2003.

40. Dan Stets, "Cianci, Garrahy Unite on Effort for Waterfront," *Providence Journal* (7 February 1983).

41. In an "only in Rhode Island" story, before he came into the Cianci administration, Collins was Wood's successor as the city politics beat reporter for the *Providence Journal*.

42. William E. Collins, interview by authors, Providence, R.I., 7 August 2002.

43. Mayor Vincent A. Cianci, quoted in Stets, "Cianci, Garrahy Unite on Effort for Waterfront."

44. Governor J. Joseph Garrahy, quoted in Stets, "Cianci, Garrahy Unite on Effort for Waterfront."

45. City of Providence, Department of Planning and Development, *Memorandum to the Members of the Design Subcommittee* (15 February 1983).

46. Kenneth Orenstein, quoted in Milly McLean, "Moving Heaven and Earth," *Rhode Island Monthly* (February 1989): 35; Orenstein interview, 14 June 2001.

47. Warner interview, 20 August 2002.

48. Warner, "Abbreviated History," 4; Orenstein interview, 14 June 2001.

49. Joseph R. DiStefano, interview by authors, Providence, R.I., 12 June 2003.

50. Warner interview, 13 December 2001; Orenstein interview, 14 June 2001.

51. Lange interview, 20 September 2002.

52. Warner interview, 13 December 2001.

53. Kenneth Payne, interview by authors, Providence, R.I., 17 September 2002.

54. Orenstein interview, 14 June 2001; Collins interview, 7 August 2002.

55. Hoxie interview, 13 September 2002; Lange interview, 20 September 2002; Wood interview, 4 October 2002; Arruda interview, 19 April 2003.

56. Joseph Paolino Jr., quoted in Charles Mahtesian, "Buddy's Town," *Governing* (October 1998): 29.

57. Warner interview, 13 December 2001.

58. William D. Warner, quoted in Dan Stets, "A Vision of Providence," *Providence Sunday Journal Magazine* (26 August 1984): 14.

59. Kenneth Orenstein, interview by authors, Providence, R.I., 22 August 2002; Warner interview, 22 August 2002.

60. Bunnell, *Making Places Special*, 181.

61. Arruda interview, 19 April 2003.

62. Kenneth Orenstein, "Providence Waterfront Study/Memorial Boulevard River Relocation Project Ingredients for Success/Overcoming Obstacles & Lessons for Other Communities" (unpublished document, 2003).

63. Warner, "Abbreviated History," 6.

64. William D. Warner, interview by authors, Exeter, R.I., 1 April 2003.

65. The type of reprogramming of funds that Senator Chafee was able to achieve for this project was the predecessor of the flexibility mandated today by ISTEA (Intermodal Surface Transportation Efficiency Act) and TEA-21 (Transportation Equity Act for the 21st Century) legislation, which guides intermodal transportation in the United States.

66. Two successive road bond issues failed to pass. In addition to the death of I-84, I-895 and an I-295 loop extension through the East Bay to Warren, R.I., were shelved.

67. Wood interview, 4 October 2002; Joseph Arruda, interview by authors, Coventry, R.I., 15 April 2003. In addition, the passage of the Nickel Act as part of the amended Federal Interstate Highway Act in 1981 provided the funds to Rhode Island that made the highway projects in Providence even more feasible. This act raised the federal gas tax by five cents per gallon.

68. Wood interview, 4 October 2002; Garrahy interview, 10 June 2003. At this time commitments were also made to undertake the Route 99 Woonsocket, R.I., bypass; the Route 4 extension project in South County; and—most significant—the building of the new Jamestown Bridge.

69. Collins interview, 7 August 2002.

70. Capaldi interview, 30 September 2003.

71. Ibid.

72. This delay would eventually result in the Old Harbor Plan, which is detailed in chapter 12.

73. Orenstein, "Providence Waterfront Study."

74. Warner interview, 20 August 2002.

75. Wood interview, 4 October 2002.

76. Ibid.; Arruda interview, 19 April 2003.

77. Capaldi interview, 30 September 2003.

78. Ibid.

79. Garrahy interview, 10 June 2003; Wood interview, 4 October 2002.

80. Samuel J. Shamoon, interview by authors, Providence, R.I., 15 June 2001; Hoxie interview, 13 September 2002; Wood interview, 4 October 2002.

81. Bunnell, *Making Places Special*, 181; Romolo Marsella, interview by authors, Providence, R.I., 30 October 2002.

82. Warner interview, 22 August 2002.

83. Joseph DiStefano, quoted in Dan Stets, "RI, P&W Clash on River Relocation," *Providence Journal* (11 July 1984): A-18.

84. Warner, "Abbreviated History," 6.

85. Bruce Sundlun, interview by authors, South Kingstown, R.I., 21 June 2001.

86. Wood interview, 4 October 2002.

87. Sundlun interview, 21 June 2001.

88. DiStefano interview, 12 June 2003.

89. Orenstein, "Providence Waterfront Study."

90. Romolo Marsella, transcript of interview with Linda and Ed Wood, 12 December 2003, 19. The negotiation and litigation surrounding this agreement was finally completed in 2003.

91. Capital Center Commission, *Design and Development Criteria Incorporating Revisions in Response to the Relocation of the Woonasquatucket and Moshassuck Rivers* (8 August 1985), 39.

92. Marsella, transcript, 12 December 2002.

93. Payne interview, 17 September 2002.

94. Orenstein interview, 22 August 2002.

95. Warner interview, 1 April 2003.

96. Warner, "Abbreviated History," 9.

97. Collins interview, 7 August 2002.

98. Hoxie interview, 13 September 2002.

99. Warner, "Abbreviated History," 10.

100. St. Florian interview, 7 April 2003. "Memory piece" is St. Florian's descriptive term.

101. Warner, "Abbreviated History," 9. Whyte is the author of *The Organization Man* (New York: Simon and Schuster, 1956) and other works such as *The Social Life of Small Urban Spaces* (Washington, D.C.: Conservation Foundation, 1980).

102. A small dispute erupted in the 1980s over whether the towering monument could be dismantled at all; a number of architects insisted to Warner that the monument could not be taken apart. Warner sought out the original plans for the monument in Philadelphia and found that it could. Warner interview, 13 December 2001.

103. Wendell Flanders, quoted in Gregory Smith, "City Park to Have Official Debut," *Providence Journal* (10 July 1996): B-1.

104. Barnaby Evans, interview by authors, Providence, R.I., 7 April 2003. H. P. Lovecraft lived in Providence and is buried in Swan Point Cemetery on the city's East Side.

105. Evans interview, 7 April 2003.

106. Ibid.

107. Ibid.

108. Barbara Ashley, Senior Vice President, Taubman Companies, quoted in "Providence Place Shoots for Autumn Opening," *Providence Business News* 10, no. 3 (1995): 7.

109. Collins interview, 7 August 2002.

110. Warner interview, 1 April 2003.

111. Providence Preservation Society, *Downtown Providence: Celebrating the Past, Meeting the Future* (Providence, R.I., 1997): 2.

CHAPTER 7

1. William E. Collins, interview by authors, Providence, R.I., 7 August 2002. This meeting was hosted by Textron CEO William Miller, President Jimmy Carter's secretary of the treasury.

2. Bernard Frieden and Lynn B. Sagalyn, *Downtown Inc.: How America Rebuilds Cities* (Cambridge, Mass.: MIT Press, 1989), 7.

3. Melvin Simon, quoted in Frieden and Sagalyn, *Downtown Inc.*, 84.

4. Frieden and Sagalyn, *Downtown Inc.*, 172.

5. Ibid., 136–37. Compressed space presents another obstacle because it requires multistory malls, making such costly items as escalators and elevators a necessity.

6. Ibid., 77.

7. Dean Schwanke, *Remaking the Shopping Center* (Washington, D.C.: Urban Land Institute, 1994).

8. In the early 1960s the same area had been established as a pedestrian mall but failed. City policy makers then reopened the streets until the 1986 *Pedestrian Plan* surfaced.

9. Kenneth Orenstein, interview by authors, Providence, R.I., 20 August 2002; Joseph R. Paolino, interview by authors, Providence, R.I., 11 June 2001.

10. Paolino interview, 11 June 2001.

11. Greg Chapman, "Persistence Pays Off for Providence Place Developer," *Providence Business News* (3 March 1997).

12. Collins interview, 7 August 2002.

13. In 1982 Guerra, who had bought the property from the Sharpe family, unsuccessfully tried to obtain financing for a similar proposal in another part of town.

14. Russell Garland, "Stores, Offices Planned at Old Brown and Sharpe Site in Providence," *Providence Journal* (25 June 1986): A-1.

15. Economic Research Associates completed the survey. ERA also had worked for a city-state task force studying the feasibility of building a convention center in Providence.

16. Joseph R. Paolino, *Inaugural Address to the People of Providence*, 5 January 1987; repeated in Joseph R. Paolino, Mayor of the City of Providence, *Third Annual State of the City Address to the Providence City Council* (January 1987), 10.

17. Edward Sanderson, interview by authors, Providence, R.I., 28 April 2003.

18. Bruce Sundlun, interview by authors, South Kingstown, R.I., 21 June 2001. At the time Simon and Associates had developed 134 shopping centers in twenty-five states and owned sixty-two malls. The Simon brothers also owned the Indiana Pacers basketball team.

19. Paolino interview, 11 June 2001.

20. Ibid.; Sundlun interview, 21 June 2002.

21. Romolo Marsella, quoted in Russell Garland, "Project Gets Upscale Push," *Providence Journal* (6 January 1987): A-3.

22. Paolino interview, 11 June 2001.

23. A separate payment of $2 million from the city to the state for river relocation was made when the city sold the Majestic Garage on Washington Street to a private developer.

24. Paolino interview, 11 June 2001.

25. Wendy Nicholas, Providence Preservation Society Executive Director, quoted in John Castellucci, "Preservationists Find Fault with Plan for the Providence Place Mall," *Providence Journal* (14 October 1988): C-1.

26. Sundlun interview, 21 June 2001.

27. The authority was created in 1974 to oversee the development of Quonset Point in North Kingstown, R.I., and to acquire land for economic development. It had the power to issue revenue bonds protecting the state taxpayer from having the burden of paying for any state general obligation debt.

28. Alexius Conroy, quoted in John Castellucci, "Builders Sign Pact to Buy 7 Acres for Providence Place," *Providence Journal* (26 October 1988): A-3.

29. Joseph R. Paolino, quoted in John Castellucci, "Panel to Allow Big Stores in Capital Center," *Providence Journal* (16 June 1989): B-1.

30. Sanderson interview, 28 April 2003.

31. Wendy Nicholas, quoted in John Castellucci, "Panel to Add Mall Site to Capital Center," *Providence Journal* (13 January 1989): C-1.

32. Frederick Williamson, quoted in Castellucci, "Panel to Allow Big Stores," B-1.

33. Joseph R. Paolino, quoted in John Castellucci, "Capital Center Shelves Guidelines," *Providence Journal* (14 July 1989): C-1.

34. Using the bonding authority of the quasi-governmental Providence Off-Street Public Parking Corporation to help build the garage was discussed in 1987. That entity had the legal authority to borrow up to $50 million in tax-exempt bonds for garages.

CHAPTER 8

1. For a detailed analysis of Rhode Island budgetary politics in this period, see Francis J. Leazes Jr. and Robert Sieczkiewicz, "Budget Policy and Fiscal Crisis: A Political Matrix," *New England Journal of Public Policy* 10, no. 2 (Fall/Winter 1994): 71–82.

2. State of Rhode Island, Department of Economic Development, *Basic Economic Statistics* (1990, 1992, 1994).

3. Darrell M. West, Thomas J. Anton, and Jack D. Coombs, *Public Opinion Polling in Rhode Island: 1984–1993* (Providence: Brown University, Taubman Center for Public Policy and American Institutions, 1994), 70. In addition to the recession and the RISDIC banking crisis, Rhode Island voters were buffeted by stories of alleged misdoings by the Rhode Island Speaker of the House and Governor Edward D. DiPrete.

4. Paolino had run against Sundlun in the Democratic primary.

5. For a short period Providence Place was renamed the Mall of New England.

6. Bruce Sundlun, interview by authors, South Kingstown, R.I., 21 June 2001.

7. Joseph R. Paolino, interview by authors, Providence, R.I., 11 June 2001.

8. They replaced RTKL Associates of Baltimore.

9. The CCC hired Harvard's director of urban design programs, Alex Krieger, to replace Taylor.

10. Rhode Island General Assembly, Senate Commission to Study and Investigate Any and All Contracts between the Rhode Island Port Authority and Providence Place Mall, *Final Report* (19 December 1994), 6–8.

11. John Sasso, quoted in John Castellucci, "Capital Center Mall Plan Alive," *Providence Journal* (12 December 1992): B-1.

12. "Another Extension Granted to Providence Place," *Providence Journal* (3 March 1992): E-1. The first extension was granted to Melvin Simon three months before he dropped out. In June 1991 an extension was granted to Pyramid.

13. Rhode Island General Assembly, Providence Place Mall Commission *Final Report*, 6–8.

14. John Sasso, quoted in Castellucci, "Renewal Projects Raise Concerns," *Providence Journal* (24 March 1991): B-1.

15. John Bersani, Pyramid general manager, quoted in John Castellucci, "DiPrete Opposes State Financing of Downtown Mall," *Providence Journal* (14 June 1990): B-1.

16. Gordon Hoxie, interview by authors, Providence, R.I., 13 September 2002.

17. Castellucci, "DiPrete Opposes State Financing of Downtown Mall," B-1.

18. Castellucci, "Renewal Projects Raise Concerns," B-1.

19. Ibid.

20. William E. Collins, interview by authors, Providence, R.I., 7 August 2002; Bruce Sundlun, interview by authors, South Kingston, R.I., 25 September 2002.

21. Collins interview, 7 August 2002.

22. Governor Dennis Roberts, Transmittal Letter To The Rhode Island General Assembly, 1958, State House Library, Providence, R.I.

23. Rhode Island Development Council, *Preliminary Feasibility Study for a Convention/Civic Center and Visitors Reception Center in Newport, Rhode Island*, by E.B.S. Management Consultants, Inc. (August 1969).

24. The Providence Foundation, *A Brief Outline of Twenty Years of Effort to Build a Convention/Exhibition Complex in Providence, RI, 1961–1981* (1981).

25. City of Providence, Office of the Mayor, *The Downtown Providence Development Strategy*, by Melvin F. Levine and Associates and Carr, Lynch Associates of Cambridge, Mass. (1984).

26. State of Rhode Island and City of Providence Convention Center Task Force, *Feasibility Evaluation of New Convention Facilities in Providence, Rhode Island*, by Economics Research Associates and Howard, Needles, Tammen and Bergendoff (April 1987).

27. Ibid.

28. R.I.G.L. Title 42, Chapter 99, sections 1–22, "An Act Establishing the Rhode Island Convention Center."

29. Act of the General Assembly, *Rhode Island General Laws Title 42, Chapter 99 (As Amended)*.

30. Mollicone's bank was forced to declare insolvency during the credit union crisis in 1991. It was discovered that his bank executed multimillion-dollar loans to friends and associates "off the books." Mollicone fled the state and went into hiding in Utah for several months after his dealings were uncovered. He then surrendered to local authorities. Fellow Convention Center Authority member Thomas DiLuglio acted as intermediary. Mollicone served ten years in prison.

31. The Convention Center Authority established ten committees to oversee the development of the structure: Site Selection, Construction, Finance, Human Resources, Operations, Hotel Negotiations, Project Development, the Arts, Channel 36 Television Station Relocation, and Food Services.

32. Richard Oster, interview by authors, Barrington, R.I., 28 January 2003.

33. Cianci had to fight his way onto the ballot. He had been sentenced to a five-year term following his assault conviction in 1984. There was some question as to whether he was permitted to run under city ordinance, state law, and the state constitution.

34. Patricia McLaughlin, interview by authors, Providence, R.I., 23 December 2002.

35. John Castellucci, "Cianci, Sundlun Consider Providence Place Subsidy," *Providence Journal* (1 November 1991): B-1.

36. Sundlun interviews, 21 June 2001 and 25 September 2002.

37. Bruce Sundlun, "Big Projects Have Been a Big Help," *Providence Journal* (16 November 1997): D-14.

38. Sundlun interviews, 21 June 2001 and 25 September 2002.

39. Named for its sponsor, State Representative Linda Kushner, a Democrat from Providence's East Side.

40. Sundlun interviews, 21 June 2001 and 25 September 2002.

41. Rhode Island Convention Center Authority, *Rhode Island Convention Center Feasibility Study*, Coopers and Lybrand (Providence, 1991).

42. Oster interview, 27 January 2003. Among these prerogatives were involvement in setting room rates and determining the length of the contract with the Westin management.

43. Sundlun interviews, 21 June 2001 and 25 September 2002.

44. Oster interview, 27 January 2003.

45. Rhode Island Convention Center Authority, *Destination, Rhode Island* (1993).

46. John Castellucci, "Building Boom," *Providence Journal* (28 November 1993): M-8.

47. John Castellucci, "It's Built: But Will They Come?" *Providence Journal* (28 November 1993); Bill Van Siclen, "Convention Center Strikes a Healthy Balance," *Providence Journal* (28 November 1993).

48. Kenneth Orenstein, interviews by authors, Providence, R.I., 14 June 2001 and 20 August 2002; Sundlun interviews, 21 June 2001 and 25 September 2002; Oster interview, 28 January 2003.

49. Rhode Island Convention Center Authority, *Financial and Fiscal Overview, FY*

1995–FY 2027, Report submitted to Mayor Vincent A. Cianci Jr. and Governor Bruce Sund-lun (Providence, 1994).

50. John Castellucci, "Convention Center Costs Rise," *Providence Journal* (23 December 1992); John Castellucci, "Bottom Line Cost Figure Depends on Where the Line Is Drawn," *Providence Journal* (28 November 1993).

51. John Castellucci, "Rumors of Gaming Continue to Surface," *Providence Journal* (28 November 1993).

52. Elliot Krieger, "Conventions Add $2.3 Million to State Coffers," *Providence Journal* (9 June 1997).

53. Timothy Tyrrell, professor of Resource Economics, University of Rhode Island, tele-phone interview by authors, 21 February 2003.

54. James Bennet, chair of the Rhode Island Convention Center Authority, "Commen-tary," *Providence Journal* (1 June 2000).

55. Warren Trafton, Inc., *Sales and Marketing Plan for the Rhode Island Convention Center Authority* (1995).

56. Russell Garland, "Hospitality Does Pay," *Providence Journal* (2 September 2000).

57. Bennet, "Commentary."

58. Sophie Morse, Carol Surprenant, and Timothy Tyrrell, *The Economic Impact of the Rhode Island Convention Center: FY 1996*, University of Rhode Island College of Resource De-velopment, Department of Environmental and Natural Resource Economics and Research Center in Business and Economics (1997).

59. Garland, "Hospitality Does Pay."

60. In addition to the actual cost of construction, the $356.4 million price tag for the Convention Center included $56.2 million in capitalized interest payable on Convention Center Authority revenue bonds; $32 million for assembling the four required land parcels; $25.1 million to establish a debt-service reserve fund; $16.5 million for Convention Center Authority consultants, bond experts, and lawyers; $11.6 million in bond insurance costs; and $1 million to establish a maintenance fund. John Castellucci, "It's Built: But Will They Come," *Providence Journal* (28 November 1993): A-11.

61. Edward Fitzpatrick, *Providence Journal* (12 February 2003): A-1.

62. The Rhode Island Economic Development Corporation leases space in the domed office building adjoining the hotel's atrium, effectively offsetting a portion of the operational deficit and making the annual average subsidy close to $21 million.

63. Morse et al., *The Economic Impact of the Rhode Island Convention Center: FY 1996*.

64. Ibid.

65. Rhode Island Convention Center Authority, *Report to the Governor and General As-sembly* (1995–2002).

66. Warren Trafton, Inc., *Sales and Marketing Plan for the Rhode Island Convention Center Authority* (1995).

67. Downtown observers have commented on the "robbing Peter to pay Paul" effect that has reduced long-standing bookings at the Providence Civic Center by event coordinators who now choose the Convention Center.

68. Richard Oster interview, 27 January 2003.

69. Krieger, "Conventions Add $2.3 Million to State Coffers."

70. Ibid.

CHAPTER 9

1. Red Alerts were paid policy advertisements sponsored by local manufacturer Tyco's CEO, John Hazen White.

2. Romolo Marsella, interview by authors, Providence, R.I., 30 October 2002.

3. Aram Garabedian, "The Right Deal Is 'No Deal': No Taxpayer Money for Providence Place Mall," Testimony before the Rhode Island Corporations Committee on Behalf of the Owners, Customers, Employees and Friends of the Warwick, Rhode Island, and Lincoln Malls and the People of Rhode Island, 20 July 1995.

4. Bruce Sundlun, interview by authors, South Kingstown, R.I., 21 June 2001.

5. Gordon Hoxie, interview by authors, Providence, R.I., 13 September 2002.

6. William E. Collins, interview by authors, Providence, R.I., 29 August 2002. HOV refers to two or more occupants in a vehicle.

7. Barry Schiller, quoted in Steve Winter, "DOT Wants 5,000 Car Garage," *Providence Journal* (12 November 1993): A-1.

8. Senator John Chafee, quoted in Winter, "DOT Wants 5,000 Car Garage," A-1.

9. Paul Barret, quoted in Peter Phipps, Jeffrey Hilday, and William J. Donovan, "Behind the Financing Change, a Changed Public," *Providence Journal* (14 August 1994): F-1; William J. Donovan and Jeffrey Hilday, "State Drops Plan to Issue Bonds for Mall," *Providence Journal* (6 August 1994).

10. The Shepard's building was owned by Richmond Square Capital Corporation, the latest owner after a number of sales and bankruptcies throughout the 1980s.

11. The building was to be occupied by the Historical Society Museum, the State Council on the Arts, the State Department of Library Services, and the Rhode Island Department of Environmental Management.

12. Mayor Vincent Cianci, quoted in John Castellucci, "SPA Votes to Buy Shepard's for State Offices and Museum of Rhode Island History," *Providence Journal* (28 October 1992): A-3.

13. Hoxie interview, 13 September 2002.

14. Dante Boffi, Rhode Island Director of Transportation, quoted in William J. Donovan, Paul Davis, and Jeffrey L. Hilday, "Key Decisions Loom for Mall of New England," *Providence Journal* (27 February 1994): A-14.

15. Hoxie interview, 13 September 2002.

16. Cushman and Wakefield, Consulting Report *The Mall of New England* (July 1994).

17. William J. Donovan, "Machtley Opposes Mall Funds," *Providence Journal* (1 July 1994): C-7.

18. The Rhode Island governorship was a two-year term until 1994, when a voter-approved constitutional amendment mandating the four-year term was implemented.

19. The third candidate was the Cool Moose Party standard-bearer, Robert Healy.

20. Sundlun interview, 21 June 2002.

21. William J. Donovan, "Port Unit Won't Back Out of Plan for Mall," *Providence Journal* (3 November 1994): A-21.

22. William J. Donovan "Committee Says Deal for Mall Is Legal," *Providence Journal* (20 December 1994): A-3.

23. Office of the Governor, State of Rhode Island, *Retail Market Analysis: Providence Place*, prepared by HSG/Gould Associates (Washington, D.C., May 1995).

24. Lincoln Almond, quoted in Michael Pare, "Mall's Fate May Influence New Prospects," *Providence Business News* (9 September 1995).

25. William E. Collins, interview by authors, Providence, R.I., 29 August 2002.

26. William Donovan, "Enduring the Mall's Setbacks," *Providence Journal* (22 October 1995): A-1.

27. Sundlun interview, 21 June 2001; Friedrich St. Florian, interview by authors, Providence, R.I., 7 April 2003; Patricia McLaughlin, interview by authors, Providence, R.I., 23 December 2002; Thomas Deller, interview by authors, Providence, R.I., 25 October 2002.

28. Michael Pare, "Wrangling Continues over Providence Place," *Providence Business News* (7 August 1995).

29. Governor Almond consolidated the Department of Economic Development and the Rhode Island Port Authority into the quasi-governmental Port Authority and Economic Development Corporation.

30. Katherine Gregg and William Donovan, "Confusion Reigns on the Mall," *Providence Journal* (19 October 1995): A-1.

31. Terrence Murray, quoted in William Donovan, Katherine Gregg, and Scott MacKay, "Fleet Chief Gives Crucial Mall Support," *Providence Journal* (25 October 1995): A-1.

32. Ibid.

33. State Representative Paul Moura, quoted in Scott MacKay and William J. Donovan, "City Offered Nothing New on the Mall Deal," *Providence Journal* (28 October 1995): A-6; Ken Mingis, "Deal Making Sometimes a Perilous Trip," *Providence Journal* (1 November 1995): A-1.

34. Ken Mingis, William J. Donovan, and Scott MacKay, "City Council Comes Out against the Mall Deal," *Providence Journal* (27 October 1995): A-1.

35. McLaughlin interview, 23 December 2002.

36. Mayor Vincent Cianci, quoted in Mingis, "Deal Making Sometimes a Perilous Trip," A-1.

37. State Representative Antonio Pires, quoted in Scott MacKay and William J. Donovan, "Mall Deal Passes Easily," *Providence Journal* (2 November 1995): A-1.

38. Collins interview, 29 August 2002; Deller interview, 25 October 2002.

39. Katherine Gregg and William J. Donovan, "Mall Tax Relief Measure Clears Assembly," *Providence Journal* (9 November 1995): A-1.

40. Lugosch earlier had offered the city other, smaller sweeteners.

41. An additional provision by which the city would receive approximately $14 million over thirty years in a PILOT payment did not materialize in the final agreement.

42. The structure of the tax deal is as follows: mall merchants pay property and sales taxes to a trustee, who pays off portions of the private bonds secured by the developer over a thirty-year period. Three million dollars of state sales tax revenue is dedicated to repay mall private bonds. To date, substantially more sales tax revenue is generating net revenue to state coffers. No tax dollars go to Providence unless sales in the middle mall stores (not anchors)

reach $400 per square foot, a figure that, if reached, would make the mall one of the most successful mall developments ever.

43. Lugosch used part of the Nomura loan to buy out the interests of the former majority owner, Congell. Peter Steingraber, the mall's leasing agent, also was a limited partner.

44. Deller interview, 25 October 2002; Marsella interview, 30 October 2002.

45. St. Florian interview, 7 April 2003. The mall's design was not the product of a single office. For example, the Filene's store was designed by the New York office of Hellmuth, Obata and Kassabaum; Nordstrom had their own architect.

46. Nora Lockwood Tooher, "Design Debate," *Providence Sunday Journal* (18 May 1997): F-1.

47. Lugosch initially did not like the wintergarden and wanted to retain the dome until St. Florian indicated that removing it would save about $1.5 million. (St. Florian interview, 7 April 2003).

48. Bernard Frieden and Lynn B. Sagalyn, *Downtown Inc.: How America Rebuilds Cities* (Cambridge, Mass.: MIT Press, 1989), 153.

49. The first comprehensive assessment of the mall is Darrell West and Marion Orr, "Assessing the Providence Place Mall," *Brown Policy Report* (Providence, R.I.: Brown University, Taubman Center for Public Policy, June 2000).

50. Nora Lockwood Tooher, "Mall Sales on Track," *Providence Journal* (12 May 2000): E-1.

51. Rhode Island generally has a very narrow sales tax base, as clothing and movie tickets, among many other items, are exempt from taxation.

52. West and Orr, "Assessing the Providence Place Mall," 5.

53. Ibid., 6.

54. Ibid., 10.

55. Ibid., 12.

56. Collins interview, 29 August 2002.

CHAPTER 10

1. Three recently published volumes provide an excellent summary of the issues that are involved in sports stadium financing: Jay Weiner, *Stadium Games: Fifty Years of Big League Greed and Bush League Boondoggles* (Minneapolis: University of Minnesota Press, 2000); Joanna Cagan and Neil deMause, *Field of Schemes: How the Great Stadium Swindle Turns Public Money into Private Profit* (Monroe, Maine: Common Courage Press, 1998); Wilbur Rich, ed., *The Economics and Politics of Sports Facilities* (Westport, Conn.: Quorum Books, 2000).

2. Charles C. Euchner, "Tourism and Sports: The Serious Competition for Play," in *The Tourist City*, ed. Dennis R. Judd and Susan S. Fainstein (New Haven: Yale University Press, 1999), 216.

3. Joseph Bast, "If You Build It, They Will Come," *Journal of State Governments* 71, no. 2 (1998): 19–24.

4. David Swindell and Mark S. Rosentraub, "Who Benefits from the Presence of Professional Sports Teams? The Implications for Public Funding of Stadiums and Arenas," *Public Administration Review* 58 (January/February 1998): 11; Tim Chapin, "Urban Entertainment Centers as Economic Development," *Journal of the American Planning Association* 65, no. 3 (1999): 339–40.

5. Ziona Austrian and Mark Rosentraub, "Cleveland's Gateway to the Future," in *Sports, Jobs and Taxes: The Economic Impact of Sports Teams and Stadiums*, ed. Andrew Zimbalist and Roger Noll (Washington, D.C.: Brookings Institution Press, 1997); John Gibeault, "Skybox Shakedown," *American Bar Association Journal* 84 (1998): 68–73; Mark S. Rosentraub, "The Myth and Reality of Economic Development from Sports," *Real Estate Issues* 22, no. 1 (1997): 24–29. William Donovan, quoting the economist Roger Noll, "Stadium Winners and Losers," *Providence Journal* (27 February 1997): A-1; Euchner, "Tourism and Sports," 216.

6. Swindell and Rosentraub, "Who Benefits," 11.

7. Darius Irani, "Public Subsidies to Stadiums: Do the Costs Outweigh the Benefits?" *Public Finance Review* 25, no. 2 (1997): 238–53.

8. Zimbalist and Noll, *Sports, Jobs and Taxes*.

9. Quoted in Euchner, "Tourism and Sports," 216.

10. Rick Burton, University of Oregon College of Business, quoted in Christopher Rowland, "Owners Want More, Communities Oblige," *Providence Journal* (1 October 1997): A-1.

11. Swindell and Rosentraub, "Who Benefits," 11.

12. Tim Chapin, "Urban Entertainment Centers," 339–40.

13. Senator John Celona, "Hearings to Begin on Stadium Prospects," *Providence Journal* (19 March 1997): F-1.

14. Rhode Island General Assembly, State Senate Commission to Study Sites for a Possible Stadium for the New England Patriots, *Final Report* (10 June 1997).

15. Governor Lincoln Almond, quoted in William Donovan, "Almond Joins Cianci in Backing Football Stadium," *Providence Journal* (11 July 1997): B-1.

16. Governor Lincoln Almond, quoted in Christopher Rowland, Scott MacKay, and William Donovan, "Rhode Island Stadium Courtship Comes to an Amicable End," *Providence Journal* (2 October 1997): A-14.

17. William J. Donovan and Tom Mooney, "Pats Deal May Hinge on High Priced Business Seats," *Providence Journal* (9 March 1997): 1.

18. Tom Mooney, "Curtain Rises on Next Act of Stadium Negotiations," *Providence Journal* (29 October 1997), A-1; A-7.

19. William E. Collins, interview by authors, Providence, R.I., 29 August 2002.

20. John Swenn, Rhode Island Director of Economic Development, quoted in Rowland et al., "Courtship Comes to an Amicable End," A-14.

21. Joan Vennochi, "Divided Loyalties," *Boston Globe* (26 September 1997): C-1.

22. Rowland et al., "Courtship Comes to an Amicable End," A-14.

23. Antonio Pires, quoted in Christopher Rowland, "Pires: No State Money for Stadium," *Providence Journal* (4 September 1997): A-1.

24. Rhode Island General Assembly, Possible Stadium Study, *Final Report*.

25. Patricia Nolan, quoted in Gregory Smith, "Council Members Demand a Place in Stadium Talks," *Providence Journal* (19 September 1997): C-1.

26. Rowland et al., "Courtship Comes to an Amicable End," A-14.

27. Market Strategies of Michigan conducted the poll 3–5 February 1997.

28. Ken Mingis, "73 Percent of Rhode Islanders Say 'Come on Down,'" *Providence Journal* (18 February 1997).

29. Patricia McLaughlin, interview by authors, Providence, R.I., 23 December 2002; Collins interview, 29 August 2002.

30. Laurie White, spokesperson, Greater Providence Chamber of Commerce, quoted in William Donovan and Tom Mooney, "State's Business Leaders Stayed on the Sidelines," *Providence Journal* (2 October 1997): A-14.

31. Ibid., quotation from James Hagen.

32. Ibid., quotation from John Swenn, Executive Director, Rhode Island Economic Development Corporation.

33. Ariel Sabar, "On Smith Hill, Relief at Stadium's Demise," *Providence Journal* (2 October 1997).

34. Barbara Polichetti and Aubrey Cohen, "Cranston, Coventry Suggest Their Own Sites for Patriots Stadium," *Providence Journal* (26 February 1997): A-7.

35. McLaughlin interview, 23 December 2002.

36. Christopher Rowland, "Almond: No Regrets for Frugal Game Plan" *Providence Journal Bulletin* (3 October 1997): A-1.

37. M. Charles Bakst, "Pats Deal Collapse: Almond Handling to Be an Election Topic," *Providence Journal* (3 October 1997).

38. Rowland, "Almond: No Regrets," A-1.

39. Scott MacKay, "Now That It's Over, Bitter Words," *Providence Journal* (3 October 1997): A-18.

40. Ibid. Cianci's reference was to the state subsidy to refurbish McCoy Stadium, the home of the Pawtucket Red Sox, the AAA affiliate of the Boston Red Sox. Pawtucket was then the home city of the Rhode Island Speaker of the House and the chair of the House Finance Committee.

41. Karen Lee Ziner, "Cianci: 'We Take Our Lumps . . . We'll Survive,'" *Providence Journal* (2 October 1997): A-14; MacKay, "Bitter Words," A-1; Rowland et al., "Courtship Comes to an Amicable End," A-14.

42. Rowland, "Almond: No Regrets," A-1, 18.

43. Rowland et al., "Courtship Comes to an Amicable End," A-14.

CHAPTER 11

1. Taubman Center, Brown University, *Public Opinion Report* 10, no. 2 (1997).

2. Joseph R. Paolino, *Second Annual State of the City Address to the City Council* (January 1986), 3, 4, 16.

3. Vincent A. Cianci, "Operation Plunder Dome: Providence Development Will Weather This Storm," *Providence Journal* (6 April 2001): A-1.

4. Vincent A. Cianci, "Capital City Is Still on a Big Roll," *Providence Journal* (27 June 2000).

5. Vincent A. Cianci, *City of Providence Budget Message* (2001).

6. Robert Mulcahy, Teresphere, quoted in "Market Builds for Pricey Downtown Housing Units," *Providence Sunday Journal* (14 January 2001): A-1, A-17.

7. Howard Cohen, president, Beacon Residential Properties of Boston, quoted in "Market Builds," A-1, A-17.

8. These indicators are suggested in Rhode Island Public Expenditure Council, *Municipal Fiscal Health Check for Rhode Island Cities and Towns, 2003* (March 2003); Sanford M. Groves

and Maureen Godset Valente, *Evaluating Financial Condition: A Handbook for Local Government* (Washington, D.C.: International City Manager Association, 1994); Ken W. Brown, "The 10-Point Test of Financial Condition: Toward an Easy Assessment Tool for Smaller Cities," *Government Finance Review* (December 1993): 21–26; Richard Larkin, "Impact of Management Practices on Municipal Credit," *Special Report*, FitchIBCA (May 4, 2000). Locally an effort is under way to develop a municipal fiscal health index for Rhode Island, to which the authors have contributed. See Rhode Island Public Expenditure Council, *Municipal Fiscal Health Check*.

9. Thomas Deller, interview by authors, Providence, R.I., 25 October 2002.

10. In 2001 a new property tax classification system was enacted whereby the homestead exemption does not apply fully to a residence unless it is occupied by the homeowner. Previously, absentee owners enjoyed the full exemption.

11. Nexus Associates, *The City of Providence: Tax Policies, Economic Outlook and Competitive Performance*, Report Prepared for the Rhode Island Public Expenditure Council (13 March 1997): 30.

12. Ibid., 13.

13. The Providence tax levy history mirrored the revenue stream derived from the property tax. During the mid-1990s the levy remained flat, and by decade's end the levy began its upward climb once again, generally outstripping inflation.

14. The statute requires certain revaluation procedures and methods to produce comparability from community to community within the state. There is a state-local cost share arrangement to encourage compliance.

15. The city does receive a share of the hotel room tax.

16. House Fiscal Advisory Staff, *Rhode Island Education Aid* (November 2000); House Fiscal Advisory Staff, *Rhode Island Local Aid* (November 2000); Rhode Island Department of Administration, *Rhode Island Budget, Executive Summary, 1991–2000* (2000).

17. The formula in place from the early 1960s through 1994 was challenged by four municipalities in 1995 and ruled unconstitutional by a Rhode Island Superior Court. The thrust of the superior court decision was that the Rhode Island legislature acted unconstitutionally by failing to equalize education aid to poorer urban communities. The judge ordered the adoption of an alternative funding mechanism. Providence and other urban community policy makers cheered lustily only to see their visions of education aid sugarplums quickly vanish when the Rhode Island Supreme Court (on an appeal by the Rhode Island Senate leadership) ruled that constitutionally the legislature is able to fund education any way it desires. A 1999 suit brought by a few rural and suburban towns challenging a state education aid formula that gave proportionally more aid to urban communities also failed for essentially the same reasons.

18. Providence Building Authority, *Official Statements*, Combined Statement of Revenues, Expenditures, and Changes in Fund Balance, year ending 30 June 2000 (2000).

19. This case is built on information contained in the Providence Building Authority *Official Statements*, Retirement System, City of Providence, 1992–1999 (1999).

20. *City of Providence et al. v. the Employee Retirement Board of Providence et al.* The consent decree established minimum monthly retirement allowances for all pensioners who had completed twenty-five years of service. All retired police and firefighters were to receive an annual COLA of 6 percent while all other municipal pensioners' annual COLA would be 3

percent. Municipal employees other than police and firefighters became eligible to retire after twenty-three years of service.

21. The high court ruled that all police and firefighters who retired as of 19 December 1991 would continue to be entitled to the consent decree 6 percent annual compounded COLAs, and all other employees who retired at that date would receive the 3 percent compounded COLAs. Police and fire department retirees after 19 December 1991 were entitled to 3 percent noncompounded COLAs on the first $12,000 of their pension. All other employees, including school employees, who participate in the state pension system will not receive any COLA.

22. *Information Statement of the City of Providence, Rhode Island*, Appendix A: City Finances—Retirement System (21 November 2001): A-24.

23. There are a number of other terms and conditions under which borrowing authority is used, including public referenda, city council approvals, mayoral vetos, issuing time lines, and others. The Providence Public Building Authority receives an annual appropriation from the city in the form of a lease-rental payment to cover payment of authority bonds or notes. The Providence Water Supply Board long-term debt also is a general obligation of the city but is treated separately as an enterprise fund. The city also issues special tax increment bonds to support projects such as the Providence Plan Housing Program and the Manchester Street power station.

24. Moody's Investor Service, "Stable Outlook for Rhode Island Cities and Towns" (February 2003).

25. John Mikesell, *Fiscal Administration*, 5th ed. (Fort Worth: Harcourt Brace College, 1999), 556.

26. Patricia McLaughlin, interview by authors, Providence, R.I., 23 December 2002.

27. Ibid.

28. Many of the indicators used in this section are suggested in Groves and Valente, *Evaluating Financial Condition; Survey of Leading Downtown Indicators* (Washington, D.C.: International Downtown Association); and Standard and Poor's *Municipal Finance Criteria* (1989).

29. Rhode Island Secretary of State, Business Incorporation Records, 1980–99.

30. The business inventory tax in 2003 is in the fifth year of a ten-year state-mandated phaseout.

31. *Official Statements, Providence Building Authority, Information Statements*, Appendix C: Economic Characteristics—Major Private Employers—City's Largest Taxpayers, 1988–2000.

32. Data were provided by the Rhode Island Division of Taxation, "Adjusted Gross Income and Tax Liability," and were available only for the period 1995–2000.

33. U.S. Bureau of the Census, *Profile of Selected Economic Characteristics, Rhode Island Statewide Planning* (2002). Per capita income was $15,525 in 2000.

34. Ibid. Non-inflation adjusted income was $32,058 in 2000.

35. Nexus Associates, *The City of Providence*, table 17.

36. U.S. Bureau of Labor Statistics, *Metropolitan Areas, Providence–Warwick–Fall River, 1998–2000* (2000).

37. See Rhode Island Public Expenditures Council, "Urban Indicators Report for Rhode Island and Its Urban Communities, Final Draft, Commercial and Industrial Value" (2003), 17.

38. Gregory Smith, "An Upscale Housing Plan for Providence," *Providence Journal* (16 October 2002): A-1.

39. Mark G. Brown, "Rhode Island Statewide Planning, Profile of Selected Housing Characteristics, 1990 and 2000" (2001). Brown based his study on U.S. Bureau of the Census, Decennial Census, 1990 and 2000.

40. Because the 1992 economic census did not disaggregate its data to the metropolitan level, there are no comparative data to the 1997 federal economic census data. The 2002 economic census is not yet published at this writing.

41. See Office of Travel, Tourism and Recreation, University of Rhode Island, *Annual Economic Impacts of the Rhode Island Travel and Tourism Industry* (2002).

42. Timothy J. Tyrrell, *Rhode Island Travel and Tourism Research Report* 17, no. 1 (June 2000): 3.

43. U.S. Bureau of Labor Statistics, *Providence–Warwick–Fall River*.

44. See Data Resources Inc.–Wharton Economic Forecasting Associates, *The Role of Travel and Tourism in America's Top 100 Metropolitan Areas*, report prepared for the U.S. Conference of Mayors, Travel Business Roundtable, and International Association of Convention and Visitors Bureaus (22 October 2002).

45. Mayor's Special Commission on Business, Tourism and Culture, "Safeguarding the Providence Renaissance in the Post–September 11th Era" (April 2002): 4.

46. Thomas Boston and Catherine Ross, eds., *The Inner City: Urban Poverty and Economic Development in the Next Century* (New Brunswick, N.J.: Transaction Books, 1997).

47. Paul Peterson, *City Limits* (Chicago: University of Chicago Press, 1981); Merrill Goozner, "City Prospects: The Porter Prescription," *American Prospect* (May–June 1998): 56–64.

48. Susan Fainstein et al., *Restructuring the City: The Political Economy of Urban Redevelopment* (New York: Longman, 1986).

49. U.S. Department of Justice, *FBI Uniform Crime Reports, 1981–1999* (2000).

50. See Rhode Island Public Expenditures Council, "Urban Indicators," Table 5.2, 47.

51. City of Providence, Office of Human Resources, Public Safety, 1999.

52. For example, see Rhode Island Public Expenditure Council, *Public School Governance in Rhode Island: Joining Hands—Not Pointing Fingers* (1987); Rhode Island Department of Elementary and Secondary Education, "Reaching for High Standards: Student Performance in Rhode Island" (various years); Rhode Island Public Expenditure Council, "Results: Education in Rhode Island, 1997" (1997).

53. Rhode Island Department of Elementary and Secondary Education, *Information Works, 1997–2000* (2000).

54. Ibid.

55. Rhode Island Public Expenditure Council, "Urban Indicators."

56. Department of Elementary and Secondary Education, *Information Works*.

57. See Rhode Island Public Expenditures Council, "Urban Indicators," Table 3.2, p. 31.

58. According to the 2000 U.S. Census, Providence has among the oldest housing stock in the country.

59. Data were provided by Rhode Island Department of Health, Office of Occupational and Radiological Health, Division of Family Health (2000).

60. Rhode Island Kids Count, *Factbooks* for 1995–2000.

61. See Rhode Island Public Expenditures Council, "Urban Indicators," Table 2.4, p. 25.

CHAPTER 12

1. Richard Florida, *The Rise of the Creative Class and How It's Transforming Work, Leisure, Community and Everyday Life* (New York: Basic Books, 2002).

2. The Providence Foundation, Organizational Futures, and the Rhode Island Economic Policy Council, "The Creative and Innovative Economy of Providence: An Action Learning Study," *Final Report* (2003), 3.

3. Ibid., 4.

4. The Foundation's report declares that tolerance is an existing strength of Providence and that talent needs to be developed.

5. Kenneth Payne, interview by authors, Providence, R.I., 17 September 2002. A number of the interviewees made the same point.

6. William E. Collins, interview by authors, Providence R.I., 7 August 2002.

7. Gordon Hoxie, interview by authors, Providence, R.I., 13 September 2002.

8. Thomas Deller, interview by authors, Providence, R.I., 25 October 2002.

9. Alan Ehrenhalt, "The School-Renewal Fallacy," *Governing* (November 2002): 6–8.

10. Daniel Baudouin, interview by authors, Providence, R.I., 11 March 2003.

11. Ibid.

12. There were also three other nonhighway contracts: a river project along the east riverbank, which is completed; minor improvements; and a west riverbank project, which is about to begin.

13. Richard Dujardin, "Embezzlement Possible Key to Masonic Temple Woes," *Providence Journal* (11 May 1997).

14. Richard Dujardin, "Awaiting a New Lease on Life," *Providence Journal* (11 May 1997).

15. Gregory Smith, "Almond Invites Ideas for Masonic Temple," *Providence Journal* (30 April 1997).

16. Richard Dujardin, "Luxury Hotel Chosen for Temple," *Providence Journal* (14 August 1997).

17. Richard Dujardin, "Curtain Rises on Sanctum," *Providence Journal* (11 February 1997).

18. Katherine Gregg, "Secrecy in Rhode Island State House," *Providence Journal* (30 September 1997).

19. Joseph Larissa, Chief of Staff, quoted in Gregory Smith, "Money Woes Sink Temple Development," *Providence Journal* (28 March 2002): B-1.

20. Deller interview, 25 October 2002.

21. Deller interview, 25 October 2002.

22. Friedrich St. Florian, interview by authors, Providence, R.I., 7 April 2003.

23. Ibid.

24. Patricia McLaughlin, interview by authors, Providence, R.I., 23 December 2002.

25. Deller interview, 25 October 2002.

26. This section is a composite of the thoughts of all of those interviewed concerning the future of the Providence renaissance.

27. See, for example, Clarence Stone, "Urban Regimes and the Capacity to Govern: A

Political Economy Approach," *Journal of Urban Affairs* 15, no. 1 (1993): 1–28; R. DeLeon, *Left Coast City* (Lawrence: University Press of Kansas, 1992); A. DiGaetano and J. Klemanski, "Urban Regimes in Comparative Perspective," *Urban Affairs Quarterly* 29 (September 1993): 230–55.

28. See Cynthia Horan, "Beyond Governing Coalitions: Analyzing Urban Regimes in the 1990s," *Journal of Urban Affairs* 13, no. 2 (1991): 119–36.

29. See M. Orr and G. Stoker, "Urban Regimes and Leadership in Detroit," *Urban Affairs Quarterly* 30 (September 1994): 48–73; A. Harding, "Urban Regimes and Growth Regimes," *Urban Affairs Quarterly* 29 (April 1994): 356–83.

Index